The History of Utopian Thought

THE HISTORY OF UTOPIAN THOUGHT

THE MACMILLAN COMPANY
NEW YORK · BOSTON   CHICAGO · DALLAS
ATLANTA   SAN FRANCISCO

MACMILLAN & CO , LIMITED
LONDON · BOMBAY   CALCUTTA
MELBOURNE

THE MACMILLAN CO OF CANADA, LTD.
TORONTO

THE HISTORY OF
UTOPIAN THOUGHT

BY
JOYCE ORAMEL HERTZLER, Ph.D.

LONDON: GEORGE ALLEN & UNWIN, LTD.
RUSKIN HOUSE, 40 MUSEUM STREET, W.C. 1

"Ah Love! could you and I with Fate conspire
To grasp the sorry Scheme of Things entire,
  Would we not shatter it to bits—and then
Remould it nearer to the Heart's Desire?"

Ninety-ninth quatrain of
Fitzgerald's "Omar Khayyam'

PREFACE

This book embodies two related and yet distinct types of sociological endeavor. It is a study in the history of social thought, a field which has only been receiving serious and widespread attention in recent years, and attempts to give an historical cross-section of representative Utopian thought. But it is also a study in social idealism, a study in the origin, selection and potency of those social ideas and ideals that occasional and usually exceptional men conceive, with particular emphasis upon their relation to social progress.

The merit that I can hope for this book lies in the fact that, to my knowledge, it is the first book that attempts to give an unprejudiced, systematic treatment of the social Utopias as a whole. Its errors and weaknesses are those which all trail blazers have; for that reason suggestion and criticism are invited.

I wish to acknowledge my indebtedness to friends and colleagues for assistance of various kinds, to my wife for her painstaking aid in the verification of footnotes and the preparation of the manuscript, but above all to my teacher and colleague, Prof. E. A. Ross, for his constant encouragement, suggestion, and kindly criticism through the years this book has been in preparation.

J. O. HERTZLER

The University of Wisconsin,
Madison, Wisconsin.
September 4, 1922.

TABLE OF CONTENTS

PAGE

CHAPTER I. INTRODUCTION. 1

PART ONE
SOCIAL UTOPIAS: AN HISTORICAL REVIEW.

CHAPTER II. THE ETHICO-RELIGIOUS UTOPIANS AND THEIR UTOPIANISM. 7

    1. The Prophets as Forerunners of the Utopians.
        a. Introduction.
        b. Amos.
        c. Hosea
        d. Isaiah
        e. Jeremiah
        f Ezekiel.
        g. Deutero-Isaiah.
        h. Summary of the Prophets
    2. The Apocalyptists
    3. The "Kingdom of God" and the Utopianism of Jesus.
    4. Augustine and his "City of God"
    5. Savonarola's Florentine Theocracy

CHAPTER III. THE "REPUBLIC" OF PLATO. 99

CHAPTER IV. THE EARLY MODERN UTOPIAS 121

    1. The Events antedating the Early Modern Utopians.
    2 The "Utopia" of Sir Thomas More
    3. The Utopianism of Francis Bacon's "New Atlantis."
    4. Campanella and his "City of the Sun."
    5. Harrington's "Oceana."
    6. Summary of the Early Modern Utopians.

CHAPTER V. THE UTOPIAN SOCIALISTS. 181

    1. Introduction.
    2. Morelly
    3. Babeuf.
    4. Saint-Simon
    5 Fourier.
    6. Cabet
    7. Blanc
    8. Owen.
    9. Conclusion

TABLE OF CONTENTS

CHAPTER VI. THE RECENT SOCIAL ANTICIPATIONS—THE
PAGE
PSEUDO-UTOPIAS. 225
1. Bellamy's "Looking Backward"
2. Hertzka's "Freeland"
3. Wells' "Modern Utopia."

PART TWO

SOCIAL UTOPIAS: AN ANALYSIS AND CRITIQUE.

CHAPTER VII. THE UTOPIANS AND THEIR UTOPIAS. . . 257

1. Three classes of people with the social outlook: those with
   backlook, the look about you, and the forelook.
   Utopians of third class.
2. Characteristics of the Utopians
   a Filled with divine discontent.
   b Critics of their age.
   c. Intellectual originality and constructive imagination
   d Faith
   e Genius.
3. The Utopians seeking a perfect state here and those expecting it hereafter are the same thing
4. Characteristics of Utopias.
   a Result of social stress and tension
   b Inventions.
   c Merely relative
5 Reasons why Utopias are ridiculed

CHAPTER VIII. UTOPIANISM AND THE RÔLE OF IDEAS AND
IDEALS 268

1. Utopianism defined
2. Utopias as expressions of idealism
3. As stimuli to the imagination
4 Ideas and ideals go back to individuals
5 Become slowly incorporated in social thought through suggestion and imitation.
6 Final acceptance comes when society has caught up
7. Ideals are realized in fact.
8 Tolerance of new ideas and idealists
9 Ideas guide and control.
10 The social ideal.
11 Utility of ideas and ideals
12 World might have progressed without Utopias but not so
   well

CHAPTER IX. THE UTOPIANISTIC CONTRIBUTION TO CIVILI-
ZATION. 279

1. The value of an ideal depends upon its contribution to
   social betterment
2. Contributions
   a Utopianism of the Prophets and Jesus

TABLE OF CONTENTS

PAGE

b. Utopianism of More.
c. Utopianism of Owen.
d. Utopias assisted men in avoiding social disaster. -
e. Breathed a fearlessness.
f. Discovered a new criterion of human value.
g. Appreciated social laws
h. Adaptationists.
i. Determinism and free will.
j. Social will.
k. Eugenics.
l. Equality of the sexes.
m Preventive medicine
n. Religious toleration and social religion.
o Social theory of property.
p. Conception of social institutions. education, Bacon's House of Salomon, the State.
q. Basic ideas of socialism.
r Sociology itself

CHAPTER X. THE LIMITED PERSPECTIVE OF THE UTOPIANS. 301

1. Could not have a perfect social perspective.
2. Limitations:
   a. Did not grasp the necessity of a sound physical and economic basis
   b. Did not grasp the full significance of life:
      Assumed men originally perfect.
      Violated the instincts
      Did not see that life is a constant struggle.
      Over-social view.
   c Failed to start with things as they are.
   d Did not use spirit of protest for reform purposes.
   e. Considered their Utopias as the last word in perfectionment.
3. Social perfection an illusion; can only have social progress.
4. The passing of Utopias.

THE HISTORY OF UTOPIAN THOUGHT

CHAPTER I

INTRODUCTION

At this moment in the history of the civilized world when social chaos and discontent are everywhere prevalent, men are analyzing social phenomena, groping about for causes, and seeking solutions for these very puzzling complications. This, however, is not the first time that the race has faced this problem; from the dawn of history at times men have known the same unrest, for it is in the nature of customs and institutions, regardless of the department of life with which they are connected, to become antiquated and corrupt; so its men of intelligence and social spirit, its prophets of all time, have devoted their talents to devising instruments of change for the better.

In the literature of social thought a numerous, but much neglected and ridiculed section consists of the so-called social utopias, which confine themselves wholly to the problem outlined briefly above. The word "Utopia" itself has its origin in the name of the ideal social state conceived and dramatically described by the Englishman, Sir Thomas More, in a book in dialogue form written in Latin in the years 1515–1516, published by Froben at Louvain, later translated and circulated throughout Europe. It is the distinctive characteristic of this work which has caused its name to become the general term for imaginary ideal societies. And that distinctive feature is this: More depicted a perfect, and perhaps unrealizable, society, located in some nowhere, purged of the shortcomings, the wastes, and the confusion of our own time and living in perfect adjustment, full of happiness and contentment.

The Utopias seemingly have never been taken very seriously,[1] nor have scholars paid them much attention. The history of literature casts them outside as curiosities or as belonging in the field of politics or statescraft; political science has given little heed to them because they are held to be fantastic and unscientific. Religion and theology have dealt with a few, but the bulk of them have fallen without the religious field, strictly speaking. It has remained for sociology, with its limitless human interest, to examine them and appraise them in the light of later social idealism.

Among these Utopias we find in most cases searching analyses of current social situations, lucid and fascinating anticipations of a better or perfect society to come, and a presentation of instruments and principles of social progress which men of succeeding epochs have sometimes adopted and used in promoting improvement. While there is in them much that is naïve and useless from the point of view of the present, they breathe a spirit and offer suggestions which the socially minded evolutionist and the philosophical historian of to-day cannot overlook.

It is the object of the first part of this work to analyze some of the more representative and better known social Utopias, examining their social background and portraying briefly their singular features, but devoting the major portion of the exposition to a careful study of the agencies and principles whereby this social perfection was to be attained. Behind the Utopias lies the utopian spirit, that is, the feeling that society is capable of improvement and can be made over to realize a rational ideal. We propose to trace it historically from its first prominent expression. Since we find the first and most significant ideas of this kind in these Utopias, we have called this spirit "utopianism," meaning thereby *a conception of social improvement*

[1] "Utopias are generally regarded as literary curiosities which have been made respectable by illustrious names, rather than as serious contributions to the political problems which troubled the age at which they appeared." Smith. "Harrington and his 'Oceana,'" p. 12.

either by ideas and ideals themselves or embodied in definite agencies of social change. From the earliest Hebrew prophets on we have more or less conscious ideals of this kind expressed, and the means whereby such rebuilding is to take place indicated with varying degrees of definiteness. We will treat of the theorizings of people as widely diverse in their training, views, and purposes as are the means proposed to bring in their ideal states.

In the second part of this work we will appraise and analyze the Utopias, their writers, and their utopianism and the rôle of ideas and ideals contained therein. This program also demands an investigation as to any contributions they have made in human advance, and any visible influence of their potency. Of course, it also necessitates an analysis of their shortcomings. Finally, it involves a treatment of the effect of the evolutionary conception and the theory of history which came with it, on the utopian idea and the consequent changes in the type of Utopias.

Throughout it is essentially a study of social ideas and ideals, —the influence of environment and events in producing them, the types of individuals conceiving them, the factors responsible for their survival, and their ability to translate themselves into fact.

PART ONE

SOCIAL UTOPIAS: AN HISTORICAL REVIEW

CHAPTER II

THE ETHICO-RELIGIOUS UTOPIANS AND THEIR UTOPIANISM

1. THE PROPHETS AS FORERUNNERS OF THE UTOPIANS

a. INTRODUCTION

There is a common impression that Plato was the first to picture a perfect future of whom we have record in literature, and that his "Republic" was the first Utopia or ideal commonwealth. This is the result of holding to a literary field too narrowly conceived. A broader reading with the search for utopian elements uppermost, will bring a different conclusion.

Among another people and in another literature which antedated that of Greece by several centuries we find numerous utopian expressions by men, who, as social critics and social architects, were the equals if not the peers of Plato. We refer to the Hebrew prophets,[1]—men of marked individuality and originality; men of rare ability in appraising their times, in suggesting lines of social reconstruction, and in depicting the perfect future. We will devote the ensuing section to their study.

Because of the practically limitless field which thus opened to us we shall concentrate our study upon the so-called "literary" prophets who form that wonderful movement which was inaugurated by Amos, the shepherd of Tekoa, about the middle of the eighth century B. C, and continued after him by an unbroken line of prophets through upward of three centuries,

[1] The prophetic period proper can be said to have begun with Samuel in the eleventh century B C, and to have extended to the fourth century B C., when it insensibly passed over into the period of the Apocalyptists.

7

before, during, and after the Babylonian exile of the Hebrews. We shall devote ourselves to them for the following reasons: first, they are in their broad general aspects characteristic prophets; second, owing to the fact that they are "literary," i. e., have left their ideas in writing, their Utopias are authentic to a greater extent than the prophetic Utopias which have been passed from generation to generation by word of mouth before being written and thus had lost many of their pristine characteristics; and third, they show most clearly the development of the utopian idea, spoken of by them as the "Messianic" state, and profess doctrines making for what we have called utopianism.

But we must even limit our field here. So we have decided to consider the works attributed to the six most important prophets of this group, namely, Amos, Hosea, Isaiah, Jeremiah, Ezekiel, and Deutero-Isaiah, who have been called the beacon lights of prophecy.[2]

Since this is primarily a sociological study we shall hold ourselves aloof from all theological and exegetical controversy and certain mooted points of higher criticism. We will, however, accept those interpretations of time and authorship of passages upon which we find almost universal unity of opinion among Biblical scholars. What we are concerned with above all else, are the contemporary social conditions which impelled the prophets to speak as they did; the fact that there were men in those early times who felt the need of reconstructing society; men who conceived of means to be employed in bringing about the ideal state free from the evils of the time, and who possessed the constructive imagination to foresee what this ideal commonwealth might be and to describe what they saw. Whether it was this familiar individual or that unknown one does not matter so much.

We will conclude our treatment of the six prophets mentioned with a brief summary of the sociological significance of the prophets, hoping thereby to establish them definitely as forerunners of the Utopians.

[2] See the book of that name by A. C. Knudson, New York, 1914.

b. Amos

The first of these prophets was Amos, a rugged, virile character who evokes our profound admiration. "Amos is one of the most marvelous and incomprehensible figures in the history of the human mind, the pioneer of a process of evolution from which a new epoch of humanity dates." [3] It was he who gave impetus to that spirit of hope which we expect to trace through the following pages,—a movement centering about a perfect future state and containing the purest elements of utopianism.

Amos lived and spoke about the middle of the eighth century B. C., in the days of Jeroboam, second, of Israel, whose long brilliant reign had been marked by peace and prosperity. [4] It was after one of Israel's periods of depression and distress when she had again raised herself to power. Her worst enemy, the kingdom of Damascus, had been decisively defeated, and was no longer dangerous; the neighboring nations had been subjected and Jeroboam II reigned over a kingdom extending from Hamath to the Dead Sea, the size and grandeur of which had not been surpassed since the days of David. Israel was the ruling nation between the Nile and the Euphrates. The internal doings were seemingly as brilliant and stupendous as they had ever been. Everything breathed of luxury and riches; ivory palaces, houses of hewn stone, castles and forts, horses and chariots, power and pomp, the luxurious and idle rich; all proclaimed the prosperity of the times. [5] In the year 760 B. C., the Autumn festival was being celebrated at Bethel, and in accordance with the spirit of the time, revelry was the order of the day. Unwonted splendor characterized the feast, and untold sacrifices were offered. People felt that all was well.

But suddenly the festival mirth was interrupted and the merry revelers were shaken out of their complacency, for Amos, a herdsman and sycamore dresser of Tekoa, a plain-looking

[3] Cornill, C. H. "The Prophets of Israel," Chicago, 1899, p. 46.
[4] Smith, H. P. "Old Testament History," New York, 1915, pp. 177–184.
[5] Amos 6.4–6

and lowly, but tremendously inspired man appeared among them, denouncing them and predicting their early destruction.

We ask ourselves, was Amos fit to speak as he did? We answer, yes! He was a man stern by nature. Furthermore, he was accustomed to the stern scenery of the wild country among the Judean hills around the Dead Sea. And so the loneliness of his life as a shepherd and the ruggedness of his surroundings deepened much the native sternness of his soul. He had time to brood and ponder, to appraise events, and contemplate consequences. At the same time he traveled much, because of his occupation, saw much, and came in contact with many people. It was with this clarity of vision and keenness of insight that he had drawn his conclusions and arrived at his solution   Beneath the shining surface of things his keen eyes saw the symptoms of rottenness and inevitable decay. The people were inflated and proud; the whole splendid structure of which the nation boasted was to Amos a tottering edifice, doomed to destruction. The times were those of false worship and social injustice; ritualism had supplanted spirituality and oppression had smothered justice.

The worship of God in ancient Israel had always been of a thoroughly joyful and cheerful character; it was considered to be a rejoicing in God. But by Amos's time it had degenerated to a Saturnalian orgy. Revelry and tumultuous carousings marked the festivals: drunkenness and indecency together with the most licentious debaucheries were common at the local shrines. And yet the contemporaries of Amos considered this the correct and fitting worship of God.[6] The spirit of the age had befogged their vision. But the prophets, especially Amos, recognized in those aberrations remnants of acquired paganism, chiefly that of the Canaanites. For him the sacrifices were not only something indifferent, they were even contemptible,—a multiplication of transgressions.[7] The sanctuaries were places of whoredom. It is for this reason that Amos cried out in protest against the ceremonies of the feast

[6] Cornill, C H. op cit., p. 38
[7] Amos 4:4

at Bethel. With true social vision, he protested against this perversion of the religious rites because the whole life of the body politic was bound up in the due performance of those rites.

"I hate, I despise your feast days, and I will not smell in your solemn assemblies.

Though ye offer me burnt offerings and your meat offerings, I will not accept them: neither will I regard the peace offerings of your fat beasts.

Take away from me the noise of thy songs; for I will not hear the melody of thy viols.

Have ye offered unto me sacrifices and offerings in the wilderness forty years, O house of Israel?

But ye have borne the tabernacle of your Moloch and Chuin your images, the star of your God, which ye made to yourselves." [8]

In the material prosperity on which the people laid so much stress the prophet saw only the social evils which prosperity had fostered. He felt it to be superficial. It was the luxury of the few at the expense of the toil of the many; consequently social injustice was rife. On the one hand the wholesale exploitation of the poor was noticeable; [9] they were swindled by being sold bad grain, given short weight, and charged exorbitant prices. [10] The courts were corrupt and venal; [11] justice was poisoned at its source by the love of money. The relations between tenant and landlord were favorable to the landlord alone. [12] Shameless oppression was to be seen at every hand.

On the other hand profligate extravagance and debauchery characterized the life of the fortunate classes. The rich idled in their sumptuous palaces lying on couches of ivory with damask cushions; gorging themselves with the choicest of the flocks; imbibing the costliest wines; and anointing themselves with precious oils. [13] The voluptuous women of whom he

[8] Amos 5·21–26
[9] Ibid. 4:1, 5:12,
[10] Ibid. 5·11, 8 4–7.
[11] Ibid. 2:6.
[12] Ibid. 5:12.
[13] Ibid. 6:4–6.

speaks as the Kine of Bashan, as always is the case in such a social system, were even more extravagant and avaricious than the men.[14]   All were swollen with foolish pride and wallowing in shameless luxury.   Life in general was corrupt, and the evils, always prevalent at such a time, were present here in a marked degree.   This corrupt condition meant a corrupt state, and a corrupt state meant corrupt individuals, and a general condition of inequality and iniquity.

It was this deplorable social corruption which incensed Amos and caused him to make the predictions he did.   The sum of the message that he proclaimed with such elemental power was that a society founded upon social injustice could not endure; and that its doom as a nation was inevitable and irrevocable. As a nation it was being broken down by its own indolent, dissolute leaders, and it was soon to be broken physically and politically by the deadly onslaught of the Assyrians.[15]   No other fate could be in store for a nation which crushed its poor, which pandered to its lust, which stifled its conscience, which rejected its preachers, and which forgot its God.   But Amos did not express the inevitableness of Israel's collapse in terms of the operation of social forces, as we should explain it to-day. The Hebrew sense of the overruling Jehovah prompted him to speak of the coming disaster as a divine infliction.   He reached out to the great truth that Jehovah is only to be served through the social relationships of men.   He admonishes men with tremendous, and what is oftentimes a terrible, earnestness.

> "Let justice flow like a river
> And righteousness like a perennial stream." [16]

But wherein lies the utopianism of Amos's message?   It lies in the social aspect of his exhortation.   The sins which Amos, like the other prophets, denounced were social sins; wrongs done to the neighbor, especially the helpless neighbor.   Jehovah does not require sacrifice but righteousness between man and man.   What Amos knew and what he thought everybody else

[14] Ibid. 4:1.

[15] The great siege ended and the exile took place about 721 B. C.—actually within thirty years after Amos had foretold it.

[16] Ibid 5 24.

ought to know was that the Almighty is ethical in his demands. |
Doing justice in society, bringing about fair play between man
and man was the end. Amos looked forward to a world in
which service and not ceremonial was the ideal; a world in
which a new era of social justice would be inaugurated.[17]

But how was society to be recast so as to bring this social
state into being? Well, his was not the message, "Down with
the rich, the aristocracy, the bourgeoisie." It was "Seek the |
Lord and ye shall live."[18] "Seek good and not evil that ye
may live." "Let righteousness roll like a perennial stream."[19]

The ideal for which Amos pleaded so passionately was that
of a well-ordered society, animated by the spirit of justice and
fair play. The new, perfect society was to come about by a
complete change both individually and nationally, in social
relationships. This in turn depended upon a moulding anew
of the social ethics, the quickening of men's innate sense of
right and justice. This was only possible as the people clung
more and more to Jehovah, followed His precepts, and brought'
their lives into conformity with His. It decreed a change of
attitude, a reconstituted group-morality, an awakened spirituality, a renewed assurance of the existence of Jehovah and of
His control of the universe for a moral purpose.

After the violent denunciation had fallen upon the people
like a thunderbolt from the midst of a tempest, and after he
had pictured to them the inevitable doom, Amos in the last
chapter [20] portrays briefly the beautiful rainbow bursting forth
after the storm had wrought its worst. It was a fleeting glimpse
of a halcyon Utopia to come.[21]

[17] In touching upon this phase of Amos's teaching A. C Knudson, op.
cit, p. 91, has said: "Amos may be regarded as standing at the head of
all those who through the ages have sought to free religion from its unnatural alliance with superstition, ceremonialism, selfishness, and tyranny,
and who have endeavored to identify it with the never-ceasing struggle
of the human mind for righteousness, truth, freedom, and social progress."

[18] Amos 5 6.

[19] Ibid. 5 14 and 5.24.

[20] Amos 9 11-15

[21] A large number of the critics agree that this last passage of Amos
may have been added at a later date by a reviser, to add the necessary
element of hope required at a time of particular social stress. This does
not materially affect our general method of presentation.

In the overwhelming ruin which was at hand the sinful members of this nation, who composed the bulk, were to perish, but there remained a residue,[22] comparable to the good grain which passed through the sieve and remained upon the thresh-ing floor. The question as to the ultimate destiny of this good grain was answered by pointing to the reëstablishment of the shattered power of the Davidic house. This house, though weakened by the invasion which overwhelmed Israel, survived the shock, took up unto itself all those who escaped, and was restored to its former integrity, splendor and power. In that reestablished Kingdom there was that abundance of physical blessing which was the natural production of a land flowing with milk and honey [23]—blessings to be shared in perpetuity.

But the Israel which is represented as restored is not the corrupt Israel of Amos's own day; it is the Israel, which, though he does not expressly say so, is implicitly conceived as worthy of being reinstated in its ancient home. It is the nation purged of transgressions, the purified, ideal Israel of the future—a paradise regained.

c. Hosea

Hosea made his contribution to prophetic literature between 738 and 735 B. C., about twenty-five years after the appearance of Amos.[24] It is in Hosea that we find the utopian elements hinted at by Amos more fully developed and also presented from a different viewpoint. It is held by some that Hosea was a farmer, and the wealth of agricultural metaphors, anal-ogies and allusions would seem to bear out this statement, but it has been conjectured, and with greater probability, that he was a priest. As will be presently shown he had an unusually high conception of the duties of the priesthood. He also re-veals a rich knowledge of the past history of his people, such as one would naturally expect of a priest;[25] then too, he is

[22] Amos 9 9   "I will sift the house of Israel among all nations, like as corn is sifted in a sieve, yet shall not the least grain fall upon the earth "

[23] Ibid 9 13, 14.

[24] Cornill, op cit, p. 53

[25] Hosea 9·9, 10·9, 11 1, 12:3; 13:1

acquainted with a written law and its requirements in which it was apparently the special function of the priest to give instruction.[26] It is therefore not improbable that he belonged to the priesthood, and was forced into the prophetic office by the degeneracy of his order.[27]

This difference of origin between Amos and Hosea is one of several marked distinctions between the two. Amos is the stern moralist—a preacher of Jehovah's awfulness and majesty —sitting in judgment on his people, pronouncing them guilty, and almost rejoicing to anticipate that justice will be done. His Jehovah is essentially a criminal judge, inspiring fear, but not love; "Jehovah is justice." But Hosea is deeply emotional and sympathetic, rich in his affections, and for him "Jehovah is love"; his is a deeply moved heart torn by grief. Not that Hosea is any less severe in his judgment of the people, but because he cannot rest content with merely a negation or threat. For him Jehovah is one whom pity overcomes, One who is merciful, who cannot cast aside the people He loves; hence He will change them, improve them, educate them so as to make them fit to abide in his presence. Whilst in Amos the ethical element is predominant, in Hosea the religious element occupies the foreground.[28] Hosea is essentially the critic of religious observance. He makes the religious corruption of his time, including idolatry, particularly prominent, laying less stress on the distinctively ethical side of his people's life. Hosea, even more than Amos, looks upon the activities of his day with that detachment which moral insight and purity of motive alone can give.

An examination of the social background shows that Israel was rapidly approaching the doom which Amos had foretold, and the evils which he denounced so vigorously had become still more flagrant and accentuated. There was considerably less prosperity than in the time of Amos, hence the wickedness took on different forms. It was a period of anarchy and dissolution. Politically the nation was rapidly approaching bank-

[26] Hosea 4:6; 8:1, 12.
[27] Knudson, op cit., p. 97.
[28] Cornill, op. cit , p. 47–48.

ruptcy. Kings were both murderers and usurpers; distrust was everywhere rife; current diplomacy was little more than intrigue.[29] Sensuality, ever the sin of the Oriental peoples, had become increasingly shameless. Robbery, murder and fornication flourished [30] The causes for this widespread immorality centered about the priests and a badly deteriorated religion and were twofold, as Hosea saw more clearly and pointed out more definitely than had Amos. First, there was the detestable vileness and hypocrisy of the priests, with whom the false prophets were in league.[31] They were not neutral but openly wicked, and when the religious leaders are torpid in callous indifference and stereotyped in false traditions, how can a nation's decadence and doom be forestalled? The priests were failing to teach and direct the people, who were consequently perishing for lack of this knowledge.[32] There is even the imputation that the priests manipulated affairs to their personal profit, and that they encouraged people to sin in order that they might impose penalties upon them and exact fines.[33] In one passage he does not hesitate to accuse the priests of sins of violence.[34] Secondly, the worship and religion had been corrupted at its source. What had come to be the conventional worship was arrant paganism, and constituted the real cancer that was eating the life out of Israel. The worship had taken on elements of the Canaanitish observances. So the ethical Jehovah worship had been perverted into a sensuous and sensual pagan nature worship These corrupt forms had been introduced through the alliance of King Ahab with Jezebel, a daughter of the usurper Ethbaal of Tyre, who had been a priest of Astarte.[35] The coarse emblems of Asherah and Ashtoreth thus brought in smoothed the way for a cultus of which the basis was open sensuality. The "adultery" and "whoredom" which are denounced so incessantly on the pages of Hosea are

[29] Hosea 8 4, 13·10 ff; 7 11, 5·13
[30] Ibid. 4:2; 6:9, 10; 7:1, 4; 9·10, 10 11–14.
[31] Ibid 5 2
[32] One of the most important duties of the priests was to interpret and teach the Law See Deut 33 10, Lev 10.10, 11
[33] Hosea 4 6, 8, 9; 6 8
[34] Ibid. 6:9.
[35] Farrar, F W "The Minor Prophets," New York, 1890, pp 79, 80

not only the metaphors for idolatry, but the literal description of the lives which that idolatry corrupted.[36] Hence at the popular festivals the orgies and debaucheries received the religious sanction. The altars on the high hills were places of iniquity. At them prostitution was regularly practiced.[37] It was for this reason that Hosea denounced the priests and a popular religion which smacked of Canaanitish origin, while Amos condemned the wealthy and aristocratic for their injustice and oppression.

Amos felt that it was his mission to tell a smug and contented people rejoicing in prosperity that their social fabric was rotten and was really tottering to its fall, while Hosea had to call a broken, troubled, corruption-ridden society back to its religious loyalty as the only hope of political and social salvation.[38]

He drew an analogy between his own unfortunate marital experience and Israel. He married Gomer, at first pure, but who later turned out to be an unworthy, profligate person, who made shipwreck of their married life. Reflecting on this, Hosea saw something which taught him the heart of Jehovah toward Israel. He himself in his mixed and harrowing feelings toward Gomer was a type of Jehovah. His loathing abhorrence of her sin, his flaming indignation at her infidelity, and, stronger than either, his tender compassion at the depth of misery to which she reduced herself, are but a reflection of Jehovah's feelings toward His people.[39] Israel's unfaithfulness was the unfaithfulness of a wife, she had given preference to another lord, Baal. As Gomer erred, so Israel as a nation erred. Jehovah has an indictment against his people, says Hosea; there is no fidelity and no knowledge of Jehovah in the land; there is naught but breaking faith and killing and stealing, and committing adultery.[40] Therefore this people must be given over to perdition. "For they have sown the wind, and

[36] Ibid p 80.
[37] Hosea 4·13
[38] Soares, T G , "The Social Institutions and Ideals of the Bible," New York, 1915 , p. 226.
[39] Cheyne, T K., "Hosea" in the Cambridge Bible, p. 21.
[40] Hosea 4:1, 2.

they shall reap the whirlwind." [41]   But Jehovah has no personal object in this judgment; He wishes thereby to lead these foolish and blinded hearts to reflection and self-knowledge.

Hosea sets forth his utopianism and his Utopia in many scattered passages throughout his book.   His utopianism centers about the principle of Divine love.   It is his purpose to set forth this love in its moral nature, as opposed to the altogether non-moral and quasi-physical union supposed to exist between a heathen deity and his worshipers. [42]   Jehovah in His infinite love will follow after His socially, politically and religiously corrupt people into their misery and degradation until they depart from their erring ways and permit Him to minister to them through the agency of His love.   Only as they assume this submission can they hope for a lasting and profitable life.   Jehovah wants pure and unadulterated love and faithfulness rather than sacrifices, and knowledge of Himself rather than burnt offerings, [43] and as the people conform themselves to this standard will they approach perfection. When the people approach Jehovah in their distress, openly confess to Him their transgressions, and become properly penitent, then will He accept them into grace and they will be His people and He will be their God. [44]   The central idea of Hosea's teaching expressed throughout his pages is that fatherly love is the foremost attribute of Jehovah and that it alone is the great reconstructing force of which society can avail itself in order to work out its redemption.   But it is not only the love of Jehovah for Israel of which he speaks, for, in catching his spirit, we feel that he also emphasizes the love of man to man as a fundamental reconstructing agency in the social organism.

Of the Utopia we obtain but occasional glimpses. [45]   It is the natural outcome of the prophet's doctrine of divine love, and an integral part of his message.   He seems to have used these various utopian fragments as a sort of lure to woo the people on to obedience to Jehovah.   It is the picture of a rehabilitated,

[41] Ibid. 8 7
[42] Cheyne, op cit , p 29
[43] Hosea 6 6
[44] Ibid. 2·21–23, 5 15, 6·1–3; 14·4.
[45] For Utopian passages see Hosea 1 10, 11; 2.14–23, 3.1–5; 14:1–8.

purified people after the Covenant. It is to be a new betrothal. Right and justice, grace and pity, love and faith will be the blessings of this new time. The bow and the sword shall be broken and the battles that had harrassed Israel so long shall be ended. The earth shall bring forth its wealth of products. It will be a righteous and peaceful people living in harmony with Jehovah and enjoying physical abundance.[46]

d. ISAIAH

Isaiah is the third historically of the prophets, the social background and utopianism of whom we are considering, his period of activity extending from about 740 to 700 b. c. He stands out in many respects in marked contrast to his immediate prophetic predecessors, Amos and Hosea. Like Amos, he was a native of Judah. But Amos was a man of lowly station; a sheep-herder and a nature-man; an inhabitant of the moorlands and hills and open places; self-tutored, and disciplined by rigorous experience. Hosea's home was in the northern kingdom, Israel, where he doubtless was a priest. But Isaiah was a noble and courtier, by some accounts even of royal birth. This we infer from the fact that he seems to have had ready access to the king and court.[47] He was an inhabitant of the capital city. Nor was he an untaught man like Amos, but was a scholar, fully acquainted with the literature of the past,— one who shared in that revival of culture and learning which seems to have marked the reign of Hezekiah.[48] Unlike his predecessors Isaiah did not hold himself aloof from the political life of his time. The ministry of Amos was apparently of brief duration; he came, spoke and wrote, and then passed away into obscurity. Hosea seems to have stood apart from the controlling forces of the nation's life. But Isaiah spent nearly half a century as the councillor, advisor and critic of kings; a statesman who took a keen interest and played a vital rôle in the politics of his day. Like the prophets of old [49] he assumed the rôle of the practical statesman, watching the intrigues of the

[46] Hosea 2.18–22.
[47] Isaiah 7 3 ff., 8·2, 22·15 ff
[48] Sayce, A. H , "The Life and Times of Isaiah," London, 1890, p 14.
[49] Samuel and his immediate successors.

rulers, seeking to circumvent their secret plans, denouncing their wicked and faithless policies, and approaching them with precise direction as to the course they should pursue in certain critical situations.[50] He had a strong and commanding personality, which he by virtue of his high social station and long public ministry, was able to bring to bear with tremendous power upon the political and religious issues of the day.

Isaiah realized in anticipation the noble ideal of a single-hearted statesman sketched four centuries afterwards by the Athenian patriot, Demosthenes: "To discern events in their beginnings, to be beforehand in the detection of movements and tendencies, and to forewarn his countrymen accordingly; to fight against the political vices from which no State is free, of procrastination, supineness, ignorance, and party jealousy; to impress upon all the paramount importance of unity and friendly feeling, and the duty of providing promptly for their country's needs.[51] ᵥ

But there were also some points of similarity. In originality Isaiah ranks along with Amos and Hosea. As Amos was the first to identify the perfect life and a perfect state absolutely with the moral law, and as Hosea was the first to make them fundamentally a matter of love, so Isaiah was the first to formulate the great doctrine of faith as a condition for their realization.

His conviction as to the social, moral and political rottenness of his times is equally as strong as that of Amos and Hosea:

> "Ah sinful nation, a people laden with iniquity,
> A seed of evildoers, children that are corrupters:"[52]

"From the sole of the foot even unto the head there is no soundness in it, but wounds, and bruises, and putrefying sores." [53]

> "How is the faithful city become an harlot;
> It was full of judgment;
> Righteousness lodged in it;
> But now murderers.

[50] Buttenwieser, M., "The Prophets of Israel," New York, 1913, p. 254.
[51] "De Corona," par. 246, p. 318,—Quoted by Driver, S R., "Isaiah: His Life and Times," p. 107.
[52] Isaiah 1:4.
[53] Ibid. 1 6.

Thy silver is become dross, thy wine mixed with water:
Thy princes are rebellious, and companions of thieves:
Every one loveth gifts, and followeth after rewards;
They judge not the fatherless, neither doth the cause of
the widow come unto them." [54]

The people have fallen away from Jehovah, whom Isaiah
has protest: "Sons have I nourished and brought up, but they
have rebelled against me. The ox knows his owner and the
ass his master's crib. Israel does not know, my people does
not consider." [55]

As in Hosea, Jehovah is particularly displeased with the
hollowness and lack of sincerity in their worship. What they
really believed in was not Jehovah, but silver and gold, vest-
ments, incense and the other flashy accouterments of worship.
"What is the multitude of your sacrifice to me, says Jehovah;
I have had enough of the burnt-offerings of rams, and the fat
of fed beasts, and I delight not in the blood of bullocks, or of
lambs, or he-goats." [56] "Bring no more vain oblations; incense is an abomination unto me." Their religion was
merely a false religiosity, a lip worship.[57]

Like Amos, Isaiah denounces the rulers and upper classes as
most to blame for the wretched spectacle of tyranny, hard-
heartedness, and degrading wickedness prevalent in the land.
The men of authority have forgotten their responsibilities, and
have given up all else but the means of enjoyment to themselves, heedless of the cruelty or injustice which may in the
process have been afflicted upon others. All the imitated classes
are shot through with cupidity, insolence and dissoluteness.
"Jehovah stands up to judge the people; Jehovah will enter into
judgment with the elders of his people, and with the rulers
thereof. It is you who have eaten up the vineyard; the spoil
of the poor is in your homes; what mean you that you crush
my people and grind the faces of the poor? says Jehovah, Lord
of Hosts." [58] The women are haughty and given to ostentatious

[54] Ibid. 1:21–23.
[55] Ibid. 1:2–3.
[56] Ibid. 1:11, 13.
[57] Ibid 29:13–14.
[58] Ibid. 3 13–15.

display, vain and extravagant.[59] The priests and prophets give themselves over to drunkenness and carousing and consequently "they err in vision, they stumble in judgment." [60] They defile the temple and make it filthy.

The common people with such examples before them have become infected with the callousness and corruption about them, have admitted gross accretions and admixtures to their religion and "say to the seers: See not; and to the prophets, Prophesy not unto us right things, speak unto us smooth things, prophesy deceit, turn from the way, go aside from the path, trouble us no more with Israel's Holy One." [61] And so he goes on pointing out their every weakness with the keenness of insight and clarity of motive of the true social reformer. Driver has admirably summarized this aspect of Isaiah's activity in the following passage: "As a reformer Isaiah labored to correct all political and social abuses. To elevate statesmanship, to purify justice, to reform religion, to fight against inconsistency, to redress social wrongs, was the aim which he set himself in life; and his book discloses to us the persistency and uncompromising earnestness with which he pursued it. No rank escapes his censure. The soothsayers, and other professors of occult arts, who found in Judah an only too ready welcome; the men of wealth and influence, who ignored the responsibilities of office or position; the leaders of opinion, who possessed weight in the government, or gave a tone to society; the irreligious, shortsighted politician, who nevertheless knew how to put forward views in an attractive and plausible guise; a powerful minister, whose policy he saw was calculated to jeopardize the State; the women, whose frivolity and thoughtlessness on two distinct occasions suggested to him his darkest apprehensions for the future, the masses, whom he saw sunk in indifference or formalism; the king himself, whether it were Ahaz, in his wilfulness and insincerity, or Hezekiah listening incautiously to the overtures of a foreign potentate,—all in turn received his bold and fearless rebuke." [62] The passage indicates with singular com-

[59] Ibid 3:10–26.
[60] Ibid. 28 7–10.
[61] Ibid 30 10–11
[62] Driver, "Isaiah   His Life and Times," pp 108. 109

pleteness the course of Isaiah's lifelong conflict with the dominant tendencies of his age,—superstition, immorality in private
and disloyalty in public conduct.

Like Amos, Isaiah considers the judgment as unavoidable.
He sees that the case is hopeless, and that the people cannot
profit by his words, he knows that they are doomed. The
nation as a whole is too utterly corrupt, apathetic, and spiritually blind for real repentance. A people who have lived· heedless of all warnings, scoffing at all attempts to teach them the
way, who continue in sin despite warnings and punishments,
cannot survive but will be destroyed. A visible and physical,
a mighty and irresistible judgment must fall upon the nation.[63]
The rotten, which is by far the greater part, must be cut off,
the people must be purified, the dross removed.[64] The people
will be punished for their sins by material suffering; privation,
captivity and death will be their lot.

Like Hosea, Isaiah sees in the judgment not the end but the
beginning of the true salvation. Yet the manner of realization
is singularly his own. He feels that not all of his people can
be justly punished, because there are some who are susceptible
of good, who can be classed as being worthy of living in the
true perfect moral state, the Kingdom of God on earth. These
are the "very small remnant,"[65] the "holy seed" from which
the future Israel shall burst forth. They shall survive alone
on the earth and develop free and unchecked and will eventually
constitute the nation Israel will be purged, but not destroyed.

This introduces to us Isaiah's theory of social reconstruction,
or utopianism, which presents a considerable variation from
that of Amos and Hosea. It is a fruitful and positive program
of salvation by faith, and centers about his own expression:
"If you have not faith, verily ye shall not endure";[66] and we
may add: "If you have faith, a perfect life lies before you."
Isaiah feels that only by refraining from action and trusting
in Jehovah, by abandoning all efforts at self-defense and per-

[63] This actually occurs in 722 B C, when Israel disappears, crushed by
Assyria.
[64] Isaiah 1:25.
[65] Ibid. 1:9; 10:20–22.
[66] Ibid. 7.9.

sonal aggrandizement, and relying utterly on Jehovah can
the people hope to attain the perfect future life. The classic
verse in which he formulates this principle and which might
be prefixed as the motto to his book is: "By repenting and
remaining quiet you would have been delivered; in quietness
and pious trust you would have found your strength." [67] In
another passage he shows that by faith, by laying the coal of
righteousness upon the lips, is iniquity taken away and sin
purged.[68]

This also applies to the material strength and political safe-
guarding of the nation. Here he advocates trust in Jehovah
as against political intrigue. This aspect of his idea of faith
is in many respects the same principle that underlies the viewpoint of all the literary prophets, but Isaiah developed the idea
more explicitly than any of the others, for he was the first to
make it clear that trust in Jehovah meant for a nation righteous government, a perfectly conducted state, a state in conformity with the divine standard of holiness and one altogether protected against entangling alliances and unfortunate obligations.
But he defines this holiness in the purely ethical sense. The
people and the nation will only be holy as they observe the
fundamental ethical precepts. When that is the case "justice
will be the rule, and righteousness the standard." [69] Furthermore, the people must cast aside their loftiness and hauteur
and recognize the exalted state and majesty of Jehovah.[70]

Isaiah, more emphatically than any other, insists that mankind endures, progresses, attains perfection, not so much by
means of material forces or the prevalent doctrine of economic
necessity, as by the purely ethical and spiritual forces. When
these essential forces are not in the ascendancy, the life of nations as well as of individuals is doomed to wastage and destruction; when they are, there will be advance, enlightenment,
happiness without end. Jehovah will guide and care for His
people.

Isaiah was also the revealer of a better mundane state to

[67] Ibid 30 15, 7 4; 8·12 ff ; 28 16 ff.
[68] Ibid. 6 3–8.
[69] Ibid 28·17
[70] Ibid. 2 10 12.

come. It might be well to state here that the conception of heaven, as the abode or final dwelling-place of the perfected people of God, so familiar to us, was unknown to the prophets. Heaven was the abode of Jehovah alone. Furthermore, the belief in a future life and future reward and punishment was also almost entirely absent from the utterances of the prophets.[71] Hence the perfect state was on earth and the perfection of the people was attained not by their being transplanted to the sphere of Jehovah's abode but by His coming down and dwelling among them. Isaiah's vision is one of a transfigured city of this kind, and a more marvelous Utopia has never been conceived.

It is to be governed by a righteous king who shall so reform the nobles and princes that they shall be a true aristocracy, the protectors and helpers of the people.[72] He is to be a descendant of Jesse, hence a Davidic king. He is to be endowed with all the gifts of the practical ruler, having strength and wisdom, the spirit of counsel and quick understanding, and a highly developed religious sense. He will be a righteous and faithful ruler, protecting and elevating the weak and crushing the wicked oppressors.[73] He will be called "Wonderful, Counsellor, the Prince of Peace." [74] Physical human sufferings and afflictions shall be no more: "Then the eyes of the blind shall be opened, and the ears of the deaf shall be unstopped. Then shall the lame man leap, and the tongue of the dumb sing." [75] There will be a moral and intellectual improvement of the commonalty. Those who are now dull shall learn to use their eyes and ears. Men in general will learn to judge truly and call things by their right names. To work iniquity and practice hypocrisy will be unknown.[76]

All nature shall be tranquil and bring forth in abundance. The wilderness and solitary places shall be tilled, "the desert

[71] See Davidson, A. B., "Old Testament Prophecy," Edinburgh, 1912, p 310; Rauchenbusch, W., "Christianity and the Social Crises," New York, 1913, p. 17.
[72] Isaiah 32:1.
[73] Ibid. 11·1–5
[74] Ibid. 9·6.
[75] Ibid. 35 5–6.
[76] Ibid. 32:3–6

shall rejoice, and blossom as a rose." [77]   Even that which
remains rough pasture will be made safe for flocks. "And the
parched ground shall become a pool, and the thirsty land
springs of water." [78]

The animal world will be regenerated. "The wolf also
shall dwell with the lamb, and the leopard shall lie down with
the kid; and the calf and the young lion and the fatling together; and a little child shall lead them. And the cow and
the bear shall feed; their young ones shall lie down together;
and the lion shall eat straw like an ox. And the sucking child
shall play on the hole of the asp, and the weaned child shall put
his hand on the cockatrice's den. They shall not hurt or destroy in all my holy mountain." [79]   All fierce and dangerous
beasts shall become tame and gentle. The lion and the serpent
will be the playmates of the child.

It shall be a day of universal peace. Nations "shall beat
their swords into plowshares, and their spears into pruning
hooks; nation shall not lift up sword against nation, neither
shall they learn war any more." [80]

It will be a wonderful time: all will be happiness and contentment. "The ransomed of the Lord shall return, and come
to Zion with songs and everlasting joy upon their heads: they
shall obtain joy and gladness and sorrow and sighing shall flee
away." [81]   This is the idyllic state, the glories of which are
to be inherited by the "Remnant," the survivors of the catastrophe.

It is in Isaiah that we really have the first true and adequate
conception of a Messianic reign. The earlier prophets do not
refer to it much, although it was current in Israel at a much
earlier time.[82]   The literary prophets took this traditional
material, purged it of its heathen elements and gave it a
distinctly ethical character. But even so the clearcut expressions are few. Amos has a single reference to it, that about

[77] Ibid 35·1.
[78] Ibid 35·7
[79] Ibid. 11.6–9.
[80] Ibid. 2:4.
[81] Ibid 35 10
[82] Knudson. op. cit., p. 156.
[88] Amos 9:11·

the tabernacle of David, and that is only an allusion to the Davidic house. It is in the prophecies of the Assyrian age, particularly Isaiah and his contemporary Micah, that the doctrine is most profoundly developed. This doctrine is probably the product of its age. The period in which it appeared was one of extreme danger. The monarchy was threatened with extinction by the pressing encroachment of Assyria on the east, and the best men, rallying about it, refused to allow the thought of its destruction to find a place in their minds. Hence we find the ideas of Immanuel, the Virgin's Son, the Mighty God, the Prince of Peace, the Everlasting Father in Isaiah [84] and that of Bethlehem Ephratah in Micah.[85] These are the first prophecies of the Messiah's glory. The essence of these predictions was the hope that in due time God would create a new and higher social and moral order in Israel and in the world. This king belonged to the latter days, the time of the final perfection of the Kingdom of God upon earth,[86] for the Kingdom of God still stood upon the earth, though, to be sure, it was a transfigured earth. Glazebrook, tells us [87] "Isaiah's vision did not reach beyond a near horizon . . . ; the king he looked for was a literal king of a small and feeble nation." But this vision became but the first stage in the development of a great thought, which, nourished by the religious experiences of ages, was afterward embodied in a larger and nobler form. And as Glazebrook further says,[88] "in the light of that development the Jewish people were justified in regarding Isaiah's words as prophetic of issues beyond his purview, and the Christian Church in applying the titles, which he designed for a prince of his own day, to another Son of David seven centuries later at Bethlehem."

One of the outstanding characteristics of the Messianic hope, due doubtless to the fact that it is to be realized in some distant future time, is its marked idealism. This idealism is fre-

[84] Isaiah 9·6
[85] Micah 5 2.
[86] Davidson, A. B., "Old Testament Prophecy," Edinburgh, 1912, p 310
[87] Glazebrook, M. D., "Studies in the Book of Isaiah," Oxford, 1910, p. 92
[88] Ibid. p. 92.

quently poetical and produces exquisite pictures of physical abundance or perfection in nature. But it is chiefly moral idealism that characterizes the representations. Freedom from evil, not only in the physical sense, but also in the moral sense, is to be attained. The ethical irregularities, now so tremendously detrimental in checkmating our efforts at social betterment, will be non-existent. People will be neither un-moral nor immoral, but will have a profound sense of their duties and responsibilities as units of a greater human whole. Hence the ideal of universal peace plays such a prominent part.

Just what the utopianistic effect of Isaiah's conception of the Messianic ideal has been and is, it is difficult to say, but it doubtless is very considerable. It surely has been effective in fixing thought on the differences between our present ways and motives and those presented in the idyllic picture; and such contrast frequently prompts to imitation of the superior. Furthermore, the emphasis placed upon this hope has brought into prominence, in a striking way, the ethical demands for realizing the Kingdom of God, making them a matter of widespread knowledge, if not of actual obligation and acceptance. What is more, the Messianic age, belonging to the future, and therefore ideal, is a weighty factor in promoting the faith and hope of a people. To have a goal, the characteristics of which are perfection in every regard, cannot but draw the glance forward and upward and provide a norm by which the present can be more accurately appraised.

e. JEREMIAH

In searching for the utopianistic elements in the prophets we find those of Jeremiah so pure and pronounced, so superior to those of his predecessors, that we can properly and justly place him at their head in this regard. But before considering these aspects of his activity we must establish him both as individual and as a representative of his time

Jeremiah, tender and emotional, stands out in marked contrast to the austere and pitiless Amos. While Amos is filled with wrath at the backslidings and mistakes of his people, Jeremiah is oppressed with grief. Mentally and emotionally he is more nearly akin to Hosea; both have tenderness and sympathy: both are preëminently devout, and after a survey of Jeremiah's utterances it is easily discernible that he was powerfully influenced by Hosea, and that he perhaps even looked upon him as his prototype.[89]

Jeremiah differs again from Isaiah. In addition to his tenderness he was by nature weak, timid, distrustful of his own powers, while Isaiah was strong, self-reliant, equal to any emergency. Nor does he compare with Isaiah in brilliancy, in literary power, or in majesty of conception. His outstanding characteristics are his depth of feeling, his insight into human nature, his power of sympathy, and his grasp of great spiritual truths.

Jeremiah, owing to his intimate and singular habit of self-revelation, has given information enabling us to speak of his life with considerable certainty. He was born about 650 B. C., at Anathoth, a small village near Jerusalem.[90] He came of a priestly family, descended through Abiothar, the high priest of David, from Moses,[91] and the impression is that he did not live in poor circumstances. Naturally Jeremiah early became proficient in Israelitish lore, trained to regard and cherish the proudest and dearest recollections of the past. Furthermore, he was carefully educated, and we see evidences of this and his social heredity in many allusions to the ancient literature and history of Israel in his book. His prophetic activity extended from 626 to 586 B. C. He was, according to Jewish tradition, stoned by an infuriated mob in the latter year in Egypt, whither a part of his people had fled to escape the invasion of Judah and the expected persecutions by Nebuchadnezzar.[92]

Jeremiah's time was one of profound internal and also of external unrest. At the beginning of Jeremiah's ministry there was an irruption of northern barbarians, the Scythians, who swept over the country, as later did the Huns over another part of the world. This invasion wrought widespread deso-

[89] Cornill, "Prophets of Israel," pp. 91, 92
[90] Jeremiah 1:1.
[91] Cornill, op. cit, p. 92.
[92] Ibid. p 107.

lation in the Assyrian empire, and doubtless was an indirect cause of the empire's end, which came with the fall of Nineveh in 606 B. C., at the hands of the allied Medes and Chaldeans. At the same time the Egyptian hosts under Pharaoh-Necho were attempting to secure for themselves certain coveted portions of the heritage of Assyria, one part of which happened to be Syria. In 605 Nebuchadnezzar met the forces of Necho and decisively defeated them. This gave Syria and Palestine to the new Babylonian empire, in whose power they remained until the capture of Babylon in 538 B. C. Judah as a small buffer state naturally suffered fearfully as the result of these epochal world movements.

Internally, however, chaotic conditions also existed. There was a constant change of world masters, which was accompanied by a change of national kings. Josiah's reign was cut short by his tragic death on the battlefield of Megiddo where his troops, Assyrians in allegiance, attempted to stay the eastward advance of Necho. His younger son Jehoahaz, proclaimed king by the people, was three months later carried away as a captive. In his stead Jehoiakim, older son of Josiah, ascended the throne as a vassal of Necho. With the subsequent change of hands, he became tributary to Nebuchadnezzar. In 597 B. C. the people revolted, and before the Babylonian army could reach them, Jehoiakim died and was succeeded by his son Jehoiachin After a brief reign of three months he was forced to surrender to Nebuchadnezzar, and along with his princes, nobles and many of the priests was carried captive to Babylon. This passionate longing for independence again asserted itself under the new king Zedekiah, and led to another revolt which resulted in the capture and destruction of Jerusalem in 586 B. C.[93]

Social, moral and religious affairs were in equally desperate straits, perhaps even worse than the deplorable political conditions. There had been a progressive deterioration of the people since the terrific pronouncements of Amos in the eighth century. The people were more hardened to their evils; they

[93] For elaboration of facts, see Smith, H P, "Old Testament History," pp 275–300; Smith, H. P, "The Religion of Israel," pp. 163–169.

were worse than their fathers,[94] and transgressed, not unconsciously, but wilfully. Jeremiah does not dwell so long upon social evils of his time as Amos did but he does mention many of the sins of which the people were guilty. Among these are vanity,[95] hard-heartedness,[96] covetousness,[97] lies and swearing,[98] deceit,[99] adultery, lewdness, unashamed licentiousness,[100] prevalence of dishonesty and cheating,[101] and murder.[102] There was widespread and insolent profligacy and impurity and a bent toward evil heretofore unparalleled. Religiously, affairs were hopelessly distracting, affording the prophet, as also Hosea, occasion for bitter mourning, but also for stern rebuke. Irreligion was sweeping the land.[103] The people were ridden with false prophets, who calumniated the true prophet, misled the nation with their false visions and slippery ways, walked in lies and committed adultery.[104] The priests were utterly corrupt, giving divinations of Baal; heathenish customs were everywhere throughout the land;[105] even child sacrifice had been reintroduced.[106] The people were steeped in a lifeless ritualism, combined with an easy-going moderatism, the end of which was utter corruption. Truly, it was a troublous age needing a "jeremiad." They were to be destroyed by sword, famine and pestilence.[107]

Jeremiah, like his predecessors, felt that the people were doomed, that the catastrophe was not only inevitable but imminent. It may be wondered why the prophets held this view in conjunction with the message of hope, common to all of them. Buttenwieser gives a reason to which we can readily

[94] Jeremiah 16·12.
[95] Ibid. 2.5.
[96] Ibid. 5:28.
[97] Ibid. 22:17.
[98] Ibid. 9 3; 23·10; 29·23
[99] Ibid 5·27, 8:5; 9 5–6.
[100] Ibid. 5:7, 8 12; 9.2, 13:27; 23:10, 29:23.
[101] Ibid. 23·13.
[102] Ibid. 7:5–9; 22:17
[103] Ibid. 11:10, 13; 22:9.
[104] Ibid 2·8; 5:13, 30–31; 14:14; 23:9–16, 25–27; 29:8.
[105] 13:27; 19:4.
[106] 7:31; 19:5
[107] Ibid 22 6–8; 29.17–18

give credence: "They were aware from the outset that they were preaching to deaf ears, for they fully realized the insuperable difference in religious views which separated them from the people; and they did not fail to make clear their belief that by nothing short of the overthrow of the whole religious-social structure could the people be brought to the realization of their delusions and superstitious beliefs.[108]   It was for the furtherance of the ultimate purpose which the prophets believed God pursued in calling them, and not because they hoped their exhortations might be heeded by their contemporaries, that they took pains to set forth how the doom might be averted." [109] And so Jeremiah despaired of the immediate redemption of the people.   Only after a long period of suffering in exile would they finally be cleansed from their errors and their corruption.[110]

We now approach Jeremiah's greatest contribution not only to prophecy, but also to the development of religion,—his utopianism.   Jeremiah, it is true, speaks of an ideal future state, which we will briefly consider, but that which demands our closest attention is this new aspect, which he has given to the prophetic form of ethico-religious utopianism, as we have termed it.   It is as an exponent of individual spirituality that Jeremiah stands without a peer.   In the earlier prophets there was a strong expression of tribal solidarity; the religion and ethics were primarily a national or group affair; a matter of group conduct and morals, a matter of collective responsibility. It was Jeremiah who first made the soul of the individual the true seat of pure religion and the individual conscience the basis of social ethics, who first explicitly formulated the new idea of moral freedom and responsibility.   He says:

> "In those days (i. e., days of future Israel) they shall
> say no more,
> 'The fathers have eaten a sour grape,
> And the children's teeth are set on edge'
> But *every one shall die for his own iniquity*:

[108] For confirmation of this see Ibid 13 23; 17·1–3
[109] Buttenwieser, M , "The Prophets of Israel," pp. 177–178.
[110] Jeremiah 13 24–27.

Every man that eateth the sour grape,
His teeth shall be set on edge." [111]

As Duhm says, "He first discovered the soul and its significance
for religion." But it can also be seen that he discovered the
idea of individual accountability. This does not mean that he
entirely gave up the national point of view, for he continued
to address the people as a nation throughout his ministry. But
it does mean that he revised the conception of religion, made
it not only widespread and pure, but also vital, and more transcendent. Its essential nature came to consist in personal
fellowship with Jehovah, an ascription also by implication of
new importance to the individual. This idea went far to clear
up the confusion between ritual and worship, between mere
conformity to convention and true ethical activity. It made
the individual the motor of social betterment, and personally
responsible for his own activities. Efforts to be utopianistic
must be such that they harmonize with the will of Jehovah and
this is attained by seeking Jehovah by "circumcision of the
heart" and by living righteously. [112] Right life and true piety
consist in the fellowship of the individual soul with Jehovah.
Jeremiah goes a step further and makes universal this individual fellowship with Jehovah—this newly perceived means
of regeneration. He pictures Jehovah as offering it to all the
peoples of the earth, as making possible the spiritual regeneration of all mankind. [113]

It is not surprising that Jeremiah should be the one to give
expression to this body of doctrine. The exigencies and trials
of his life—a ministry of strife, suffering, loneliness, villifi-
cation, imprisonment and martyrdom—were such as would
lead him to seek companionship, comfort, and hope elsewhere
than among men, who denied him these. Hence Jeremiah in
his solitude and affliction, in his travail of spirit, developed a
conscious, personal relationship to Jehovah,—a more spiritual
relationship than we have evidence of in the case of any of his

[111] Ibid. 31: 29–30. See whole passage 31 29–34 Italics mine.
[112] For further evidence on facts expressed see Ibid 4:3, 4.
[113] Ibid. 16:19–21.

predecessors. Furthermore, he illustrated his new conception in his own life, and by his loyal adherence served as a noble and inspiring example.

The Utopia of Jeremiah belongs to the later discussion of utopianism. The picture he draws is not the superlatively beautiful one of Isaiah, to be sure, and yet it is sufficient to show that he believed in an ideal future social state which was to come to a socialized people who should passionately desire it. With wonderful insight he saw that this would come about as a result of individual and social regeneration and that united endeavor which comes when individuals are stirred by participation in a great common enterprise. It will be a marvelous restoration of the various remnants of Israel brought together from the ends of the earth,[114] and they shall be governed by a righteous branch of the house of David,[115] who shall execute judgment and justice on the earth,[116] and they shall be ministered unto by a purified family of Levites; [117] and they shall walk by the rivers of waters in a straight way, wherein they shall not stumble.[118] Mourning will be turned into joy and both young and old will rejoice and be merry.[119] The temporal blessings will be profuse: [120] goodness and prosperity shall be abundant; palaces shall be rebuilt and communities restored; [121] and Jehovah of righteousness shall keep watch over His own, and the people shall all know Him from the least unto the greatest.[122] Thus does Jeremiah, in his conception of the future, share in common with the other prophets the view that there was to be a marvelous interposition of Jehovah resulting in the establishment of a new social, moral and religious order.

[114] Ibid. 23: 8, 30 3, 8; 31: 8, 33: 15.
[115] Jeremiah, it is seen, also introduces the idea of a Davidic king and alludes to Messianic times, as did Isaiah before him.
[116] Ibid. 23·5
[117] Ibid. 33:22.
[118] Ibid 31 9
[119] Ibid. 31:13
[120] Ibid 31.12
[121] Ibid. 30 18–20.
[122] Ibid. 31.34.

f. Ezekiel

Perhaps the most influential of the characters of the prophetic cycle we are considering is Ezekiel.[123]   He was the son of the priest Buzi of the Temple of Jerusalem and had doubtless received his youthful training in the Temple and later himself served as a priest. He manifests by his tastes and interests an intimate acquaintance with the Temple and its ceremonial institutions. He was also well acquainted with the earlier history and literature of his race as his peculiar literary style and figures so well indicate. He was among those "good figs," to use Jeremiah's expression, who were carried off to Babylonian captivity by Nebuchadnezzar in 597 B. C. He and his fellow exiles formed an organized community, presided over by elders, at Tel-Abib, on the banks of the canal Chebar—the great Khabaru Canal which, as we learn from contemporary inscriptions, ran from the great city of Babylon eastward to Nippur.[124] In the year 593 B. C. he assumed the rôle of a prophet which he maintained for at least twenty-two years. He was thus the first prophet of the exile and his messages are in many instances colored by the circumstances of his field of labor.

Ezekiel was one of the most striking and dramatic characters in the history of Israel. In temperament he was stern and severe, strong and relentless, never permitting the tenderer tones of the heart to come into play, in this respect resembling Amos and Isaiah rather than Hosea and Jeremiah. In personality he also resembled Isaiah, being a man of a thoroughly practical nature with a wonderfully sharp perception of the problems and needs of his age, and with the same terrible yet lofty moral earnestness. He was harsh and resolute in his condemnation of the sins of his nation, tremendously intense in his zeal for righteousness, and bold, almost dogmatic, in proclaiming his convictions. His idealism, though profound and almost sensational, never was poetic, although it was portrayed

---

[123] Smith, H. P , says of Ezekiel, "Taking him all in all he is the most influential man that we find in the whole course of Hebrew history."

[124] Kent, C. F., "The Kings and Prophets of Israel and Judah," New York, 1909, p. 276.

with a wealth of dramatic imagery and symbolism. His was a wonderful capacity for grand and impressive conceptions, combined with an unusual proficiency in mathematical calculation and exactness of detail. His work, like that of the other prophets, was to a considerable extent a transformation or elaboration of that of his predecessors. Particularly did he enlarge, revise, and present with tremendous force Jeremiah's doctrine of religious subjectivism and individual responsibility, the discussion of which, as it touches upon our utopianistic hypothesis, will occupy our attention here.

However, before taking this up we must again orientate ourselves in his social background as we gather it from Ezekiel's pages. The charges which he brings against Israel are in many respects practically the same as those found in the preceding prophets, though in some cases more severe. On the whole, princes, priests and people were an abandoned race. The people and especially the princes had been guilty of oppression and immorality. Gross acts of injustice were committed upon the poor, the defenseless and the godly patriots. The nobles shed blood "every one according to his power." Men sold testimony against the truly innocent that led to murder; they carried on sharp, greedy business practices; they exacted usury and were harsh and unjust to debtors. The strong oppressed the weak; orphans and widows were abused and cheated; filial duty had been wanting; horrible immoralities, lewdness, sexual abomination and murder were flagrantly rife.[125]

Idolatry and other heathen abominations profaned their true worship. They ate flesh with the blood in it, disregarded the Sabbath, polluted the Temple with ceremonial and moral defilements, worshiped strange gods in the high places.[126] False prophets prowled about like jackals, lying to the people, misleading them by concealing the actual frightful condition of their social structure.[127] And so we might go on; this, however, is enough to show the deplorable condition of things.

But Ezekiel offers one singular exception to the other proph-

[125] Ezekiel 9:9; 11: 6, 22
[126] Ibid 6·1–14; 8:1–18; 16:1–43.
[127] Ibid. 13:1–7.

ets. We find in his book no vitriolic polemic against cere- monialism. He places ritual offenses alongside of the moral [128] and devotes much of his work to a detailed explanation of the externals of religion. Ezekiel here followed out a line of de- velopment begun by the author of Deuteronomy, who felt that the best way to promote the interests of true religion was not to repudiate the sacrificial cult altogether, but to moralize it and make it a medium for the expression of religious truth. In commenting on this, Knudson makes a statement which has sociological significance, that is it indicates the necessary place of ritual in religion. He says,[129] "Ritual, in and of itself, is no necessary part of genuine religion. On the contrary, it frequently carries with it much that is materialistic and un- spiritual. But over and against this, it should be borne in mind that there are many non-essential things in religion that are essential in order to make religion effective in the world. These non-essentials vary from age to age. But they exist in every age. And it is an evidence of true religious statesman- ship to be able to single them out and make them the efficient means of religious culture." This power and insight Ezekiel possessed, utilizing the ritual as a core about which he attempted to wind the moral precepts, hoping in that way to keep the people stable in the time of the extreme stress and strains of national prostration.

On the basis of the social situation just described, Ezekiel like the other prophets, predicts the doom of his people. [130] But Ezekiel's message of doom was delivered under different circumstances than those which attended the preaching of the others, since his auditors were already in exile, and expected a speedy return to their native land. This made them even less disposed to listen with favor to a prediction of Jerusalem's fall.

Jeremiah, it will be remembered, in the new Covenant,[131]

[128] Ibid. 22.

[129] Op. cit , p. 203.

[130] Ezekiel 7 2–4; 30 7

[131] This is a new Covenant which Jehovah made with the people accord- ing to Hosea 2·18–22 as distinct from the one made by Jehovah with Moses.

in which Jehovah wrote His law in the hearts of the people and evoked in them a passionate loyalty and obedience, claimed that Jehovah had established an immediate relation with each individual. He thus created the foundation of a true ethico-religious individualism and proclaimed the law of individual retribution. But while Jeremiah little more than mentions it, Ezekiel makes it the dominant feature of his work.[132] He even goes further. In pre-exilic times the individual had not been, and could not be, thought of apart from his family and nation, and his soul had been conceived of as the property of family and nation, but Ezekiel asserts that the individual soul is a unit of absolute worth in itself.[133] There is no wholesale condemnation and no salvation wholesale of men, for every one is judged by himself.

If social perfection comes to pass it will not take place by wholesale, but each individual must be dealt with separately. He takes one more step in advance and shows that the individual himself must consciously desire this change, that he must undergo a complete change of character. Furthermore, he goes on to say that it is within the power of every individual to change his own character and so determine for himself what his own lot is to be.[134] Ezekiel gives us here the first expression we find of the idea of a new birth, of the need of complete regeneration. Our study shows this idea of a new birth arises in the course of the evolution of the idea of individual responsibility.

Another significant idea introduced by Ezekiel, is that the welfare of the individual after he has undergone this complete change, is in no wise affected by his own past or by the sins or righteousness of his fathers.[135] He can throw off the shackles that bind him to the past, and make a new beginning totally different from that of the past. "The son shall not bear the iniquity of the father, neither shall the father bear the iniquity of the son." [136] His own righteousness raises him above the

[132] Ibid 3 16–21; 14.12–20; 18.1–32; 33.1–20.
[133] Ibid. 18:4
[134] Ibid 18: 21–32; 33·10–20
[135] Ibid 14.12–20; 18.20–28.
[136] Ibid 18 20.

sweep of the doom that befalls the sinful individual or the sinful nation. And since this righteousness is open to his own achievement he possesses moral freedom, and his destiny is the shaping of his own will; he is the master of his own fate, the conqueror of his own soul. Thus the community and nation as a moral and religious unit disappear and its people become self-willing moral agents, each of which pursues independently his own way, wholly unaffected by the rest, responsible only for his own acts, working out his own salvation or his own doom, his outward lot harmonizing with his inner character.

We must now pause long enough to consider a criticism or two. Subsequent study of the individual has shown that Ezekiel's doctrine of the individual responsibility is much too rigid and severe. The degree of regeneration of which the individual is capable is always conditioned in some degree by his own past and by both the physical and social heredity of his fathers. There are elements in every man's nature and lot which lie outside the sphere of his own volition. The individual cannot be accurately and justly judged unless we do know his actual physical, mental and spiritual constitution. Secondly, it inevitably follows from Ezekiel's view that a man's outward fortunes are the infallible witness to his internal character and to the actual condition in which he stands before Jehovah. This is obviously false and served as a continual stumbling-block in the two great popular Jewish handbooks— the Psalter and the Book of Proverbs—which both echo Ezekiel's doctrine. Misfortune and pain were incontrovertible evidence of sin. Hence a man though seemingly righteous, but now suffering some affliction, was *per se* an example of hidden wickedness at length unmasked and drawing upon him a fitting retribution. These incongruities were questioned and subsequently rejected in Job and Ecclesiastes.[137]

It may be asked, "What is the utopianistic course to be pursued according to Ezekiel?" Ezekiel states it concisely: "If the wicked will turn from all his sins that he hath committed,

[137] Charles, R. H., "Eschatology: Hebrew, Jewish and Christian," London, 1913, p. 64 ff. Also Job 19:25–27.

and keep all my statutes, and do that which is lawful and right, he shall surely live, he shall not die." [138] This statement is broad enough to embrace all the religious, moral and legal phases of conduct, and Ezekiel desires to have them all included, and demands even more, for there must also be a new heart and a new mind. All violations of the law, all injustice between man and man, all infringements of the legal codes are punished by earthly suffering and misfortune, by a righteous God. To refrain from all these and to be regenerated ethically and spiritually is to live the ideal life in conformity with the will of Jehovah.

But now what sort of an ideal world are these reborn, perfect individuals to live in? This introduces us to Ezekiel's Utopia, or Holy State—a real theocracy. But before taking this up we must briefly consider certain Messianic elements found on his pages. In Chapters 34 and 37 we have Ezekiel's prophetic conception of a future Messianic state which in its main outlines does not differ materially from that of the preceding prophets. It is a glorious restoration of both Israel and Judah [139] to their former land which also it again blessed with great productivity and abundance [140] The people will be cleansed of all their abominations and transgressions and all will be blessing, security and happiness. They shall be shepherded forever by David, the servant of Jehovah.[142] "My tabernacle also," Jehovah says, "shall be with them; and I will be their God, and they shall be my people." [143]

Chapters 38 and 39, which may be regarded as a supplement to the preceding chapters, present a new view of the Messianic era, an element absent in the other books discussed. After Israel has for some time been dwelling in her restored native land she is to be attacked by the peoples of the land of Magog under the leadership of Gog. The invading hosts are to be defeated and destroyed with terrible slaughter upon the

[138] Ezekiel 18: 21.
[139] Ezekiel 37:15–28.
[140] Ibid 36.1–15.
[141] Ibid. 37 23
[142] Ibid. 34: 24; 37: 24, 25.
[143] Ibid. 37 27

mountains of Israel. After Gog and his multitude have been
buried and the débris cleared away, then shall the final and
universal reign of peace be ushered in. While this idea of an
attack upon Israel by the nations of the world was not new,
since it formed part of traditional eschatology,[144] Ezekiel was
the first to date it in the distant future after the Messianic era
had been introduced. This conception of Ezekiel exerted an
important influence on the Apocalyptic, which we will presently
consider.

In Chapters 40 and 48 we have the famous description of Ezekiel's future Kingdom of God or New Jerusalem. Here he
gives us an elaborate sketch of repatriated Israel, which is not
so much a political commonwealth as it is an ecclesiastical organization or state. The community of worshipers, their
priests and the physical and mechanical sides of their worship
are vividly in the foreground and are presented with an elaboration of architectural and administrative details characteristic
of the later Utopians of the Middle Ages. Prominent is the
Temple and its services. The minutest details as to size, position, and surroundings are given. Methods and place of sacrifice are closely described. Precise information as to the priesthood, its selection, duties, and maintenance are given. Rules
are laid down to insure the purity of the ceremony, correctness
of the elaborate ritual, and the proper observance of the feasts,
seasons, and the Sabbath. In fact, everything necessary to
insure the formal holiness and prescribed purity of the people
of a common faith is provided for in this Holy State   Some of
the old social convictions also still exist in it. The nation was
to be ruled by a prince (not of the Davidic line) who was to be
a tyrant no more;[145] the nobles were to "remove violence and
spoil, and execute justice and righteousness"; harsh exactions
were to be abolished and absolute fairness was to obtain: [146]
The land was to be equitably divided among all the people, and
the stranger was to share as the homeborn.[147] And yet the
pleas for the abandonment of injustice, oppression and moral

144 Ibid. 38:18.
145 Ibid 46:18.
146 Ibid. 45. 9–12.
147 Ibid 47. 22–23.

bankruptcy so much stressed by the older prophets are here dim and shadowy. Here holiness is the fundamental requirement, and by holiness is meant chiefly ceremonial correctness and attention to minutiæ. The ideal state is completely absorbed in the church.

In this theocracy we find the presence of an element, though not explicitly expressed, which was altogether wanting in the earlier views. It is that of religious fellowship.[148]   Ezekiel was the first to notice how essential union and cooperation are in all great undertakings, hence he regarded it as part of his mission to educate his compatriots to live together as members of a community ought to live.

The Hebrew nation as such had ceased to exist before Ezekiel had started to work out the details of his theocracy, and with its passing the emphasis passed from the great national and human interests to an ecclesiastical attitude of mind. Hence knowing that his generation would never see Jerusalem he occupied himself in preparing for his countrymen a new constitution for the reorganized, perfect nation which should ultimately come   He conceived it as being inhabited only by those purified and regenerated men and women, who being instructed in His commandments, and versed in His laws, were fit to live in this God's world, hence he called it "Jehovah is there." [149]

g. DEUTERO-ISAIAH

Deutero-Isaiah is the last of the prophets we are to treat individually, and he in many respects is the crowning point of this prophetic cycle   Deutero-Isaiah is the unnamed exilic and post-exilic prophet whose prophetic period began about 540 B. C. and extended for an uncertain period of time, perhaps even into the period of the freedom of the Israelites.   The prophecies assigned to him are found in Chapters 40 to 66 of Isaiah, hence the name, Second or Deutero-Isaiah.   Scholars are now practically unanimous in assigning these chapters to an

[148] This is the spirit which pervades 37: 22-27, also Chapters 40-48 Similar interpretations given by Cornill op cit, p 120, and Baldwin, E C, "Our Modern Debt to Israel," Boston 1913, pp 64, 65
[149] Ezekiel 48 35

author during the time of the exiles,[150] some even going so far as to divide these chapters up among two writers, Chapters 40–55 being thought to be the work of a writer at the end of the exile, and Chapters 56–66 those of a writer of the period immediately following the exile, this being their inference from the context. But this does not necessarily imply a difference of authorship, though the conflictions suggest that we have works written for a different purpose and under different conditions. We will treat these two sections as the work of the same author writing at different times, considering Chapters 55–66 as the work of the same author during his residence in Jerusalem after the return from the Babylonian captivity.

Of the life of this author we know nothing, since he did not attach his name to his writings, nor did he give them any title or superscription, nor did he anywhere give us those intimate extracts of his personal life that we found among some of the other prophets discussed. Furthermore his works are singularly lacking in local coloring so we will make no attempt to add to the numerous distracting assumptions on this score; but will devote ourselves largely to the exposition of his idea of universal restoration and the presentation of his eternal commonwealth.

Deutero-Isaiah realized that the message the people needed in their national humiliation and depression of spirit was one of comfort and encouragement and not rebuke, and he opens his book with words of this nature.[151] But this does not mean that he took no account of their transgressions and shortcomings. They were far from perfect as a people. They were reminded repeatedly that their sufferings and misfortunes were the result of their own sins.[152] They had dealt treacherously from birth[153] and had eyes that saw not and ears that heard not.[154] Insincerity, obstinacy and idolatry were among their

[150] Among the famous scholars holding this view are: Canon Cheyne, in his "Commentaries", Driver, S R, in "Isaiah His Life and Times": Davidson, A B, in "Old Testament Prophecy"; Smith, G. A., in Expositor's Bible on "Isaiah"; Cornill, C. H., in "Prophets of Israel."

[151] Isaiah 40·1, 2

[152] Ibid 42: 24–25, 43 27; 50:1.

[153] Ibid 48: 8.

[154] Ibid. 42: 13–20

faults.[155] But Deutero-Isaiah, unlike the other prophets, had no message of doom to give to his people. There was no threat of invasion or destruction, no doctrine of the remnant. This was due of course to the altered circumstances of Deutero-Isaiah's ministry. His people were already in exile doing that penance which the earlier prophets had foretold. The purpose of his 'message was rather to arouse the indifferent, to reassure the wavering, to expostulate with the doubting, and to announce with certainty the imminent broad redemption and restoration of the people. Israel was to be delivered from Babylon and her seed was to be gathered from all the corners of the earth where they were now held. They were to be led back through the wildernesses to Jerusalem where the universal kingdom, the new Jerusalem, was to be set up in all its glory.[156] Then Deutero-Isaiah adds another element unknown or at least unmentioned among his predecessor prophets. The new Jerusalem is to be eternal and joy is to be everlasting, world without end.[157] This is the first striking distinction made between the temporal and eternal. And still another new element is the fact that the advantages and privileges of this new Jerusalem are to be participated in by Jew and Gentile alike, by all peoples and all nations.[158] It embraces all men, not the chosen people only as was the case with the former prophets. It is in the addition of these two factors that Deutero-Isaiah has made such tremendous strides forward. Instead of the future hope being confined and exclusive, temporal and passing, he made it broad, catholic and everlasting—truly an unparalleled contribution to the utopian literature of the race.

His description of the new ideal commonwealth differs little from that of his predecessors, particularly Isaiah, but when we remember the nature of its composition and its period of existence, it becomes hallowed with new and unsurpassed glories. Another peculiarity about it is that nowhere does Deutero-Isaiah speak of a future Messiah of the house of David who will rule; he is always concerned simply with Jehovah on the

[155] Ibid. 48: 1-5.
' [156] Ibid. 40 3, 4, 17-20, 43.5, 6, 19-21; 54:11, 12; 55 12, 13.
[157] Ibid 45:17, 51:11
[158] Ibid 42 6; 43·9; 56 1-8; 66·19.

one hand and the selected peoples of the earth on the other.[159] Here then we have the first transition from a quasi-political state under a Messianic king to a truly divine state, in which the people are completely spiritualized. In this ideal nation violence and destruction will be no more, and assured peace and tranquillity will reign throughout the land.[160] Rivers and fountains will break forth and the waste places will be like Eden and the deserts like gardens.[161] Instead of the thorn shall come up the fir tree, and instead of the brier shall come the myrtle tree.[162] The days of mourning shall be ended, for death will be no more. Happy man shall live forever.[163] Labor shall have its just reward.[164] The animal world shall be at peace. As in Isaiah, "The wolf and the lamb shall feed together, and the lion shall eat straw like the bullock: and dust shall be the serpent's meat. They shall not hurt nor destroy in all my holy mountain, saith Jehovah." [165] The inhabitants will all be righteous, possessing the land forever, and thriving upon it like a branch planted and tended by Jehovah, whose growth redounds to His honor. Heaven and earth will be made new again.[166] "All flesh shall worship before me, saith Jehovah." [167]

The utopianism of Deutero-Isaiah is not unlike that of the other prophets in its primary details. But in addition to these it is universal in its scope and application, and eternal after once accomplished. The external restoration, which he so uniquely and brilliantly depicts, reposes entirely upon the internal redemption of the people. There must be individual change of viewpoint, that purging the self of all unrighteousness and corruption and that conscious acceptance of the ways of Jehovah, that Jeremiah and Ezekiel portrayed so splendidly. "Let the wicked forsake his way, and the unrighteous man his thought: and let him return unto the Lord, and he will

[159] Vide Cornill, C H, "Prophets of Israel," p. 135, for confirmation.
[160] Isaiah 53.17.
[161] Ibid. 41.18, 19; 43:19; 51:3.
[162] Ibid. 55 13.
[163] Ibid. 60 20
[164] Ibid. 65:23.
[165] Ibid. 65.25.
[166] Ibid 65 17: 66 22.
[167] Ibid. 66.23.

have mercy upon him; and to our God, for he will abundantly pardon." [168]   But, as was characteristic of Deutero-Isaiah, this essential yet pleasurable relationship with Jehovah, this salvation from a world of evil, and this installation in a world of righteousness was open to all mankind.[169]   Furthermore this salvation offered was to be eternal.   Jehovah said, "My righteousness shall be forever, and my salvation from generation to generation." [170]   The redeemed people were to live lives of righteousness forever.   And this, in its last analysis rested upon the favor and compassion of a God who was both omnipotent and eternal; [171] and the one and only God, [172] knowledge of whom shall be universal.   Thus have we attained the exalted summit of the evolution of prophetic utopianism.

We are perhaps led to ask ourselves, "How are the Gentiles, the people of all nations, to be introduced to and prepared for this perfect life, which, among former prophets, has been the reward of the Hebrews alone?"   This presents another new element in Deutero-Isaiah, of particular interest to the sociologist.   It is service which he portrays as Jehovah's highest call to any people.   In the successive passages in which the prophet speaks of the "Servant of Jehovah" he without question refers to Israel, idealized and personified, as his elect representative and witness among mankind.[174]   In order that Israel might better serve as Servant, in order that it be more fit to give than receive, it has been trained in the hard school of adversity and suffering.   And it is this people prepared by many trials which is to minister to and redeem all peoples.[175]

In this manner is the altruistic note struck by the prophet —the idea of the watchman over others, the brother's keeper— a concept absolutely necessary in any utopianistic scheme.

Thus did Deutero-Isaiah attain to heights which successive

[168] Ibid 55·7, also see 56.1, 2.

[169] Ibid. 49 6

[170] Ibid. 51 6, 8.

[171] Ibid. 40 8, 15–17, 22, 23, 28; 48:12; 55 8, 9; 57.15

[172] Ibid 43 10, 11; 44.6; 45:5, 22

[173] Ibid. 45:23.

[174] Ibid. 41 8–14, also Smith, H P., "The Religion of Israel," p. 257, and Baldwin, E C, "Our Modern Debt to Israel," p. 79 f.

[175] Ibid 49:5, 6

prophets could not excel and which were only surpassed in the first century by one who builded better than we can know and who used the priceless heritage we have discussed as the foundation upon which to erect his magnificent structure.

h.   SUMMARY OF THE PROPHETS

The Hebrew prophets shared the fate of all men who are ahead of their time.   They had caught a glimpse of a larger social and religious purpose in life; of the great ethico-religious aspects of a regenerated mankind and of a constructive program; and consequently looked forward instead of backward; let hope take the place of regret; adopted progress for a watchword instead of conservatism.   These visions and this spirit they attempted to convey to their people.   But these people were so seeped in a past, which at its closing yet scintillated the more brilliantly, and were so enchained by a present which held them enrapt as it blinded and befuddled them, that they refused to strive for that idyllic future when Jehovah shall reign and when justice and righteousness shall be the common attributes.

We must not think that the prophets were hopeless, impractical mystics or visionaries yearning for some world to come; for one and all stand in an intimate relation to the history of their time.   They cared for the world about them with its perplexing social and political, national and international problems.   It was upon this world that they believed the ideal society would eventually emerge.   Whatever the truth was that they had to announce, it was never presented in abstract form, but was based on the condition of the people of their time, the elements of their life, the current moral or political situations, the dangers that threatened and on their attitudes toward prominent forces then existing.   The aim of the prophets was to influence men; therefore they dealt with them as members of the age in which they lived.   Their primary interest is bound up in the needs of their own generation, but their significance was not exhausted after they had done this work, for the principles they asserted were and are fortunately capable of a much wider range of application.

The problems the prophets had to face were essentially those connected with the breaking down of an old moral order—one called upon to endure the breaking up of the social, economic and political systems of the time. This may be due to the intrusion of a pagan people, the expansion of a nation, or the collapse of a governmental or religious system, and the consequent absorption of foreign ideals along with the corruption of the traditional mores. This disintegration resulted in the innumerable evils that we have described in connection with our study of the individual prophets. It is of these predominantly moral evils that the prophets wanted the people purged, hence their messages are essentially ethical messages, tingling with a clearcut conception of righteousness. But the phase of the prophets that interests us the most is the indomitable optimism which led them to speak of an abiding and unfaltering faith in the ultimate triumph of righteousness and justice. This centered about an ethical, social, political and cultural rehabilitation.

The unit to be rehabilitated changed with the course of Hebrew history, again illustrating the adaptation of their teachings to the times. During the time of national stability the prophets conceived of their people as a gigantic personality which sinned as one and must be reconstructed as one. The figures of speech they used expressed this organic and corporate social life. But when the Israelitish nation was crushed and scattered by the foreign invasions, and its people carried into exile or forced to flee into strange lands for protection the emphasis changed The prophets then began to address themselves to the individual life and placed importance upon individual changing of character and individual responsibility. With Deutero-Isaiah we again have a new emphasis Here it is not upon the particular nation or race, nor upon the individual of any nation or race primarily, but it has become universalized, extending to the individuals of all races. Coincident with these changes, but probably not causally related to them, we find another evolution of emphasis taking place. The demands of the earlier prophets were ethical in nature; they demanded spontaneous righteousness and freedom from social corruption. As time passed the prophets stressed this less and began to insist upon correctness of ceremony and upon formality of worship. It is true, this may have been done to give the people something concrete about which to center their religion and their nationalistic hopes in time of national and racial distintegration, but we have no grounds for dogmatically asserting this.

But whatever the emphasis, the purpose of the prophets was the same, viz., to prepare the people for residence in the ideal future state conceived in ethical and social terms. This ideal state with the development of prohpecy came to center about the Messianic hope [176]—the hope for the Messiah or coming Deliverer through whose instrumentality the glories of the future age were to be realized. To prepare themselves for residence in this perfect state, the people had to undergo an evolution, a change which was essentially moral in its nature and which was attainable as the people permitted themselves to come into intimate relationship with Jehovah. This relationship was possible as the people adopted the theocratic law and consciously lived lives having the attributes which Jehovah demanded —righteousness, justice, holiness This implied at first a collective and later an individual effort directed toward the attainment of those qualities, hence it was utopianistic to a very high degree. This utopianism, of course, varied in the stress which was put on one element or the other, but the general principles are as outlined above.

The important thing about this utopianism of the prophets is that it demands not only proper human relations but also an extrahuman, supramundane, theocratic relationship. It implies a change of human character, but also the recognition by the human group, collectively or individually according to the different prophets, of a divine Being, Jehovah. The regenerated individuals are the product of the combined efforts of themselves and Jehovah. Hence the change must be not only ethical, but ethical-religious.

Another fact that has not been over-stressed thus far is that the prophets considered this process of regeneration as natural

[176] Not mentioned by Deutero-Isaiah, however. Vide Deutero-Isaiah above.

and realizable and that they expected the nation, having overcome the adverse conditions of their own day, to be eventually
restored to this perfect and transfigured Messianic state. This
was a broad, general conception, fitted to sustain the hearts of
the men of their time. It, in itself, probably acted as a stimulus to right conduct.

In the centuries that followed the period of the prophets we
have a change taking place in Hebrew writings, a change which
expressed itself in the so-called apocalyptic writings. Although these differed widely in their details, they all agreed in
one essential. Despairing of any such natural development
and restoration as the prophets had foretold, they looked for a
deliverance through miracle. Either by the agency of a supernatural Messiah, or by the direct action of Jehovah, the old
order and the existing race of men was to be destroyed, and
a new kingdom of Israel was to be established in a renovated
world. Their brief study will occupy us in the next section.

2. The Apocalyptists

A study of social Utopias would be incomplete without some
allusion to the writings of the Apocalyptists, since among them
we find clear-cut Utopias, although of a remarkable naïve and
transcendent character. The Apocalyptists [177] are generally
thought to be a class of almost entirely unknown Jewish and
Christian writers whose works appeared between 210 b. c. and
1300 a. d., the bulk of them, however, appearing during the first
four centuries of the period mentioned and serving to fill that
gap in the history of Jewish thought between the prophetic
teachings and the acceptance of Christianity. [178] The apocalyp-

[177] Apocalypses are not confined entirely to Jewish and Christian
writers. Case, in his "Revelations of John," states that they were
present among other peoples, in their mythologies and philosophies, even
before their contacts with Judaism or Christianity He gives as examples,
among others, the eleventh book of the Odyssey, Virgil's description of the
Cumæan Sibyl, the Vision of Er in Book X of Plato's "Republic," Cicero's
account of the dream of Scipio, and Virgil's descriptions in Book VI of
the Æneid of the revelations to Æneas on the occasion of his visit to
the lower regions Pp 100 ff.

[178] The most important of the Apocalypses are found in the Bible and the
Apocrypha and are as follows· Apoc of Daniel, Apoc. of Enoch, Book of
Jubilees, Psalms of Solomon, Assumption of Moses, Testament of Twelve

tic writings are essentially of a predictive and miraculous nature and treat of a future which is highly artificial, unusual, unhistorical and yet symbolic and imaginative in character.

There are several factors responsible for this peculiar coloring which the Apocalyptists gave to the future; the same factors also partially account for the characteristics inherent in apocalypses alone. In the first place, the period most productive in apocalypses was one of reverses and discouragements for the Jews. They passed through the persecutions under Antiochus IX, later through the unsuccessful revolt of the independent Jewish kingdom of the Maccabees against Rome, then the destruction of Jerusalem and the end of the separate political existence of the Jewish community. These were times of adversity due to the great political, social and religious upheavals, and the people found themselves overwhelmed by misfortunes and plunged in perplexities. Therefore, pious seers resorted to apocalyptical visions as a source of inspiration for the faithful in this period of sore distress. The apocalypses were tracts for the times.

Furthermore, during the exile previously, the Israelites had become steeped in the myths, and symbols and other rich imagery prevalent among their Babylonian conquerors. At the same time they were a scattered people of a highly religious nature, separated from the realities of civic life. This resulted in an amazing development of what may be called religious imagination. The exiles were inspired by great hopes for the future, evidences of which are shown in Jeremiah, Ezekiel, Zechariah, Habbakuk, etc. After the return from the exile the Jews came under the influence also of Hellenistic culture which led them to research and the expression of aesthetic conceptions. Moreover, under the Jewish Law literature was the only form of æsthetic expression (except music) which was open to the art impulses of the Jews. All of these various factors combined to produce an ornate literature at this time abounding in symbols, æsthetic imagery, prophetic lore, and elements of re-

Patriarchs, Ascension of Isaiah, Apoc of Ezra (2nd Esdras), Apoc. of Peter, Apoc. of Abraham, Apoc. of Baruch, Sybylline Oracles, and Revelation of John. Most of these will be discussed here

ligious faith, constituting a singularly unique mosaic of the future.[179] But we must not forget that the fundamental purpose of these accounts of the future was to comfort the living and encourage faith in Jehovah. The apocalyptist was picturing a coming victory for the righteous as the reward of present endurance. Apocalypses also serve as vehicles to present a solution of the difficulties connected with a belief in Jehovah's righteousness and the suffering condition of His people on earth,[180] or to bring to the people various conceptions of the Messiah, the Messianic Kingdom, resurrection, cosmogony, causes of sinfulness, etc.

Further characteristics of apocalyptic writing can be shown by comparing it with prophecy. First, the work of the apocalyptist is pseudepigraphic. He assumes the name of some ancient seer or other worthy long since dead, such as Enoch or Daniel, and lets on that one is the speaker. The prophet, on the other hand, maintains and asserts his own individuality. Second, the apocalyptist is imitative. He simply takes conceptions handed down from the past and reshapes and recolors them. But the prophet is creative. He is a pioneer, exploring new territory and originating new conceptions. Third, the interest of the apocalyptist is primarily eschatological. His glance is directed toward the future entirely. On the basis of a tradition or a visionary experience or both he depicts the marvelous things to come with fantastic and bookish calculation and shows a woeful lack of insight into the affairs of the present he is satisfied to leave degenerate. The prophet, however, plants himself firmly on the earth, dealing with the forces about him and showing the inevitable outcome of a certain course of conduct. Fourth, the ideal future of the apocalyptist could only be inaugurated by awful convulsions, catastrophes or some other miraculous deliverance. The sign of its nearness was not the likeness, but the unlikeness of the present to it; whereas the Utopias of the prophets were, on the whole, the

179 For expressions of the various elements mentioned see, Rauschenbusch, W., "Christianity and the Social Crisis" pp 35, 112; Baldwin, E. C "Our Modern Debt to Israel," p. 58, Matthews, Shailer, "Apocalyptic Literature," N Y 1907; Art. on Hastings' One Volume Dictionary, p. 39.

180 Charles, C H , Art on "Apoc Literature," in Hastings' D. B , Vol 1

outcome of ordinary political processes of history and of certain ethical activities.[181]   It is only in the primary purpose that the prophets and apocalyptists are similar.

The first of these pseudonymous works was the Apocalypse of Daniel which is commonly held to be the parent and model of Apocalyptic and also the representative apocalypse in the Hebrew Canon, most of the others being found in the Apocrypha.   It appeared by the almost unanimous consensus of scholars in the year 166 B. C., at a time when the Maccabean revolt was at its height, and was doubtless published to encourage patient endurance on the part of the pious Jews during the persecutions of Antiochus Epiphanes, who attempted to root out the Jewish religion and forcibly convert the Jews to the Greek religion.   It really marked the transition from prophecy to apocalypse.   From this time on for several centuries we find a continuous stream of apocalypses each marked by a strange combination of pessimism as to the present and hope as to a miraculously established future.   It was this literature which, as best it could, was henceforth to play the prophet's part in comforting, inspiring and guiding the nation.

The writer wrote in the name of a Daniel, a seer of the Exile, mentioned in Ezekiel, an extraordinarily righteous and wise man, belonging to the same class as Noah and Job, whose piety availed with God on behalf of their unworthy contemporaries. The exiled Jews knew of this Daniel,[182] famous for piety, righteousness and wisdom, and around his name, in the course of the ages, stories illustrative of these qualities had gathered, and the author of our book worked up this material afresh with renewed skill.   Through Daniel he expressed his own convictions, authenticating his story by the correspondence of the vision ascribed to Daniel with the actual course of history.

This unknown writer was intensely sure of the truths which he uttered and to him the historical setting which he employed was but a framework upon which he displayed his message of faith and piety.   Although not claimed to be by him, this

[181] Similar views in part expressed by Knudson, A. C., "Beacon Lights of Prophecy," p. 50 f; Matthews, Shailer, op. cit. p. 39; Smith, H. P., "The Religion of Israel," p. 294 f.
[182] Ezekiel, 14.14–20; 28:3.

message of the writer of this apocalypse is utopianistic in natuie. He shows by means of myths [183] built around the traditional character that the Jews through implicit adherence to Jehovah are superior to other peoples. He contended by means of the stories of dream interpretations [184] that the Jews, due to their peculiar relationship to Jehovah, were more proficient in the acts of astrology than were the Babylonian Magi themselves. Daniel and his friends lived at the court of a typically licentious heathen ruler and stood high in authority, yet because of their great faith and pure ethics resisted temptation and were not defiled, nor did they become disloyal. This goes to re-enforce further his indirect emphasis on the living of a perfect life. The deliverance of the three from the fiery furnace and the protection of Daniel in the lions' den—phenomena which impress even the heathen monarchs with the uniqueness of Israel's God—are simply the last word in an appeal for that type of life idealized by the prophets of old. To live righteously, to have faith in Jehovah and to obey minutely the mandates of the Hebrew Law was the height of perfection. The writer of Daniel must surely have inspired his people to such a life, although they were unconscious of his methods. We have here a very fine specimen of teaching by example and illustration. Consider how steadily these stories from the Book of Daniel are still used for the same purpose today and we perceive how well this ancient writer fulfilled his task.

For the prophets, such a utopianism would eventually have led to life in an ideal earthly commonwealth, or Kingdom of God. But not so in an Apocalypse. Here the Utopia is only the result of a miraculous intervention of Jehovah, and it is the duty of the faithful to wait in resignation for this divinely ordained collapse of earthly affairs and principalities. To this end the writer introduces the illustration of the image [185] and the vision of the four beasts,[186] which picture the passing of the nations and their kings as they are one after another

[183] See Smith, H P., "The Religion of Israel," p. 300.
[184] Daniel 2.4.
[185] Daniel 2:31–47.
[186] Ibid. 7.

swept from the scene by the mighty hand of Jehovah. This image was made of gold, silver, brass, and iron and clay, the metals being interpreted as standing for the great Babylonian, Medo-Persian, Grecian and Roman heathenish world empires, which were to rise, one after another, beat down and destroy their predecessor by force, violence and cruelty, fill the earth with tears, misery and desolation, only to have the world scepter, in turn, wrenched from their grasp almost before it was gained. In the long vista of the ages the writer saw empire succeeding empire until suddenly the great stone, Jehovah's instrument, loosed itself from the mountains, rolled down and demolished all things earthly,[187] and itself became the eternal Kingdom of God. Here, then, we have the view that the world's history will terminate in the ascendency of evil, and that Israel will be delivered by supernatural help to live gloriously and exert her dominion forever [188]—a view which which became a permanent feature in Jewish Apocalyptic.

There are a few outstanding qualities about this future state portrayed by the writer of Daniel which must be briefly discussed. The scene of the kingdom is on earth, for "all peoples, nations and languages" are its subjects.[189] It is to be an eternal world-empire of Israel. There is no Messiah, nor is mention made of an earthly ruler, but the "Ancient of days," [190] an angelic character, was to have dominion. A resurrection which embraces all Israel is to take place at the time of the universal collapse, in which some are to have everlasting happiness and some everlasting shame and contempt; [191] the former enjoying their bliss because of their exemplary lives.[192]

One of the most representative of the Jewish Apocalypses of the Apocrypha was that of Enoch which was a collection of passages written by a group of orthodox Jews between 170 B. C. and 64 B. C. It also was doubtless called forth by the

[187] Ibid. 2:35, 45
[188] Ibid. 7:14.
[189] Ibid. 7:27.
[190] Ibid. 7.13.
[191] Ibid. 12 2, 3.
[192] For comment on utopian characteristics see Charles, R. H., Art on "Eschatology," in Hastings, D. B.. Vol. 1.

unhappy experiences of the righteous during that turbulent period of Maccabean times, previously mentioned. Here, as in Daniel, an ancient worthy is utilized as the assumed proclaimer of the truths found therein. This time, Enoch, the antediluvian patriarch, is selected as the appropriate teacher of religious lessons, for according to tradition, he had been translated to the presence of Jehovah where he had abundant opportunity to learn divine wisdom, and obtain knowledge concerning the mysteries of the angel world, the forces and operations of nature, the future judgment and the consummation.

This book, like others discussed later, abounds in angelology, [193] describing and naming them, as it also does in demonology, [194] origin of sin [195] and other elements foreign to our purpose. There are some subjects treated, however, which we must consider. One of the authors refutes Ezekiel's doctrine that a man's earthly condition corresponds to his moral desert.[196] The writer perceived that the wicked often enjoy prosperity in life, and die in honor, while the righteous fare poorly and die in darkness and tribulation. But the righteous, nevertheless, are encouraged to be of good cheer, for in the next life a new balance will be drawn and the sinners will receive their due recompense, for they shall "descend into Sheol . . . and into darkness and chains and a burning flame where there is grievous judgment" shall their spirits enter for all generations of the world.[197] And those who had been put to shame through ill and affliction and who died in righteousness, shall in due time 'shine as the lights of heaven,' and 'the portals of heaven shall be opened' to them, and they 'shall become companions of the hosts of heaven.' [198]

This doctrine, of course, must rest on a theory of resurrection and future life, and it is in connection with the discussion of these that we discern utopianistic elements. As in Daniel some of these must be taken from the spirit of the writing

[193] Enoch (Charles version) 20 1–8; 40; 81 5, 87.2, 3, 88·1; 90 22, 23
[194] Ibid 6; 15 3, 8–11; 16·1; 19, 54·6; 69·2–3; 86, 90:7; 106:13–14.
[195] Throughout Chapters 6–36.
[196] Ibid Chapters 91–104
[197] Ibid 103 7, 8
[198] Ibid. 103:3; 104:2–6.

rather than from express statements. For him the life after
death is the organic development of the life on earth. Only
the righteous dead of Israel will be raised to take part in the
kingdom to come.[199] The Messiah will appear amongst them
and all the righteous will be transformed into His likeness [200]
and, as we noticed above, the wicked and sinful will suffer
their everlasting contumely and rebuke. This then is the
perfect life attained in the old, old way, namely, via the
spiritual righteousness path. As Enoch is supposed to say,
there is no man more honorable or greater than he that
feareth Jehovah [201] and consciously conforms to those demands
which express this fear.

In the 94th chapter in his admonitions to the righteous, the
writer, however, gives some very definite statements:

> "Walk not in the paths of wickedness, nor in the paths
> of death,
> And draw not nigh to them, lest ye be destroyed.
> But seek and choose for yourselves righteousness and an
> elect life,
> And walk in the paths of peace,
> And ye shall live and prosper." [202]

Following these, six chapters are devoted to a portrayal of
the many sins which prevent men from enjoying the companionship of the Most High.

The concept of the Kingdom of God undergoes a considerable change during the course of the writings combined in the
Apocalypse of Enoch. In Chapters 6-36 we have presented
a type similar to that of the Old Testament prophets, being
highly sensuous in character. The Kingdom of God was to
be established on the purified earth in magnificent splendor
with Jerusalem as its center. The righteous were to live
patriarchal lives and have a thousand children each. The land
was to be full of abundance and blessing; vines and olive trees
would bear abundantly and all seed a thousandfold. All

[199] Ibid. 90:33.
[200] Ibid. 90:38.
[201] Ibid. 66:2-3.
[202] Ibid. 94:3-4.

children of men were to become righteous and God was to come
down and dwell with men.

In Chapters 83 to 90 the writer or writers have progressed beyond the naïve and sensuous ideas described above.   They have
now become more spiritual. [203] The climax, however, is reached
in Chapters 91-104. Here the hope of the eternal kingdom
on the present earth is now absolutely finally abandoned. The
faithful are to be lifted bodily out of their sinful and materialistic environment and shall be placed in a spiritual region far distant from the sins, temptations and curses that in-
veigle men and bind them to eternal discontent and woe. The
spirits of the righteous shall live and rejoice, and become
companions of the hosts of heaven, and they shall be united with
Jehovah. Here the emphasis is not so much on a Messianic
kingdom, but upon the future spiritual life of the righteous,
giving us the first clear expression in Jewish literature of
heaven as the abode of the spirits of the righteous.

Among the less significant Apocalypses which we will discuss very briefly are the following. The Secrets of Enoch,
written in the Christian era before 70 A. D., receives its name
from the fact that it purports to disclose particularly the
secrets of God as revealed to Enoch. It is full of the punishments imposed upon sinners and the great and varied blessings
awarded the righteous, seen by the seer as he was taken thru
the various heavens. The last part contains admonitions of
an ethical nature, in which emphasis is laid on justice and
charity, patient forbearance and endurance, and sincerity in
all one's service of God. These duties are enforced by the
expectation of a coming judgment, which will introduce the
world to come, and in which the individual conformists will
enjoy a blessed immortality.[204] These elements are seen to
be vastly different from those discussed in the pre-Christian
Enoch Apocalypse.

The assumption of Moses, written 4 B. C. to 10 A. D., protests
against the division of Israel's interests into political channels,
and encourages piety while awaiting the personal intervention

[203] Spiritual evidences particularly noticeable in Chapter 90.
[204] Case, T J, "The Revelation of John," Chicago 1919, p. 88, Porter,
F C., "The Message of the Apocalyptical Writers," London 1905, p. 333

of God on behalf of the righteous. An attitude of patient
endurance, even to martyrdom and retirement from the world,
is advocated, confident that God himself will vindicate the
righteous in the heaven which is to come after the earth is
miraculously destroyed.[205]

The Apocalypse of Ezra was called forth by the destruction
of Jerusalem in 70 A. D., and the condition in which Judaism
was left by that dreadful calamity. The event tended to detach many Jews from the national and legalistic side of the
Jewish religion, and the writer of Ezra was one of them. It
is on a high plane of religious feeling and reflection throughout.
In one place a millenarian age of four hundred years is mentioned. At the end of this the Messiah himself dies with all
other men so as to emphasize the fact that the new creation,
the heavenly Jerusalem, which follows, wholly supersedes the
national hope, by something more catholic far in its inclusiveness.

The Book of Baruch purports to record the visions experienced
by Jeremiah's scribe, Baruch, soon after the first destruction
of Jerusalem by the Babylonian king, Nebuchadnezzar, but it
is very evident that the real author, or authors, whose identity
is unknown, lived in the Roman period and wrote to cheer
afflicted Jews in the latter part of the first century A. D. Case
in describing it says, "The purpose of the book is similar to
that of all apocalyptic writings. Even though sinners may
seem to be temporarily triumphant, the righteous are admon-
ished to persist in their piety, believing that God in His own
good time will come to their assistance in order to bestow upon
them a glorious reward and to mete out terrible punishments
to their enemies." [207]

The Apocalypse of Peter, an uncanonical apocalypse of the
Christian era, is of epoch-making importance in that in it there
appears for the first time detailed descriptions of heaven and
hell. Porter holds that as the result of this writing, this theme
became the ruling subject of apocalyptical speculations in

[205] Case, op. cit., pp. 86–87; Porter, op cit., p. 330.
[206] Porter, op cit , pp. 334–339.
[207] Op cit., p. 92.

early and mediæval Christianity.[208]   Peter is taken to see heaven, the abode of the glorified ones, with all its magnificence, and opposite it to the region of punishment, vividly described.

The Apocalypse of Abraham, written late in the first century or early in the second century A. D., is a description of Abraham's visit to the celestial regions.   In it occurs a judgment, followed by punishment for the largest number, and reward of the pre-determined faithful.

But rather than devote ourselves longer to the depressing task of considering various particular apocalypses, of minor significance, let us consider briefly some of the more salient characteristics of apocalypses in general and then pass on to the crown of apocalypse—the Revelation of John.

One writer in speaking of the ethics of the apocalyptists has said: "In the more typical apocalypse there is no moral exhortation whatever." [209]   If the writer meant that there are no violent diatribes against the evils and shortcomings of this time such as we find among the prophets, he is correct, but moral exhortation and the expression of moral precepts is present in profusion among nearly all the Apocalypses.   They were essentially ethical, rooted in an ethics based on the essential righteousness of God, which assured the good and the noble that this righteousness would ultimately prevail.   Let the doubter recall the strong ethical spirit of Daniel or let him refer to Chapters 94 to 105 of Enoch which are almost exclusively ethical precepts of purest quality, equalling those of any prophet, or the twenty-first chapter of Jubilees or the thirteenth chapter of the Testaments of the Twelve Patriarchs.   Not only are ethical teachings present in abundance; they are presented in a less vituperative manner, and are more spiritual in quality than many of those of the Old Testament.

The concept of the Messianic kingdom of the apocalyptists is also of a more sublime quality than that of the prophets. The center of the prophets' hope is a restored and glorified kingdom on earth brought about largely as the result of a

208 Op. cit., p 352
209 Thompson, J. E. H , in the International Standard Bible Encyclopedia Art , "Apocalyptic Literature," p. 163.

moral transformation. The apocalypses, on the other hand, look through and beyond any such temporal realization of the Messiah's kingdom to an entire reconstitution of the conditions of life. Rather than expecting that Jehovah's righteousness and glory will be completely vindicated on earth, they have come to the expectation that it will be vindicated finally and completely in heaven. Thus, the concept has become supramundane and spiritual.

There is another aspect of the older apocalypse of importance, due to the effect it had on Christianity. Among some of the Apocalypses, notably, the Book of Jubilees and the Apocalypse of Enoch, we find a millenium mentioned—a Messianic age of a thousand years during which its members are to live in happiness free from the influence of evil. Just when this is to be is not clear, but in general this millenial period is to immediately precede the final judgment after which the eternal heavenly kingdom is to be instituted. For example, in Enoch in Chapters 91–93 [210] time is described as a week of seven days, each of 1000 years in length. These 6000 years are said to have elapsed from the time of Creation to the Judgment. Then will come a "sabbath of rest" of 1000 years, and then an eighth day follows which is timeless. The same idea with some added characteristics is found again in the Apocalypse of John which will be considered presently. Shailer Matthews feels that it is not impossible to trace this conception back to Babylonia or Persia. [211]

In passing from Judaism to Christianity in the first century of the Christian era, we are brought face to face with the great Christian Apocalypse—the Revelation of John, supposedly written between 81 and 96 A. D. Several marked differences between the previously studied apocalypses and this one must be noted. This Apocalypse is neither anonymous nor pseudonymous, but is authentically stamped in several places by the name of its author, one John, whom most recent evidence shows to have been either John, the Apostle of Jesus, or John

[210] Charles' version
[211] Art. on "Millenium" in Hastings' One Volume Dictionary of the Bible, p. 618.

the Presbyter.[212] Thus it made no claim to have been written by a great prophet or religious leader of the past, but was a product of the pen of a contemporary of those to whom it first came. Secondly, this man was not merely an adapter and interpreter of earlier apocalyptic visions, as were his immediate predecessors, but was conscious of being himself a prophet,—one of the new order of prophets who made their appearance following the activities of Jesus in the first century, We must not think that this Apocalypse, in itself, is so diverse from that of the general type, for it has many of the characteristics common to apocalypses as a class. Like the other apocalypses it was written at a time when the true religion of the writer and his circle was threatened both by bad environment and by the violence of the ruling heathen power. The book is full of that weird symbolism so noticeable in older works of the kind and is doubtless drawn from them. Here this symbolism is used to picture contemporary characters and actual historical events, and has a very definite meaning for the writer's own time. The "beast" (commonly interpreted as representing Rome), and horns, and dragons are mentioned repeatedly. In the fourth and again in the twenty-first chapters we have a wealth of imagery set forth with technical exactness. The whole book is based upon visions, equalling in singularity and inexplicability those of all other apocalyptists. This is shown by the lack of unanimity of opinion among Bible scholars on various points in their interpretation. Another heretofore unmentioned new element in it may be ascribed to the new Christian spirit.

The purpose of John—like that of the other apocalyptists—was to reveal the overthrow by and final victory of God and righteousness over forces of evil, in this case the Roman Empire, and to portray the blessings of the Messianic expectation to be enjoyed by His followers. Here, as heretofore, the latter element is our chief concern. John's Utopia also is to be preceded by a Millenium. But his description of the Millenium is different from that of other apocalyptists in that a new char-

[212] See Matthews, Shailer, Art. on "Revelations" in Hastings' One Volume Dictionary of the Bible, p 799.

acter, Christ, is introduced. After Satan has been bound, the martyrs, and the martyrs only (i. e., those who had been beheaded or killed in any other wise for their activities in behalf of Christ), are raised in the first resurrection, and are to live and reign as priests with God and Christ personally on earth for 1000 years with Jerusalem as the center of the kingdom.[213] The Millenium of John like that of Enoch, leads eventually to the eternal kingdom of God, only John introduces a second resurrection and a second judgment in the interim, the dead being judged, every man according to his works as written in the book of God. Those whose names were not found written in the "book of life" are cast into the lake of fire, but those whose names are, become His people and dwell with Him.[214]

This dwelling of the redeemed of Israel is the holy city, the New Jerusalem, a strictly spiritual community.[215] One of its most striking characteristics is the omission of nearly everything corresponding to the experience of enjoyment on earth. True, the city is described in terms of great splendor, the foundations are garnished with all manner of precious stones, the gates are of pearl, the streets of pure gold; the whole is iridescent with the radiance of God's glory. And the tree of life yields her fruit every month; there is no more death or pain or night or curse. But beyond this the entire atmosphere is religious and spiritual. "The tabernacle of God is with men," [216] hence they need no earthly temple, for they shall live in perfect fellowship with God and the Lamb. It is this doctrine of the Lamb of Christ that places John's Utopia on a different plane from that of his predecessors, for according to it "flesh and blood cannot inherit the kingdom of God," hence the distinctly spiritual quality of the heavenly bliss. It is a Messianic kingdom governed by the One, whom John conceives to be the true Messiah.

The purpose of the utopianism of John is simply to prepare his people for this eternal spiritual residence in the Divine

[213] Revelation 20.1–6.
[214] Ibid. 20:12–15.
[215] Ibid 21·1–27; 22:1–8.
[216] Ibid. 21: 3.

presence. Hence he emphasizes the overwhelming worth of things spiritual as contrasted with things material. "He that overcometh all things that prevent him from drinking freely of the fountain of the water of life, shall inherit all things 'and I will be his God, and he shall be my son.' 'But the fearful, and unbelieving, and the abominable, and murderers, and whoremongers, and sorcerers, and idolaters, and all liars, shall have their part in the lake which burneth with fire and brimstone.' " [217] The demand is for a life not only righteous, but purged of material interests. The glance must at all times be directed God-ward, in an effort to approximate His ideals. Hence this Apocalypse involves not only the mystical and transcendental rather than the ethical and practical elements of religion, but also of life.

On the whole though it may be said that the Revelation of John in its whole outline of the future, its philosophy of history, and its eschatological doctrines, is in the closest way parallel to those of Jewish Apocalypse. The changes, in spite of their identification with Jesus, are far less than one would expect.

Thus have we traced religious utopianism from the days of Amos, when the emphasis was primarily ethical, to John in the Christian era, where the demands upon the individual to attain the ideal set before him are infinitely greater and more difficult, becoming almost purely spiritual.

But how can we appraise the apocalyptists from the sociological point of view? They stand out as markedly inferior to the prophets. While they breathe religious fervor and pious learning, they are childish, fanciful, ornate, unreal and highly emotional, almost useless from the social point of view. Their fancies and figures make their appeal to the uninstructed imagination alone, with its love of the fantastic and mysterious. Then too, they are fraught with inconsistencies and are illogical and unconnected in themselves. They abound in angelology and demonology,—grotesque and of no avail. They in no way assist in bridging the gulf between "that which is" and "that which ought to be." They are not stern social reformers such as the prophets, struggling with their feet firmly

217 Ibid 21:6–8.

planted on the ground, and laying down elements of idealism and principles of life which will hold for all time, nor do they seem to be aware of the laws of life. As a moral stimulus they are practically *nil*.[218]

The Apocalypses were written purely for their own time and throw little or no light on the problems of the present, as the teachings of the prophets or Plato do. If one goes to apocalyptic literature for edification one does not get it; the most one arrives at is a sort of patronizing approval for the ethical and spiritual elements embodied in them. There is none of that stimulus to thought and action which surges through Amos or Isaiah.

They are anticipations of an end with little attempt to delineate means whereby the end is to be attained, other than the catastrophic or miraculous intervention of the Most High. They seemed to have no sense of a possible development, of a march of events, due to the constructive efforts of men. They looked forward merely to the approaching judgment and the roseate end for the elect. Theirs were doctrines of "Ends" and not of "Means," hence their impotency.

Yet we must grant that in them one finds a universal scope, a sort of philosophy of history, which is new. They grasped the great idea of human history as a unity, as proceeding according to a rational plan and bound to issue in a worthy consummation. Only men were insignificant; it was all His unity, and His plan, and the consummation He desired. Therefore they did not influence the efforts of social constructionists. The present rule of evil was divinely decreed, and the day of its end was set. Good men had nothing to do but to wait for the next move of the Almighty.

Their strong point is their passionate belief in the New Age. They had an unconquerable hope in the future, a hope against hope that God would make all right in the end, an unquenchable

[218] Porter, op. cit., p. 64, says, "That which they claimed to do, viz, to unveil the heavenly world, and the future age, they really did not do. We cannot accept their descriptions of heaven, of God's throne, or of the angels, their names and functions, as a revelation of hidden realities. They are at most figurative and imaginative representations or symbols of faith in God and a spiritual realm."

conviction that God would not altogether allow His chosen people to perish in their struggles with the civilization of the heathen world.   But the hollowness of this hope leads to despair.

Finally the Apocalyptists, because of their naïveté and lack of strength, have not succeeded in impressing themselves on the ages as have the prophets.   To-day they are almost unknown, and practically inconsequential as far as influence upon present-day life is concerned.   On the other hand, the bold and sublime pronouncements of the prophets still reverberate from many a rostrum, and their idealism has been embodied in many of our social institutions.

3. The Kingdom of God and the Utopianism of Jesus

While we have, in our treatment of the Apocalypse of John, shown more or less imperfectly some of the changes wrought in utopianism due to the influence of Christianity, we have, nevertheless, been dealing with what we might almost term a corruption of some of the true doctrines of Jesus, and it is our duty to correct these and place them in their true light.   Furthermore, because of the tremendous importance of the doctrines of Jesus on all subsequent thought and events it behooves us to briefly consider them in their pristine condition as found in the utterances and activities of Jesus during his ministry in the first century.

Jesus of Nazareth, was a peasant, often spoken of as the "Son of a Carpenter," and he himself was a carpenter, having been taught the trade by his father, as was the Oriental custom.   Of his father we know very little, the probability being that he died early.   Of the mother we have only glimpses, but she seems to have been the ideal type of womanhood and motherhood, combining a rare force of character and an unusual degree of intelligence with a marked devotion to her religion and her children.   Nor was she altogether untutored, for her Psalm [219] shows that she was well-read in the Scriptures and had acquired a marked ability of expression.   Jesus himself had none of that scholarly training which Jeremiah or Ezekiel,

[219] Luke 1 : 46–55

or Paul, Jesus' immediate successor, had, nor did he receive any of the benefits which come from the influence of family or official or social position. Nor was he dependent on such things. As Henry Ward Beecher said, "Only the lower natures are formed by external circumstances. Great natures are fully developed by forces from within." Jesus' was one of these great natures, surely an inspired genius, from whom emanated some of the most sublime and yet practicable doctrines ever conceived of by man.

Jesus, like his predecessors, was a product of "Bad Times," —times during which his people were under the Iron Rule of Rome and the brazen rule of their own stilted, decayed and deceitful religious orders. The nation was bound hand and foot by the Roman conqueror who extorted their every penny from them by a system of taxation the like of which the iniquity of man has since been unable to devise, seventeenth and eighteenth century France notwithstanding. The gathering was farmed out, and the tax gatherers, paying a fixed sum to the central government, took from the wretched inhabitants "all the traffic would bear." The peasantry was lodged in miserable hovels. They attempted to eke out a living on a soil which had been depleted by centuries of earth-robbing and torn by the battles and by the tramp of heartless legions. It was a time "when equal rights were unknown; when half the population of Rome were slaves, holding life itself at the sufferance of their masters; when in Rome education was confined to the higher circles, and in the higher circles to a knowledge of elocution and gymnastics; when a wife might at any time be dismissed by her husband, as a servant with us; when law was habitually an instrument for oppression, taxation was a form of robbery, and liberty was another form of lawlessness." [220] The people lived in stolid despair.

The religious leaders did very little to lift this cloak of despair. They themselves were divided into three antagonistic schools of thought, from whom instruction or inspiration could not be expected. The cynical and sceptical Sadducees,

[220] Abbott, Lyman, "Christianity and Social Problems," Boston, 1896, p. 16.

who composed the large proportion of the priests, practiced the ritual of the religion while openly disavowing belief in its doctrines. The Essenes were the ascetics of their time and believed the world was going hopelessly wrong; therefore they withdrew from it in despair. The hypocritical Pharisees knew no road to righteousness except that of conformity to external statutes, a doctrine which made it unnecessary to attempt to throttle moral transgression or to instruct people along lines of right living; formalism was sufficient. It was upon this scene of oppression and degeneracy that Jesus came, consequently the ideal which he presented was one of a new and better social order—one relieved of the aristocracy in the state, and the hierarchy of the church.

Jesus was both sociological and revolutionary in his point of view. He was interested in folks and their relationships and not in theology or ritual or ecclesiastical orders. He propounded one of the first bodies of social and ethical precepts the race is heir to, but never a creed, or confession of faith or body of divinity. He intimated that there was to be a church, but he gave almost no instructions respecting its constitution or its laws. He fought all that belittles and degrades human beings, all that breaks up society into opposing classes and clashing creeds, and attempted to cultivate all that makes for the realization of self and the knowledge of the divinely ordained social order, with its pure, noble, and beneficent life. Because of this spirit which burned in him he expected a great reversal of the world's standard of values. Not only the learned, the rich, the aristocratic, the few at the top; not only the members of a small favored nation, the Jews; but the whole human race,—rich and poor, Jew and Gentile, conqueror and conquered, Pharisee and publican,—were to be levelled, educated, transformed, enfranchised, enriched! [221] "The first would be last and the last would be first." [222] "He that is greatest among you shall be your servant." [223] He saw that what was exalted among men was an abomination before God, [224]

[221] Matthew 9.10–13.
[222] Mark 10·30
[223] Matthew 20:26; 23:11.
[224] Luke 16:15.

hence the things man made to glitter had no glamor for his eyes. He taught that wealth consists in character, not in possession.[225] This revolutionary note also runs through the beatitudes[226] for there we see that henceforth those were to be blessed whom the world had not blessed.

He extended his revolutionary viewpoint to the religious leaders and authorities of his day with an unparalleled holiness and thoroughness. Quoting the late Professor Rauschenbusch:[227] "He called the ecclesiastical leaders hypocrites, blind leaders who fumbled in their casuistry, and everywhere missed the decisive facts in teaching right and wrong. Their piety was no piety; their law was inadequate; they harmed the men whom they wanted to convert.[228] Even the publicans and harlots had a truer piety than theirs.[229] If we remember that religion was still the foundation of the Jewish State, and that the religious authorities were the pillars of existing society,— we shall realize how revolutionary were his invectives. . . . His mind was similarly liberated from spiritual subjection to the existing civil powers; He called Herod, his own liege sovereign, 'that fox.' "[230] "Ye know that the princes of the Gentiles exercise dominion over them, and they that are great exercise authority upon them. But it shall not be so among you."[231] Jesus was neither a theologian, nor an ecclesiastic, nor a socialist, nor a reformer, as many affirm, but a great revolutionist and a real man. His teachings were not poetic, allegorical or fanciful, but plainly spoken truths, struck straight from the shoulder, by one who knew whereof he spoke.

Jesus' doctrines are an outgrowth, or better still a continuation of those we have discussed. In fact the Bible and the other works of a similar nature, such as the Apocryphal books, embrace within themselves a single process of evolution. But Jesus' doctrines are also revisions and improvements of those of his predecessors. He made them tangible and applicable;

[225] Ibid. 12:16-21.
[226] Matthew 5:1-12.
[227] "Christianity and the Social Crisis," p 86
[228] Matthew 23
[229] Matthew 21:23-32.
[230] Luke 13:32.
[231] Matthew 20·25-26.

purged them of their narrowing group characteristics, and made them catholic and universal.

Theoretically, Judaism gave a complete and perfect scheme of social and individual reconstitution. Its Jehovah was a powerful actor in the redemption of the people. Its Messianic state seemed to offer relief from the much-suffered social and political deficiencies. And yet both were unreal, intangible, abstract. If any foreign people had desired to practice the utopianism of most of the prophets and apocalyptists they would have had to renounce their political integrity and merge themselves in Israel, due to the highly nationalistic nature of this utopianism—a move manifestly impossible, especially where race feelings ran as high as they did in Asia Minor. The utopianism of the prophets did not displace politics but reinforced it. Furthermore, the prophetic identification of Jehovah with morality meant little or nothing to the Gentiles, who had no interest in this strange tribal God of a people steeped in race pride. Then, too, the utopianism of the prophets had in some cases become so mechanized and involved with other complicated and characteristically Judaistic conceptions and appurtenances, especially after the Deuteronomic reform and under the stimulus of Ezekiel's ritualistic emphasis, that it prevented not only the participation of mankind generally, but even the whole-hearted acceptance of some of the Jews. Finally, the mystical and catastrophic view of the apocalyptist could not appeal to many people, particularly those of races deficient in imagination and vision, it appearing to them as something fantastic and improbable.

Jesus' contribution was the conversion of these abstractions, these circumscribed conceptions and these vague generalities into concrete, realizable facts and actual practice. He gave us a practicable and universally applicable plan of social and individual redemption and centered it in his own superior and tremendously effective life. In his teachings we find the summit of utopianism and no higher peaks have been discovered in the nineteen centuries since his time.

The utopianism of Jesus has as its purpose the attainment of a definite ideal—the Kingdom of God. As an Utopia this differs from the prophets and apocalyptists. The prophets conceived of an earthly kingdom as a political organization inhabited by the select of Israel, governed by an idealized Davidic King, and permeated with the spirit of Jehovah. It was to be the rule of the world by the chosen people after their earthly enemies had been subdued. The future state of the apocalptists tists was for some an earthly state, for others a supernatural commonwealth, but whether one or the other, it was to be miraculously and catastrophically instituted by Divine intervention in our earthly affairs. We also have the government shading from a strictly political organization under Messianic rule to a Jehovah-controlled state. Among all, the inhabitants were to be those select individuals who abided by the will of Jehovah. But for Jesus the Kingdom was to come not by outward force, or social organization or apocalyptic dream, but by the progressive sanctification of individual human beings. When the interests, purposes and ideals of individual men were brought into conformity with the Divine Will, then we would have the Kingdom of God. It would become an external social order as soon as it was realized internally in the individual. To separate the inner lives of individuals from the social order was really impossible, for they react upon one another always and inevitably.

He had no place for superficial or imaginative schemes, but gave full recognition to the law of development in human life. He had caught the vision of a gradually established regenerated society, looking not only to personal perfection,[232] but also to the establishment of a Society, pure, blessed and world-wide. When all things which now cause stumbling in life [233] are eliminated, when all people shall be drawn together in a perfect harmony of brotherly love and mutual coöperation, when all good is come, when all lives are atune with the Infinite, then will that perfect community be realized. The Kingdom of God is thus seen to be an evolving—a gradual process of social and spiritual progress. It begins in the hearts and lives of men and does not end until the spirit of God rules in every

[232] "Ye shall be perfect as your heavenly Father is perfect." Matthew 5:48

[233] Ibid. 13·41

institution and relation of life. It is both a subjective state of the soul and an objective social order. It is a growth, a development, the unfolding of a principle of life, in its subjective as well as its objective phases. It is a kingdom in which man should be governed, not by the baser, but by the nobler motives, not by threat of punishment or by the fires of hell; not by force or fear, or by the hope of selfish reward here or hereafter; not by the desire for pleasure or fame; but by the spirit of God working in the hearts of men, by the common understanding of that which is best and by the love of righteousness and truth. This means no war, no oppression in state, no injustice in industry, no constant struggle and enmity and exploitation anywhere.

This Kingdom of God is both present and future. It is present now [234] for he saw the reign of God being set up in men's lives;[235] publicans and harlots, supposedly the most sinful of all people, were entering into it.[236] God's rule, even now, is displacing the rule of evil.[237] Now we perceive only the small beginnings, as men one by one turn to righteousness and brotherhood and as evil is slowly overthrown. But it will come in its fullness and power in the future, the relative remoteness of which depends upon the zeal with which individual men adopt and promote its requirements. The exact moment of its complete manifestation is unknown to all, even Jesus himself, although we have some means of estimating the possible time of its fulfillment.[238] But the growth, quiet and almost unnoticed, is yet continuous and certain. This is assured in the three parables.[239] The seed that God's followers were scattering was growing slowly and there were the tares, but it was growing surely and both would some day be harvested. The Kingdom was only a mustard seed now; it would be a tree by and by. Now it was like hidden leaven but it would permeate the whole lump after awhile. The Kingdom has as its very essence the capacity for expansion. "The earth beareth fruit

[234] Mark 1 5; Matthew 6 10; 10 7; Luke 10:9.
[235] Matthew 17 26; Mark 2: 19.
[236] Matthew 21 31, 32.
[237] Ibid 12:22-29.
[238] Mark 13 28-32.
[239] Matthew 13·24-33.

of herself; first the blade, then the ear, then the full grain in the ear.[240] The ideal would eventually be realized, and the Kingdom would at length come in all its perfection and purity.

There is a seeming paradox connected with Jesus' discussion of the Kingdom, he appearing to indicate that it is both of an earthly and a heavenly society. He explicitly states "My kingdom is not of this world," [241] and also speaks of the "kingdom of Heaven." [242] On the other hand, he says: "Behold, the kingdom of God is within you"; [243] while he taught us to pray: "Thy kingdom come. Thy will be done on earth as it is in heaven." [244] There really is no inconsistency here, as Professor Peabody states: "The ancient paradox disappears . . . Jesus . . . views the world from above. He sees in it the movement of the life of God on the souls of men. Wherever, then, this spirit of God finds welcome in a human life, there, immediately, unostentatiously, yet certainly, the Kingdom of God has already come." [245] It is simply a case of being in the world and yet not of it—of being a citizen of a regenerated society among men of the world who are not yet perfect. Heaven is theirs who are fit for it.

The fact that it is called a "Kingdom" does not necessarily imply the connotation of autocracy or arbitrary control. It really is a republic in which all have equal rights and equal privileges. The King of this Kingdom is King by Divine right, but also by the sovereign election of every citizen of the Kingdom. The power of the King is absolute, but every citizen is free. The King's throne is in the hearts of His people. The law of the Kingdom is no arbitrary command from without, but wrought within the souls of the citizens. It is a society resting on love, service and equality—and more democratic principles cannot be conceived of.

The sociality and universality [246] of the Kingdom must also

[240] Mark 4 26–28.
[241] John 18:36.
[242] Matthew 7:21.
[243] Luke 17 21.
[244] Matthew 6 10.
[245] Peabody, F G , "Jesus Christ and the Social Question," N. Y., 1900, p 100
[246] Matthew 6:10

be emphasized. As we shall presently see, its duties are largely social, and, of course, its relations are of this nature. The purpose of the Kingdom is the social redemption of the entire life of the human race on earth. It is a reign of mutual service and help, with an unselfish devotion to others as its impelling power, inspired by the rule of God in the hearts of entire humanity. One of Jesus' great contributions was this social aspect of the Kingdom which he placed in the fore.[247] His Kingdom was also spiritual in nature,[248] to be sure this being its essential characteristic, but he never spiritualized the vitality out of it, as his predecessors did. It was never for him a disembodied ghost, but a truly attainable end. Jesus also speaks of an eternal life which cannot be enjoyed apart from the Kingdom.[249] If the requirements for entrance into the Kingdom have been fulfilled, then eternal life is assured. One implies the other; "to inherit the kingdom" and "to inherit life" are synonymous,[250] except that we must remember that eternal life is the good of the individual, while the Kingdom is that of the community.

Now, having discussed the ideal, how is it to be attained? What is the rôle of the human mind, acting subjectively or objectively, in reconstructing society in conformity with this ideal? The Kingdom, we have seen, was social, but the utopianism was individual and subjective.[251] Jesus recognized the evils of his day, but saw that behind them all were men, hence he held that they were not social evils, but individual sins. And since the sins were individual, reconstruction must also be individual. His appeal was made not to the class or the nation, or the race, but to the individual, proceeding on the

[247] Rauschenbusch, W,—"The Social Principles of Jesus," p. 192 says: "By having such a social ideal at all he draws away all who are stationary and anchored in the world as it is, from all who locate the possibility of growth and progress in the individual only; and from all whose desire for perfection runs away from this world to a world beyond the grave."

[248] Matthew 4 8–10; 5:3–12; 11:12, Mark 10:23; Luke 17·20–21; John 18:36.

[249] Matthew 18.3, 8, 9; 25:34; Mark 9:43–47

[250] It is only in modern times that men, through much pain and labor, have learned that redemption may also be objective or institutional.

[251] Matthew 25 15

assumption that as individuals do right, become virtuous, and are regenerated, the world will progress toward righteousness and regeneration.   Therefore his purpose was to teach men to establish individually proper relations to God; to learn to discriminate between that which is evil, degrading, demoralizing, and that which makes for welfare, happiness and brotherly relations; and to instill in men that integrity and strength of character that will enable them to stand by their convictions. After all, the excellence of the Kingdom of God, or the perfectibility of any social group, depends in the last analysis, not on its religious appurtenances—splendid cathedrals, gorgeous ritual, beautiful music, scholarly and inspired divines; nor on its economic state—amicable relations between capital and labor, freedom from graft and corruption; nor on its political conditions—democratic institutions and government, peace within or without; nor upon its social situation—welfare, charity, philanthropy, excellent alleviative and corrective agencies— but upon the character of its members.   The teachings of Jesus keep this truth constantly in the foreground.

The emphasis on individual men did not mean that Jesus thought that all men were equal or that all were to render the same service or receive the same rewards.   In his parable of the Talents he says, "Unto one he gave five talents, to another two and to another one, to every man according to his several ability," [252] and the attainment he expected in return was "every man according to his several ability."   "His purpose was to develop the highest, noblest, and divinest quality in each individual, and therefore the highest and noblest quality in the aggregate of individuals.   For character is the end of life, and all that we live for is manhood and womanhood." [253]

Jesus gives us his message of utopianism in concentrated form in his reply to the Pharisee: "Thou shalt love the Lord thy God with all thy heart, and with all thy soul, and with all thy mind.   This is the first and great commandment.   And the second is like unto it, Thou shalt love thy neighbor as thyself.

[252] Matthew 25:15.
[253] Abbott, Lyman, "Christianity and Social Problems," p. 367.

On these two commandments hang all the law and prophets." [254]
Love, in its Godward and in its manward aspect; love of God
and humanity, is the basis of Jesus' utopianism. All that follows is but an elaboration of these principles. The second
commandment is really the big contribution of Jesus to the
utopianism of the Jews. He himself says: "A *new* commandment I give unto you, That ye love one another; as I have loved
you, that ye also love one another." [255] The first commandment
had been repeatedly emphasized by the prophets and apocalyptists, as we have seen, but this second had only been hinted
at. With Jesus we have its repeated enunciation, and a great
body of doctrine based upon it. "Christ taught the infinite
worth of every human individual, and our endless mutual obligation. . . . The distinctive feature of Christ's teaching from
the human standpoint is the exaltation of man, carrying with
it universal benevolence as a supreme law of conduct. Christ
thus furnishes a strange contrast to all who ever went before
Him, and became literally the first philanthropist." [256] But
these commandments are inter-dependent and inseparable.
Both must be accepted and followed. John attested to this
fact when he said: "If a man say, I love God, and hateth his
brother, he is a liar; for he that loveth not his brother whom
he hath seen, how can he love God whom he hath not seen?
And this commandment have we from him, That he who loveth
God love his brother also." [257] God can only be served and
loved by serving and loving our fellow men. The test of our
devotion to God, is the practice of the Golden Rule seven days
a week.[258] In the Fatherhood of God and the brotherhood of
man we have the whole doctrine. To deny the one is to deny
both.

In order to examine the utopianism of Jesus more carefully
we will divide the discussion into "duties to God" and "duties

[254] Matthew 22·34–40 —Dr. Ely, speaking of this passage, says· "This is
a most remarkable, and at the same time a most daring, summary of the
whole duty of man " "Social Aspects of Christianity," p 1.

[255] John 13 34.

[256] Ely, R. T , "The Social Law of Service," N. C , 1896, p 30.

[257] I John 4 20–21

[258] For an expression of this idea see the famous passage in Matthew
25 31–16.

to our fellow men," attempting to portray under each the more important phases of the efforts demanded. It must be understood, however, that the division is not arbitrarily made, for some of the duties apply to both God and men.

Doubtless the most important duty of man to God, as of man to man, is to *love* Him. Love being the great quality manifested by God toward men, their fundamental duty is to love Him in return with all their heart, and with all their soul, and with all their mind, and with all their strength.[259] Jesus himself set the example in this: "But that the world may know that I love the Father; and as the Father gave me commandment, even so I do." [260] The true test of progress on the part of the individual toward the consummation of the utopianistic ideal is this warm and unfaltering love toward the Infinite.

A duty of almost equal importance with love is to have *faith.* "And Jesus answering saith unto them, Have faith in God." [261] With this implicit faith all things are possible, for if it is sufficient to remove mountains,[262] surely the small and inconsequential obstacles met by man in his daily life can be surmounted. Faith in God, the Father, and in the eventual fulfillment of the Divine Law must be a voluntarily assumed duty of all who would abide in the Kingdom.

Closely bound up with faith, as an essential condition, is *penitence.*[263] "Repent ye and believe the gospel." To sin is not the greatest evil, but to refrain from repenting, for "Except ye repent, ye shall all likewise perish." [264] Therefore a sensitive conscience is highly desirable since it is the basic essential in restitution, and enables the individual to quickly make that restitution worthy of repentance.[265]

Among the other means of testing the fitness of the individual by means of his relations of God, are his *obedience* and *humility.* "Therefore by their fruits ye shall know them.

[259] Mark 12 30; Luke 10:27.
[260] John 14·31
[261] Mark 11·22.
[262] Ibid 11:23–24.
[263] Mark 1:15.
[264] Luke 13:3.
[265] Matthew 3.8; Luke 3:8, "Bring forth therefore fruits worthy of repentance" See also the great classic on repentance, Luke 15.11–32.

Not everyone that saith unto me, Lord, Lord, shall enter into the kingdom of heaven; but he that doeth the will of my father which is in heaven." [266] There must be no self-deception, no going about and crying "Lord, Lord!" but obedience to the Divine Will. Only such compliance will stand the crucial test.[267] Such obedience is not simply a preparation for the Kingdom; it is of the essence of the Kingdom, for the rule of God thus brought about in the life of individual men means the righteousness of man: "Seek ye first the Kingdom of God and his righteousness; and these things shall be added unto you." [268] This is an exaltation of spiritual values—not an exhortation to faultless observance of a set of rules imposed by some self-important school-master or vain precisionist, nor to obedience to the arbitrary and vexatious commands of some proud ruler,— it is a searching after the highest good, conformity to the Divine plan.

It is the duty of men to submit in humility and patience to God's command: "Whosoever, therefore, shall humble himself as this little child, the same is greatest in the kingdom of heaven." [269] It is a sense of humility arising from a sense of need, akin to that of a child which is cast upon others for the supply of its wants. At another time Jesus asks us to admire the publican, who, in contrast to the self-satisfied Pharisee, confessed his unworthiness and his need of mercy. Yes, *humility* is also an essential aspect of our relation to God.

This relationship must, however, *be free from all hypocrisy and deceit*. Jesus ridiculed those who were so punctilious about ritual and other church observances, and so indifferent to their spiritual and moral relations. He was especially incensed at the Pharisees, who faithfully gave a little of everything to religion, down to the mint, anise and cummin in their gardens, but forgot judgment, mercy and faith, the very foundation of the law; who strained the milk lest they swallow a drowned gnat and so transgress the law and yet were doing much worse; who wiped the outside of the platter, but permitted the

[266] Matthew 7:20–21
[267] Ibid 7·24–27.
[268] Ibid 6.19–34.
[269] Ibid 18:4.

inside to be full of extortion and excess. Ah, for such is not the Kingdom of God, but the damnation of hell.[270] The Divine relation must be frank and true and without ostentation.[271]

Furthermore, to maintain this relationship with God unimpaired, man must be *free from Mammonism.* "Ye cannot serve God and mammon." [272] The cares of this life and the deceitfulness of riches will choke the pure communion with God, even as rank weeds appropriate soil and sunshine for their own growth.[273] As soon as men accumulate earthly treasures, these are likely to distract their attention from inner things, "For where your treasure is, there will your heart be also." [274] Covetousness and wealth are delusions; "for a man's life consisteth not in the abundance of the things which he possesseth," [275] but in "faith, hope, love, these three; but the greatest of these is love." [276]

The supreme fraternal obligation, like the filial, is *love.* "These things I command you, that ye love one another." [277] It is to be extended to all men: "Thou shalt love thy neighbor as thyself." [278] By our neighbor we are to understand all who are in need, and whom it is in our power to help. Our love is not to be exclusive and narrow but broad and cosmopolitan as was that of the Good Samaritan.[279] The test is, not in loving our friends but our enemies. "Ye have heard that it hath been said, Thou shalt love thy neighbor, and hate thine enemy. But I say unto you, Love your enemies, bless them that curse you, do good to them that hate you, and pray for them which despitefully use you, and persecute you; That ye may be the children of your Father which is in heaven. . . . For if ye love them which love you, what reward have ye?

[270] Matthew 23.23–33.
[271] Ibid 6 1–6, 16.
[272] Ibid 5:24
[273] Ibid 13:18–32.
[274] Ibid 6:19–34; Luke 12·34.
[275] Luke 12:15
[276] I Corinthians 13:13.
[277] John 15 17.
[278] Mark 12:31.
[279] Luke 10:30–35.

do not even the publicfans the same ?" [280] If one of our fellows
smites us on one cheek we must turn the other instead of returning the blow.[281]   The fraternal relation which binds men
dare not be sundered.   To love our fellow men without qualification or exception is a true expression of our fitness to enter
the Kingdom.[282]   The maxim by which to gauge our activities
is: "Whatsoever ye would that men should do to you, do ye
even so to them." [283]

This fraternal love expresses itself in a multitude of ways.
Devotion to the welfare of our fellow men is one of its aspects.
Not only devotion to our equals and superiors but to children [284] and outcasts,[285] for in order to inherit the Kingdom "ye
must do it unto the least of these my brethren."   Here Jesus
gives us the assurance that there is no distinction between least
and much or between aristocrat and pauper, but that each is
worthy as he *serves his fellow men.*   "Whosoever will be great
among you, let him be your minister; and whosoever will be
chief among you, let him be your servant." [286]   Jesus made
this law of service the fundamental law of his Kingdom and
made it a potent practice in his life.[287]   And in this Kingdom
where love and not selfishness rule, those who have most must
serve those who need most.[288]   The spirit of Jesus' law was
not the abolition of inequalities, but the utilization of superior
gifts as instruments of service.   All greatness anywhere must
rest on this basis.   Not receiving but ministering makes man

[280] Matthew 5 43–46, Luke 6:27–28.
[281] Matthew 5: 38–24.
[282] John 13.35.
[283] Matthew 7 12.
[284] Ibid 10·42; 18 5
[285] Ibid. 25:34–40.
[286] Ibid 20 26–27, 23:1–11; Mark 10 43.
[287] Luke 22 27

[288] "Intelligence can attain its highest and broadest development only
in imparting its wisdom to the ignorant; virtue can approach its ideal
of perfection only in the effort to save the vicious. Official dignity and
rank can manifest its true dignity only in the service of its subjects.
The highest social class is not that which gluts its pride in its contrast
with the lowly, but it is that class which stoops in service to refine, to ennoble, and to purify those who are beneath   Wealth can never purchase
for its possessor the best gifts and the highest happiness until it is used
to bless those who have it not "—Howerton, J R., "The Church and
Social Reform," New York, 1913, p 113

capable of perfection. But let him beware of ostentatious display.[289]

Another phase of this manifestation of brotherly love is *self-sacrifice* and *unselfishness*. "He that hath two coats, let him share with him that hath none; and he that hath food, let him do likewise." [290] "Whosoever shall compel thee to go a mile, go with him twain." [291] Other great social thinkers have recognized the same truths. Carlyle says: "It is only with renunciation (Entsagen) that life, properly speaking, can be said to begin," [292] and Lecky holds that "The first condition of all really great moral excellence is a spirit of genuine self-sacrifice and self-renunciation." [293] Neither Jesus nor these other writers, however, advocated asceticism, which is self-denial for its own sake; they believed in that conscious, free-will offering of self for the good of others. To do this is to suppress selfishness and to enlarge the self.

Akin to service is the spirit of *humility*. Jesus gave us a striking object lesson in this himself, when he arose from the supper table, took a towel and himself washed the feet of his disciples,[294] showing the immeasurable loftiness of the subordination of self to the service of the community; yes, even amongst the lowly. In connection with this striking example of service and humbleness we must also speak of the forceful manner in which Jesus repudiated the spirit of self-righteousness. The self-styled pious scribes and Pharisees brought to him an object of contempt and abhorrence, a woman taken in adultery, and said: "This woman was taken in adultery, in the very act. Now Moses in the law commanded us that such should be stoned: but what sayest thou?" After a moment Jesus gave an answer which in its simplicity, but also in its all-inclusiveness and tremendous force, is unparalleled anywhere: "He that is without sin among you, let him cast the first stone at her." [295] And the woman's accusers, thoroughly

289 Matthew 6·2–4.
290 Luke 3:11.
291 Matthew 5·41.
292 Carlyle, Thomas, "Sartor Resartus," Macmillan Edition, p. 173.
293 Lecky, "History of European Morals," Vol II, p 155.
294 John 13·1–20.
295 John 8: 3–9.

rebuked, and ashamed of their vaunted goodness, slunk away like the mean persecutors that they were.

Another quality which Jesus emphasized, not so much by express statement, as by frequent indirect allusion, is the sense of *individual responsibility*.[296]   Jesus realized that the chief responsibility for a very large part of social disorder lies in the passions and ambitions of individual men, and that no social arrangement can guarantee social welfare, unless there is brought home to individuals singly a profound sense of personal accountability for both the acts of omission and commission, even "every idle word that men shall speak, they shall give account thereof "[297]   He would have none of that flimsy fatalism which regards character as the creature of circumstance, but appealed to the will of men.   The social solidarity which would be the natural outcome of his two great commandments demanded this knowledge of personal responsibility. He seemed to realize in a way, the great law since discovered, that the most infinitesimal molecule cannot be moved an inch without affecting the balance of the entire universe.

Jesus also commends to us by his actions a spirit of sociability *or cosmopolitanism*. He often fell into conversation with people, sometimes in calm disregard of the laws of propriety. When his disciples returned to him at the well of Samaria, they were surprised to find him talking with a strange woman.[298]   He recognized no class lines, frequently associaing with those whom society had ostracized.   He accepted the dinner invitations of tax-collectors, and even invited himself to their houses, thereby incurring the sneer of the reputedly respectable as a friend of publicans and a glutton and winebibber.[299]   He also on occasion broke bread with the socially elect, the Pharisees.[300]   Jesus wanted all men to live as neighbors and brothers, and himself set the example.

Finally, Jesus demands a *forgiving spirit* in every person. Some of the transgressions for which he suggests forgiveness

[296] Luke 15:18; 18·15.
[297] Matthew 12·36–37.
[298] John 4·27
[299] Matthew 11·19.
[300] Luke 14 1. For an expression of the spirit discussed above, also see Luke 14 21, 22.

are injury to person,[301] loss of property,[302] defamation of character,[303] "For if ye forgive men their trespasses, your heavenly Father will also forgive you: But if ye forgive not men their trespasses, neither will your Father forgive your trespasses." [304] If one of our fellows has wronged us we must not permit that to tear our fraternity asunder, but we must forgive, and forgive not the Pharisaic thrice nor Peter's seven times but seventy times seven times.[305] If, while extremely busy with some important task, we remember that we have offended and our fellow is now alienated from us, we are to drop everything and go and restore fellowship.[306] For if we forgive not, we shall suffer that torment which a guilty conscience and a righteous-loving God provide, as Jesus shows in that most human parable of the unforgiving servant,[307] but if we do forgive we are truly expressing that love, upon which rests all the law and the prophets. The extremely important spirit of forgiveness is not only a manward duty, but also a Godward obligation, for it is a case, as Paul says, of "forgiving one another, even as God hath forgiven you." [308] Our real motive to forgive, and our power, lie in our forgiveness first by God. Finally our true relation to God depends on our success in fulfilling these obligations toward our fellow men, especially that of forgiveness.

This is Jesus' program of regeneration or utopianism, and, like every ideal, is beyond our perfect practice; but, like every true ideal, it is the point toward which our endeavors may growingly converge and approximate. Its most outstanding characteristics are its emphasis on individual character and the means to its perfection; these means being certain very definite and closely interwoven moral and spiritual demands consummated by a human life full of righteousness, justice and love brought into harmony with the Divine life.

It really is the doctrine of a true religion, since it is no

301 Matthew 5·39.
302 Ibid. 5:40.
303 Ibid. 5:11.
304 Ibid 6:14–15.
305 Ibid. 18:21–22.
306 Ibid 5 23–24.
307 Ibid. 18:23–35
308 Ephesians 4:32.

mere emotional effervescence, or mystical ecstasy, or occult vaporing; nor is it a question of mechanical performances, ecclesiastical institutions, rituals, or creeds; but it is an affair of the soul; it is spiritual and ethical, and is based upon a simple, childlike communion with a beneficent and loving Father-God, and expresses itself in daily fraternity and service; it makes for happiness and peace and satisfying life for all humanity. It is a doctrine of optimism and hope, for it looks to the future, not to the past, to human possibilities and not miraculous occurrences, to the perfection of all and not to the glory of a remnant. As utopianism it stands without parallel.

4. Augustine and his "City of God"

The lineal descendant of the ethico-religious utopian conceptions that we have been tracing is Augustine's "City of God." To make complete this division of our study a brief examination of the epochal work is essential. It was written by Aurelius Augustinus (354–430 A. D.), born at Thagaste, a small Numidian (now Algerian) proconsular municipality. Its author is familiar in history as St. Augustine, the greatest of the post-Nicene Latin fathers of the Christian Church, and Bishop of Hippo Regius, now Bona. The "City of God" was written between the years 413 and 426 A D., a decadent time when the world was being sorely tried and when Christianity was experiencing a tremendous crisis which demanded the best efforts of its greatest apologists. Augustine stepped forward to fill this need in the years of his maturity and produced this work, his masterpiece. It has played an important part in the plans of kings and popes, and the schemes of empires and hierarchies. To understand the book, we must begin with an examination of what was going on in the world at the time.

The age immediately preceding the appearance of the "City of God" was one in which extreme political and social confusion prevailed. The Roman Empire, nominally one, was practically two, and the people of the East and West were becoming rapidly alienated from each other. The inhabitants of the outlying provinces,—Britons, Gauls, Hispanians, and Africans,—never assimilated, but merely held in check by the complex and highly adaptable organization of control,—were in continual revolt. The semi-barbarous peoples on the Empire's edge,—the Ostrogoths and Visigoths, the Huns and Alamanni, the Vandals and Moors,—were continually pressing in upon the Empire, harrassing it, plundering its outskirts, keeping the people in continual uncertainty and terror. And yet, in spite of this, the Roman World deluded itself into feeling that the imperial might, the invincible sovereignty of the Empire, was unimpaired, and that Rome, the Eternal City, was secure.

In the religious and intellectual world a similar chaos reigned. Paganism, Christianity and Judaism were struggling for power, with Christianity in supremacy. But Christianity it-self was in a critical condition. Its ardor was cooling under the influence of the prosperity, pomp and prevailing corruption of the times. The Christian clergy of the age were often per-fidious, or without a high sense of their responsibilities. A thousand philosophical cults had their fanatical adherents, who were sacrificing depth and philosophic outlook to polish and sophistry. Learning was becoming more and more a thing of conventions. Old institutions and religions were passing away. New religions, new systems of thought were pressing forward for recognition and regnancy. All was turmoil and discord.

In the year 410 A. D. this terrible confusion terminated in the capture and plundering of Rome by Alaric the Goth and his hordes. When this occurred men felt that the solid earth was giving away beneath them and that the powers of heaven were shaken, for the mighty city which had enthralled the world had fallen. Roman and barbarian, Christian and pagan alike, were filled with inexpressible excitement and ter-ror, chiefly of a religious nature. Christians by multitudes began to lose faith and looked for the end of the world to fol-low forthwith. Pagans saw in this fall of Rome the vengeance of Rome's neglected gods. For centuries these ancient deities had defended the city and given her unprecedented power. At length, amid the frittering away of their worship and the rise of an enervating and humiliating religion, their patience was exhausted, and it was they who had visited this catastrophe upon the empire. Everywhere Christianity was excoriated as being the factor influential in explaining this disaster. Nor were these complaints confined to the unthinking multitude. Thoughtful men detected in the very core of Christian teaching principles incompatible with the maintenance of states. If the dominant religion forbade resistance to evil, how could the barbarians fail to carry all before them? Rome grew great under the old religion, but perished in Christian times. Hence there was a widespread plea for the restoration of the old religion.

These various and serious objections failed not to strike Augustine's consciousness with vivid force, and he attempted to answer them. His original object was simply to show that it was not the renunciation of the old gods that had ruined Rome. Neither was it any inherent defect in the Christian religion which caused it, but the natural growth of barbarian ambition. Christianity, if duly carried out, would secure far the best and most inviolable state. But this was not all. As he pondered upon the vanished glory of the earthly city, there seemed to hover over the ruins the splendid vision of the City of God, "coming down out of heaven, adorned as a bride for her husband." He saw the Church in its fullest and most ideal manifestation furnishing a haven of repose for the world in upheaval. But he was led even further to give a comprehensive survey of history. It was Christianity itself, as a renovating force in the world, and his own particular conception of Christianity that taught him to conceive of the history of human society no less than the course of individual life, as the continuous unfolding of the Divine purpose, and impelled him to interpret all the forces of time as working harmoniously onward to the final consummation in the City of God. He really made a strenuous attempt to create a philosophy of history as Ozanam has said.[309]

Augustine has divided his treatise into twenty-two books. Of these the first five are given to an attack upon paganism; the following five books are more philosophic in nature, the moral impotence of the systems of Varro and Plato among many other subjects coming in for unsparing criticism. In

[309] Ozanam, "History of Civilization in the Fifth Century," II, p. 160.

the remaining twelve books, which form the second half of the work, Augustine presents a full treatment of his own convictions on various religious and theological subjects, chief among which is his doctrine of the two cities,—the City of Men and the City of God, in respect to their origin, their history, and their destiny,—and a treatment of the "last things." The "City of God" is a monumental work covering a great variety of subjects. In fact, it was called by Poujoulat, [310] "the encyclopedia of the fifth century." We, of course, are interested primarily in the discussion of the ideal city and the means of instituting it and hence will devote ourselves primarily to the part of the work in which these are treated.

Augustine sets the "City of God" in contrast to the "City of Men," showing that they represent diametrically opposite principles. The one consists of those who wish to live after the spirit and is founded upon the love of God and contempt of self; the other is made up of those who wish to live after the flesh, is based upon the love of self and contempt of God, and is the embodiment of evil.[311] The individual then is the inhabitant of the one or the other of these cities as he lives according to man, or according to God.[312] Augustine's utopianism centers about this life according to God. It consists in the first place of freedom from the baser passions and lusts and the practice of a religious, specifically Christian, ethics.[313] In advising about the abstention from the baser life he calls attention to a passage of the Apostle Paul which expresses the idea for him perfectly: "Now the works of the flesh are manifest, which are these: adultery, fornication, uncleanness, lasciviousness, idolatry, witchcraft, hatred, variance, emulations, wrath, strife, seditions, heresies, envyings, murders, drunkenness, revellings, and such like: of which I tell you before, as I have told you in time past, that they which do such things shall not inherit the Kingdom of God." [314] It is a matter of desiring the good, for "the man who lives according to God, and not

310 Quoted by Dod's, Marcus, "City of God," p. xiii.
311 "City of God," Marcus Dod's Translation, XIV, Chapter 1, p. 28.
312 Ibid. XIV: 4.
313 See discussion of Utopianism of Jesus
314 Galatians 5:19–21.

according to man, ought to be a lover of God, and therefore a hater of evil." [315]   Augustine holds no doctrine of original sin but rather maintains the opposite: "Since no one is evil by nature, but whoever is evil is evil by vice, he who lives according to God ought to cherish towards evil men a perfect hatred, so that he shall neither hate the man because of his vice, nor love the vice because of the man, but hate the vice and love the man." [316]   And then he optimistically states "For the vice being cursed, all that ought to be loved, and nothing that ought to be hated will remain." [317]   In another passage [318] he states "There is a nature in which evil does not or even cannot exist; but there cannot be a nature in which there is no good." To become perfect, then, man must revert to his original natural state of sinlessness. Imperfection is merely perversion of original perfection through sin. Another element of his utopianism is connected with that laid down by Jesus and expressed by Augustine as follows: "He who resolves to love God, and to love his neighbor as himself, not according to man but according to God, is on account of this love said to be of a good will." [319]   This right will or good will is, according to his analysis, well-directed love, and the wrong will is ill-directed love. But he carries this analysis further. This good will must be directed to others, not through fear of punishment for not doing so nor for reward for doing it, but for the love of righteousness; [320] it must be freely and happily given. "For he who loves rightly, without doubt rightly believes and rightly hopes, but he who loves not believes in vain. Little love is little righteousness; great love is great righteousness; perfect love is perfect righteousness." Finally the bond of agreement in the divine city is the love of God as is shown when he defines a state as: "An assemblage of reasonable beings bound together by a common agreement as to the objects of their love." [321]   Through humble love of God, we renounce self and

[315] "City of God" XIV 6.
[316] Ibid XIV·6
[317] Ibid XIV:6
[318] Ibid. XIX:6
[319] Ibid. XIV.7.
[320] Ibid XIV 10
[321] Ibid. XIX:24

lust and receive God and His law and thus unitedly by means
of this Divine beneficence are prepared for the City of God.
This is a beatific vision of a social life in which the personality
of the individual is bound to that of other individuals through
God, truly the highest stage of moral perfection.

The corollary of this mutual love or good will is peace between
man and God and man and man.   The peace between God and
man is through the well-ordered obedience to and faith in eternal law.   Peace between man and man is well-ordered concord.
Domestic peace is the orderly obedience of those who obey to
those who rule.   The entire peace of the celestial city is to be
the perfectly ordered and harmonious enjoyment of God, and
of one another in God.[322]   This peace is maintained by the
universal good will.   He says, "And this is the order of this
concord, that a man, in the first place, injure no one, and, in
the second, do good to every one he can reach."[323]   This is
simply a statement of the law of service—another element of
his utopianism.   He goes on to show how this must begin
within the family, for the law of nature and society give the
member of the household ready access and greater opportunity
of serving there, and, furthermore, the family is the unit of
the State.   Those who rule serve those whom they seem to
command, but they must rule, not from a love of power, but
from a sense of the duty they owe to others—not because they
are proud of authority, but because they love mercy.

The supreme service, however, is to obey and serve God, for
only by so doing can the soul and the reason be brought into
proper authority over the body and the vices.[324]   How, he
asks, can the mind which is ignorant of God, and prostituted
to the most corrupting influences, properly control the body
and the vices?   True, there are some who are able to restrain
themselves without any reference to God in the matter, but
these are not cases of virtues but rather of splendid or *virtuous
vices.*   "That which gives blessed life to man is not derived
from man, but is something above him; and what I say of man

322 Ibid. XIX 13.
323 Ibid. XIX:14.
324 Ibid. XIX:25.

is true of every celestial power and virtue whatsoever." [325]

Augustine shows that complete enjoyment of felicity cannot be expected in this life, for this is to come in the future; but yet all efforts must be devoted to the perfection of virtues and seeking the remission of sins, or in brief, the attainment of righteousness. His whole utopianism centers about this righteousness, the method of acquiring which he summarizes as follows: "In this, then, consists the righteousness of man, that he submit himself to God, his body to his soul, and his vices, even when they rebel, to his reason, which either defeats or at least resists them; and also that he beg from God grace to do his duty, and the pardon of his sins, and that he render to God thanks for all the blessings he receives." [326]

Finally, all else is of no avail if man does not have faith in God. Augustine states that "it is written, 'The just lives by faith,' [327] for we do not as yet see our good, and must therefore live by faith; neither have we in ourselves power to live rightly, but we can do so only if He who has given us faith to believe in His help does help us when we believe and pray." [328] Augustine, though not indifferent to the necessity of ethical life and good works, yet felt that man was utterly helpless in himself, not having strength to work out his own salvation; hence he gave predominant emphasis to this regeneration by faith. His was a Utopianism, which, despairing of self, cast all its hope on God. Augustine has frequently been called the father of mysticism, and here we have the example of a mysticism demanding a high degree of ecstasy and internal self-repression, but withal a clear intelligence. For Augustine, like Jesus and some of the prophets, made this regeneration depend on the activity of the individual in the achieving of his unity with God, doing away with nationalistic or priestly mediation. And yet he gave the Church, spoken of as a "sanctified congregation," a very important place since he conceived it as the very essence of God and the gospel of regeneration on earth.

---

[325] Ibid XIX:25.
[326] Ibid. XIX:27.
[327] Habakkuk 2:4
[328] "City of God," XIX.4.

Therefore the individual must stand in eternal communion with it. It was through the Church—its teaching, worship, and sacraments—that people found the way of life. The Church was the door through which the soul passed to the knowledge of God. In fact he wrote the "City of God" to free the Church from the reproach of under-mining the Empire, to reëstablish it, and disclose it as the spiritual institution through.which God was building His city. He was doubtless led to this extreme championship of the spiritual and ecclesiastical phases of Christianity by the intense opposition of the times and the competition of other highly ornate and passionate religious systems, which were receiving the acceptance of highly impressionable people.

We ask, "What does Augustine really mean by the 'City of God'? Is it an earthly assemblage or is it supramundane?" We find no direct, clear-cut statement, but rather a confusion of meanings, making various interpretations possible. The exact significance of the phrase in any part of the book must be divined from the context in which it occurs. Sometimes it refers to a city-state, neither in the world nor of it, yet vitally related to it,[329] a city which represents an ideal most truly. At other times a city on earth is meant, inherited by pilgrims, who through their faith and godliness will eventually come into perfect citizenship in the heavenly city.[330] A third meaning included both of the above, the Church militant and the Church triumphant.[331] A fourth is that of the historic visible church on earth, not all of whose members can attain heavenly citizenship, for some do the things which exclude entrance into it.[332] This interpretation is most widely accepted as representing Augustine's real meaning.

But the fact that his statements carry such diverse meanings does not necessarily imply that he held so many different conceptions of the "City of God." Upon closer examination they will all be found to contribute to the same complete ideal. Augustine's purpose was to lead men to final perfection and

[329] Ibid. XV:11; XIX:11, 14.
[330] Ibid XIX:17, 27
[331] Ibid XIV:28; XV·1: XX 24.
[332] Ibid XIX:21, 26, XX 9, XXI 23.

his different conceptions of the "City of God" are clearly steps along the route to this final goal. He first wishes to call the attention of men to the fact that there is another kingdom on earth—"a city which hath foundations, whose builder and maker is God," and which is almost transcendent in its nature. From the first the city of God, or community of God's righteous people, has lived alongside of the kingdoms of this world and their glory and has been silently increasing. These righteous people, because of their superior morality and their adherence to the true doctrine as revealed by God, and above all due to their desire for a common social life,[333] have been gradually consolidated through Divine direction into a common organization—the elect of God. These elect finally triumphed and the Christian Church was brought into being. It was eventually to become universal and include all the kingdoms of the earth.

Augustine devoted himself primarily to the church of his time. It was the ecclesiastical organization which to him stood out in the world visibly, as the City of God,[334] and he was attempting to vindicate its existence. Though at present the "City of Men," or State, and the "City of God," or the Church, are of an opposite nature and purpose,[335] he was the first who was keen enough to perceive that there could be no final and visible separation of them, for the two cities depend on one another; the "City of God" is wanting in power and resources to make it secure without the protection of the state, and the state cannot obtain its purposes without the aid of justice and other moral influences to be found only in the heavenly city. But the true state in the ultimate and real sense is the Church.[336] "The State . . . merges . . in the Church, and the civil power becomes the weapon of the Church, the legislator and the magistrate are but sons of the Church, bound to carry out the Church's aims. . . . The Empire becomes the instrument and vassal of the Church."[337] Thus did Augus-

[333] Ibid XIX:5.
[334] Ibid XIX 21
[335] Ibid XIX·13.
[336] Ibid XX:9.
[337] Robertson, Archibald, "Regnum Dei," p. 212.

tine meet the universal demand for absolute authority of a
capricious age. Hitherto the religious movement and the
political movement had existed side by side. But the fall of
the imperial city made way for this spiritual predominance
"Thus in its impressive organization, in its institutions, and
above all, in its great councils, the City of God presented to
man the aspect of a world-wide Holy Empire."[338] The
thought of an empire was a welcome one at that time to Romans and barbarians alike; in fact, people could think in no
other terms. Hence Augustine's commanding message of a
hierarchical Church, universal and enduring as the empire itself, gained the ears of the people at a time when the rending
of one world order made the existence of another a necessity.

But frequently in Augustine's work we perceive that he felt
the Church to be only a fragment and beginning of the true
city of God. Augustine is willing to admit that there are
individuals belonging to the Divine city outside of the Church.
Furthermore it embraces also the departed, the unborn, and the
angels.[339] He also denied that the Church now existing was
intended to be coextensive with the final and glorious Church,
and referred his opponents to the parables of the "Tares" and
the "Dragnet."[340] However, it was not in this broad sense
that posterity accepted it, but rather as that of an ecclesiastical paramountcy, which through the efforts of Gregory VII and
Innocent III was to become "an omnipotent hierarchy set over
nations and kingdoms, to pluck up and break down and to
destroy, and to overthrow and to build and to plant,"[341]—
the great theocratic system of the Middle Ages.

Of the immediate effect of the "City of God" on its own age
it is difficult to judge; but there can be no doubt of its popularity and widespread influence in later ages. As a thinker
Augustine occupies a great place in political theory and
practice. The entire political, as well as the ecclesiastical,
movement of the Middle Ages was dominated by him. Mr.
Bryce gives us to understand that the Holy Roman Empire

[338] Osmun, G. W., "Augustine. The Thinker," New York, 1906, p. 179.
[339] "City of God," XI:7; XX:9
[340] Ibid. XX:9
[341] Robertson, op cit, p. 222.

was built upon the foundation of the "City of God." [342] And we know that it was no accident that the book was the favorite reading of Charlemagne. It takes its place among the few significant books of all time.

From the specifically sociological point of view, however, it does not have this profound significance. Augustine's utopianism had almost no original elements about it whatsoever; and as a collection or revision of that of his ethico-religious forebears, it shows marks of retrogression or even corruption. The clear-cut statements and the sound doctrines of the prophets and Jesus lose much of their buoyancy and elemental power because of the wordy, involved and sometimes platitudinous treatment of Augustine. They are further corrupted by a mysticism necessitating a high degree of emotionalism and ecstasy, which also makes them flabby and weak. While we cannot deny the political and religious effect of Augustine's work, particularly its influence in furnishing the ideas about which the hierarchical church was constructed, we must also use caution against overestimating the work as a fruitful source of social idealism. It has very little originality about it, and is, in most cases, a poor expression of that which has gone before. We must not give it too great a significance.

5. Savonarola's Florentine Theocracy

Of all the actual attempts to establish a theocracy on earth, the most striking was doubtless that of Fra Girolamo Savonarola (1452–1498) in Florence in 1494 and the years immediately following. A brief description of this occupies an essential and fitting place in a study of ethico-religious Utopias.

The last half of the fifteenth century was a time of unusual significance in the history of the world, since it was an age of transition. The soul of the new was struggling to break away from the traditions and practices of the old. In Italy the intellectual life was feeding on the newly found glories of the Renaissance. The study of the humanities was universally hailed with enthusiasm, and the classics commanded the thought of all who laid claim to scholarship. Art and archi-

[342] Bryce, J., "The Holy Roman Empire," New York, 1904, pp 93–99.

tecture, language and literature were everywhere undergoing profound changes due to this strange wave of unrest which was sweeping across the world. Nor were statecraft and government remaining unchanged under this agitation. All was in a state of unrest. And Florence, no less than the rest of Italy .and the western world, was suffering its pangs of a new birth.

The famous rule of the Medici came to an end in Florence with the expulsion of Piero de Medici and his retinue, after a reign of singular brilliance, which displayed open contempt for the middle class now growing in strength and importance, and brooking no subjection. This expulsion also, of course, involved the abandonment of all the principles of government which had been in operation during the period of the Medici ascendancy. If the state was not to fall into anarchy it was essential that a new system of government should be evolved as rapidly as possible. The times were favorable for a liberal constitution, for the Florentines, by overthrowing their despotic rulers, supposed that they had regained their ancient heritage of liberty. All that was needed was to formulate a system under which this newly recovered liberty could be enjoyed.[343] Events were of such a nature as to make immediate action necessary. Pisa and other dependencies had revolted against their Florentine conquerors during the time of Florence's unsettled state. Internally the city was in danger since many partisans of the Medici were still within the city ready to seize upon any opportunity presented by the temporary and makeshift government, to secure the return of Piero and the continuation of the old system. Accordingly all efforts were directed to the creation of a new constitution and the establishment of a stable, democratic government.

It was at this time that Savonarola, Prior of San Marco, foremost preacher, and the most influential personage of Florence, came forward with his vision of a theocracy. During the months that the Signory, the temporary elected rulers of Florence, were deliberating and attempting to bring the Republic into being, Savonarola had dreamed of an order of things in Florence and the glamor of its appeal to his enthusiasm

[343] Horsbough, E L. S., "Girolamo Savonarola," London, 1911, p. 125.

constantly waxed stronger. Finally his feeling that interposition on his part would be misplaced was overborne by the
rising political impulse which compelled him to interpose, and
soon his version was sent broadcast from the pulpit of his
church, the Duomo, to the eager multitudes. The dream he
spoke of was a theocracy, a strictly ordered Christian state,
in which immorality should be suppressed, in which social and
civic life should be ruled by Divine precepts, in which charity
and righteousness, equality and liberty should reign supreme,
in which private interests should be sacrificed to the common
good, and in the hearts of whose citizens God should reign.

Now that he held the extraordinary position of virtual
arbiter of the city's destinies through his tremendous hold upon
the great rank and file, he was encouraged in believing that the
time had come to translate his great dream into a reality. The
vision itself of Florence as a holy city made him certain that he
was justified in his participation in the affairs of state. The
sermons, preached mostly from prophetic texts, were a curious
intermingling of politics and religion. He recommended the
Venetian Constitution as a model of the holy city, because, as
was held, the Venetian Constitution was given the Venetians
by God. At the same time he summoned the citizens of
Florence to put down vice with a vigorous hand, to sweep
obscenity from their streets, to reform their manners, lay aside
their luxury, their indecent attire and gaudy finery, and instead of pursuing frivolity and pleasure, to give themselves in
humility to the worship and service of God.[344] This brought
rapid response, for with the political excitement there now
blended a strange religious fervor, and Savonarola was able to
effect many remarkable and heretofore unheard-of reforms
which were the means of transmuting his dream into temporary
reality. Florence was at this time the victim of most degrading
vices. The most vicious practices were prevalent among
all classes. "Your life," said the preacher, "is the life of
swine,"[345] and the testimony of historians is evidence that the
charge was apt. Savonarola succeeded in getting the magis-

[344] MacHardy, George, "Savonarola," Edinburgh, 1901, p 109
[345] Quoted by Crawford, W. H, "Girolamo Savonarola," New York, 1906,
p 161

trates to effect Puritanic reforms. He himself delivered the
poor from the excessive extortions of the Jewish money-lenders
and provided a means of obtaining loans at moderate and
reasonable rates. He aimed to give education a more earnest
moral and religious character. He adopted every means in
his power to purify the literature used in the schools. He
succeeded in withdrawing the rising generation from frivolous
pursuits and sensuous pleasures. And the transformations in
the social life of Florence, from 1495 to 1497, read like a story
of miracles, as is attested by a contemporary scholar who states
"The whole aspect of the city changed. Finery and jewelry
were cast aside; women dressed plainly on the streets; money
which had before been spent for ornament and display was now
given to the poor; theatres and taverns were empty; cards and
dice disappeared; the churches were crowded; alms-boxes were
well-filled; tradesmen and bankers restored their ill-gotten
gains; purity, sobriety, and justice prevailed in the city, and
the Prior of San Marco was everywhere hailed as the greatest
public benefactor." [346] Furthermore, the Constitution adopted
was modeled upon that of Venice which Savonarola had recommended, and through it men attempted to reëstablish the old
principles of free government and the new principles of righteousness and justice. Savonarola was supremely happy and
regarded the events about him as a triumph of God's kingdom
on earth. Florence, he felt, was not a republic but a theocracy,
and infidelity to the Constitution which he had recommended
and sanctioned became in his view infidelity to God.

But Savonarola's beautiful edifice contained within itself
the forces of its own destruction. As his reforms increased
in austerity and severity, many who believed in popular
government and liberty lost sympathy with him. The adherents of the Medici were once again coming to the fore under
the stimulus of this dissatisfaction. The papacy under Alex-
ander VI, the most corrupt pope the Catholic Church ever had,
rose to strike down the bold reformer who had dared to expose
and oppose its vicious practices. But perhaps the most potent
factor was human nature itself. The standard of conduct on

[346] Ibid p. 163

which Savonarola insisted was too monastic; it left scant room for the healthful play of natural human feeling.   There was too much repression, too much dependence for practical efficiency on the influence of legal prohibition and on the coercion of supernatural fears.   The changes he wrought were in a certain measure spasmodic and forced and lacked those elements only brought by slow evolution which give human progress solid depth and abiding reality.   Human nature cannot be pressed into goodness as he expected to do, nor can society be regenerated by the austere methods of asceticism.   As Calvin afterward found in Geneva, a strong and masterful mind wielding dictatorial ascendancy, may for a time, by painting the glories of the ideal and the terrors of hell-fire, obtain visible acquiescence, and yet fail to control the people permanently.

The reaction against Savonarola swept away his beautiful fabric and eventually doomed him to the fagots where "the martyr's soul went out in fire"   We can say of Savonarola as Carlyle did: [347] "We will praise the hero-priest . . . who wears out, in toil, calumny, contradiction, a noble life, to make a God's kingdom of this earth.   The earth will not become too godlike."

[347] Carlyle, "Heroes and Hero-worship," chapter on "The Priest"

CHAPTER III

THE "REPUBLIC" OF PLATO

Plato, although by no means the first Utopian, may, never-theless, be regarded as the father of idealism in philosophy, in politics, and in literature, and the captain or leader of that long train of brilliant secular and philosophical genuises, who have given us the current conception of the term "Utopia" by a long series of social anticipations; for very important elements in most of them may be traced back to his "Republic." The "Republic" is the expression of the ideal of a classical philoso-pher, the representative of the highest culture of his age, writing in his prime and consequently representing the best secular thought of the age. In contrast to this we have the visions of the prophets, previously discussed, expressions of the same idealistic nature, although the products of an intensely religious group. It is this difference in original sources and racial ideals which accounts for the varying nature of the Utopias. Therefore, we are treating the two types separately. Furthermore, there seems to be no connection between them whatever; the spirit and content are wholly different. The prophets preceded Plato by several centuries, and we know that he had access to great stores of literature through his many travels. But nothing is to be found in the "Republic" to indi-cate that he was in any way influenced by them, though there are singular similarities of a general nature. These, however, are readily seen to be accidental.[1] The sources are wholly different.

Plato (427–347 B. C.) was the pupil and disciple of Socrates,

[1] For a scholarly treatment of these similarities see E C. Baldwin, "Ezekiel's 'Holy City' and Plato's 'Republic'" in Biblical World Vol. 41:365 ff. Plato was, however, doubtless influenced by Hesiod, the Greek didactic poet, who, about 700 B C., protested against social injustice and described the Golden Age.

the truest and most intelligent, and yet the most independent of his followers. Imbued, as he was, with the doctrines of his master, he was nevertheless able to stand apart and create something distinctly his own. The "Republic" is a work of an original hand, entirely and wholly the product of its creator. The exact time of its appearance in book form is unknown, but its content certainly had been early discussed by Plato with his fellows, for in 393 B. C. some of his ideas were ridiculed in the Ecclesiazusæ of Aristophanes. It appeared at a time when the dissolution of Greek political life was taking place. The popular philosophy of the times proclaimed the exaltation of the individual to the detriment of the state. This, combined with the disastrous termination of the Peloponnesian War, gave to the powerful oligarchical party the power to rule which they did in such a way as to cause atrocities to be commonplaces. Plato, then in his maturity, after a life of close attention to these social and political conditions, after the unjust execution of his master by a misguided people, was led to distrust all existing political systems, all philosophies which exalted the individual. He conceived of a state free from the corruption of extreme license and the dangers of tyranny, and embodying in its laws and institutions the principle of fundamental unity of the moral individual with the socialized state. He used the myth of an ideal republic in which future mankind was to blissfully abide, as a vehicle by means of which to express these ideas which he could not otherwise openly utter. The "Republic" is a combination of politics and dialectics; at the same time a philosophical estimate of the highest good, and a treatise on communism and the theory of the state. But above all its main argument is the search after justice.

The Platonic state was and is regarded as an ideal or chimera impracticable of realization among men. In fact Plato himself held this conception when he said that it "exists in our reasoning, since it is no where on earth, at least, as I imagine. But in heaven, probably, there is a model of it." [2] At another time when asked when his ideal state would become

[2] Plato's "Republic," Bk IX, p 315. All references will be to Spens' translation in "Everyman's Edition"

possible he ironically replied, "When one son of a king becomes a philosopher," [3] referring to his own famous paradox in the "Republic" that until kings are philosophers, or philosophers are kings, neither cities nor the human race will ever cease to suffer ill.[4] And yet Plato was unaware that a century before his time, a son of a king—Buddha—had become a philosopher.[5] But Plato did not think of the "Republic" as a mere exercise of fancy, nor is it merely a collection of abstract theories, expressed without any practical purpose. The philosopher cannot transcend his age, but can only see it and appraise its true significance. This Plato did. His standpoint was his own age, and he took the life as he found it, exalted it to its ideal, and expected it to suggest broad lines of progress. Nor did he feel that his own generation would travel very far along the road he pointed out. When asked whether there was any way of making citizens believe a certain theory, he replied, "None to persuade these men, themselves; but I can contrive how that their sons and posterity, and all mankind afterwards, shall believe it." [6]

But a thought of the complete consummation of the ideal never entered Plato's mind. Such a conception was impossible to an inhabitant of the world at that time for it implied a vision of progress entailing advance step by step throughout the ages. The idea of progress 'is of modern rather than ancient date. In ancient times they had but a vague conception of antiquity, and no philosophy of history, or means of comparing one age with another. The idea first dawned upon the human mind after the epochal social and political changes wrought in the world by the Roman Empire, the Christian Church, and after the many new inventions and discoveries, the idealism of the French Revolution and the tremendous material prosperity of the last few centuries. It was by means of such events that man has become "the spectator of all time and of all existence" and has been able to look back through the vista of the ages and contemplate their purpose, and look ahead and by

[3] "Laws," Bk V.
[4] "Republic," p. 174.
[5] Garnett in Intro to "Republic," p xiv
[6] "Republic," III, p 105.

analogy of history lift the veil a bit and peer into the future.

Plato represented a state built upon the background of his own age and it was a philosopher's vision throughout. This ideal commonwealth took, for Plato, the outward form of a city-state, much copied in later anticipations. The city-state was peculiarly adapted to this use. Like most early reformers, he hoped for social regeneration and betterment through the organization of a closely aggregated social group, self-sufficient and isolated. The city-state of his time provided an excellent example on which to improve. It was unlike the nation-state, as spoken of by Bernhard Bosanquet [7] and Ernst Barker [8] for in it the state was not an external, alien force,—something which the average citizen feels to be something apart from himself,—but a closely knit, small community in which "it was easy for each citizen to feel that the State was but himself writ large." [9] It was a thought which conceived of the state, not as a governing and corrective body, but as an association of ethically minded individuals, bound together by thoughts of a common purpose and serving in their fit places.

The most prominent characteristic of the Hellenic conception of the state, before Greek political life had fallen into decay, was the constraint upon personal subjective freedom, the sacrifice of individual interest to the absolute sovereignty of the state. Plato in a measure revived this ideal, and, in opposition to the ruinous tendencies of his age, made the state supreme, but it was a supremacy tempered, not by political, but ethical motives. For him the state holds this supremacy because of its utterly indispensable character in the realm of human welfare. Men are not self-sufficient, but dependent upon one another; and human perfection is both impracticable and impossible unless this ethical unity, the state, is taken as the basis of organization. [10] The efforts of the moralist are discernible throughout in the ethical aspect given all phases of the work. Ethical values and standards illuminate for him the whole circuit of human life. The state is not the end of

[7] "Philosophical Theory of the State," pp 320 ff.
[8] "Political Thought of Plato and Aristotle," p. 8.
[9] Barker, op. cit., p. 8
[10] "Republic," II, p. 50.

all but rather the means to an end and its task is to present the ideal of humanity and educate the citizen to that particular virtue which will make him most happy and therefore of greatest service to the state. "We are forming," says Plato, "a happy state, not picking out some few persons to make them alone happy, but are establishing the universal happiness of the whole." [11]

To secure this virtuous happiness of all in the state [12] each of the principal functions and corresponding virtues of the soul is to be represented by a particular class of citizens, automatically selected according to their characteristic capacities. These essential virtues of the state, as of the individual soul, are wisdom, bravery, temperance and justice. Wisdom is conspicuously necessary in the state in order that it be denominated wise and well-counseled. [13] The state must also make war and fight in its own defense, and assist in preserving and inculcating the opinions of the wise counselors. Hence there must be bravery and fortitude. [14] Further, there must be in every state a harmony and symmetry of government demanding temperance. [15] If these are present in the state then justice reigns. [16] In this imaginary commonwealth there are to be three classes:—the teaching and ruling class, the warrior class or guardians, and the working class. It belongs to the first class alone, the cultured,—a very small class, to be sure,— to guide the state and to rule, to give laws and watch over their observance. The virtue proper to this class is wisdom. With the keen insight of true philosophers they are to labor only for the realization of the truth and the good of all. Plato believed in the collective good sense of the cultivated, most spiritually minded, most delicately perceptive people in the state. In support of these we find a second class, the public officials, guardians and warriors whose supreme virtue is valor or fortitude. They must fearlessly perform their duty in maintain-

[11] Ibid. IV, p. 109.
[12] For his development of the state see "Republic," Bk. II and Bk. VI.
[13] "Republic," IV, pp. 118–120
[14] Ibid. IV, pp. 120–122.
[15] Ibid. IV, pp 122–124
[16] Ibid. IV, p. 125.

ing the order of the state both within and without. The third
class is made up of the great mass of people, the manual laborers (slaves), farmers, artisans and tradesmen, who have to care
for providing the external means of the state by their labor and
industry. The virtues of this class are self-restraint and ex-
plicit obedience. When each class does its duty and maintains
its appropriate virtues the nature of the state corresponds to the
ideal of justice and happiness. Justice, then, is social coordination and the consequent harmony of the whole,—a harmony effected because every individual is doing his work in
the station of life to which he is called by his capacities.

Plato totally excludes from political life the workingmen,
which, for him, exist in the state only as a means. It was
not necessary to make laws or care for the rights of this portion of the community. But the separation between the ruler
and the warrior class is not so sharp. These ranks are suffered to interpenetrate each other, it even being possible for
the oldest and best of the warriors to rise to the dignity and
power of rulers. In reality Plato makes but two classes, the
subjects and the sovereign.

This, it will be seen, really makes for an ethical aristocracy. All individual self-will and selfishness must be sub-
ordinated to the common will and common good as dictated
by the spiritual and intellectual guides. And these rulers can
only govern as they become capable of contemplating the Idea
of Good,—not the moral but the metaphysical good. It is
the highest idea, the ultimate limit of all knowledge, and the
ground of all ideas. Justice and the other virtues are only
useful and advantageous as they use it for a model. Wisdom is
only truly wisdom, beauty only real beauty when they are in
conformity with the good. [17] Truth, knowledge, beauty—all
things "which are known have not only this from the good, that
they are known, but likewise their being and essence are given
them by it, whilst the good itself is not essence, but above essence, superior to it both in dignity and power." [18] Science and
truth are not good, but of a goodly nature, for the good is

[17] Ibid. pp 211–212.
[18] Ibid. VI p. 216.

superior to them. Again he says, "The idea of good, . . . if it be seen, it is to be deemed as indeed the cause to all bright and beautiful, generating in the visible world light, and its principle the sun, and in the intellectual world, it is itself the principle producing truth and intelligence, and that this must be beheld by him who is to act wisely, either privately or in public." [19] The idea of good is another mode of conceiving of God, for, as Plato says, only those are philosophic geniuses who "are always desirous of such learning as may discover to them, *that being which always exists,* and is not changed by generation or corruption." [20] They are truly to be individuals in tune with and like unto the Infinite. Then will the state be guided aright.

It also implies the complete assimilation of the individual in the state, for the ethical ideal becomes, for Plato, the political. The individual may lay claim only to that happiness which belongs to him as a constituent element of the state, and moral virtue becomes political virtue. The virtues of the individual soul are the same as those of the state.[21] The virtue of the cognitive part of the soul is wisdom or prudence, which is the directing or measuring virtue; that of the courageous part is valor or bravery, the helpmeet of wisdom, which consists in preserving correct and legitimate ideas of what is to be feared and what is not to be feared; the virtue of the appetitive or sensuous part is temperance, moderation or self-control whose function is to restrain within its proper limits the worst parts of the soul; justice, finally, is the universal virtue brought about by the regulation and mutual adjustment of the other faculties of the soul, forming a unified personality. This parallel between virtue in the state and in the individual soul is introduced by Plato with the remark that in the former we read in larger characters the same writing, which in the latter is written in smaller ones. Not only has the individual the same virtues as the state, but they must be fused into the body of the state. Justice for the individual is doing his duty in his appointed place; and the justice of the state thus becomes

19 Ibid. VII, p. 233.
20 Ibid. VI, p 186, Italics mine.
21 Ibid. IV, pp. 136 ff.

the composite of the sense of duty of its citizens. Plato here has approached the idea of a great fraternity based upon a feeling of brotherhood, and has tended to ennoble and elevate the notions of the aims of government and of the duties of citizens. He has made social ethics universal and firmly established their existence He has emphasized the inherent solidarity of society showing that the welfare and happiness of the whole depend on the welfare and happiness of each individual; he has also by means of his identification of ethics and politics given definiteness to ethics showing them to be simply the politics of the individual.

On the other hand, we cannot say without qualification, that the characters of nations are nothing more than the sum of the individuals who compose them, because there are tendencies of the group as a whole which can never be the tendencies of the individuals separately. When we deal with human beings the whole is not always the sum of its parts. As Jowett says, "A whole nation may be wiser than any one in it; or may be animated by some common opinion or feeling which could not equally have affected the mind of a single person, or may have been inspired by a leader of genius to perform arts more than human." [22] The character of the state is really the character of the majority of individuals acting in common.

With Plato all individual interests whatsoever are forbidden the citizens, and they are required to form in the strictest sense a family in the mass. Everything individual and particular falls away. Private property and domestic life, education and instruction, the choice of rank and possession, the arts and sciences, all these must be placed under the exclusive and absolute control of the State. The social life must be, as it were, the life of one man. This social life, the utopianistic consummation of his ideal of justice, is to be attained by two great institutions. One is a system of communism; the other a system of common education by the State. Both of these are practical proposals, induced by contemporary conditions, and meant for the remedy of those evils which Plato detected in existing

[22] Jowett, Intro. to his Trans of Plato's "Republic," p lxiii.

states. Both, he felt, were reactions against ignorance and selfishness, and made for knowledge and unselfishness.

He would have community of women, children and property, and complete control by the state of the marital relation. Plato felt that in community of women and children he had discerned the greatest good to his perfect city.[23] The family he conceived to be the natural enemy of the state, since it thrust itself and all its ties between the individual and politically organized society. He entertained the hope that a universal brotherhood might take the place of private interests,—a brotherhood free from lawsuits, and accusations and all other "disturbances which men raised about money, children or relations,"—a unified brotherhood with community of pleasures and pains, not torn by disagreements of " 'mine' and 'not mine,' 'his' and 'not his!' " [24]

Here we have the case of one of the wisest and best of men entertaining ideas of morality wholly at variance with our own. But we must observe that the relations between the sexes are for him the reverse of licentious, being of almost impossible strictness. There is to be no sentiment or imagination in the connections which men and women form, but all arrangements of marriage are directed to the one end of improvement of the race and strengthening of the state. As in animals the best are chosen for breeding, so there must be a selection made of the human beings whose lives are worthy of being transplanted into the future.[25] To this end at special festivals partners for temporary matrimony are chosen by lot; [26] but of these couples only those who are found fit by the magistrates (both male and female) can procreate and produce legitimate offspring for the state. Procreation and its supervision is strictly an affair of the state. Children must be born, not of love, but of science. Lot was resorted to in order that those who were ruled out of the privilege of parenthood might blame their own ill luck and not the guardians who manipulated the lot. The marriages were made at festivals so as to make them sacred,

23 "Republic," p 162.
24 Ibid. V, p 160.
25 Ibid. V, p. 155.
26 Ibid V, p. 156.

but the most advantageous are the most sacred.[27]   The state furthermore gives special liberties of embracing women to those men who have distinguished themselves in war or anywhere else.[28]   Otherwise men and women are to live separately having all in common.   To insure vigorous offspring, they must be born of parents in their prime, hence he would only have those men between twenty-five and fifty-five beget and those women between twenty and forty bear children to the state.[29]   The children of these unions are likewise to be common; "that neither the parent know his own children, nor the children their parent."[30]   They are to be received by magistrates, either men or women, appointed for these purposes, and placed in the nurseries where they are especially cared for by nurses and keepers instructed "to be wakeful, and to take every necessary toil."[31]   With Spartan-like severity Plato would permit no exhibitions of physical degeneracy or weakness to be tolerated within the state.   Hence the possiblity of offspring in all irregular and unsupervised unions, especially those men and women not within the prescribed age limits, must be prevented by secret means, such as abortion or infanticide, for the birth would be unconsecrated and uncertified.   And all children suitably born but deformed or sickly were to be abandoned and exposed.

It is strange that the greatest of ancient philosophers, and at the same time one of the greatest of idealists should have permitted such streaks of animalism to adulterate his ideal. Like the Spartans, he seemed to have forgotten that man is first human and then animal; that morality transcends the physical.   In fact he falls into a grave inconsistency here when he actually denies what he has himself proved, namely, that mind and reason are not subjected to the baser parts of the individual but rule them.   The improvement of the human race consists not merely in physical soundness, and excellence, but also in sturdy morals and enlightened mind.   Hence in

[27] Ibid V, p. 155.
[28] Ibid. V, p 157.
[29] Ibid V, p. 158
[30] Ibid V, p. 154
[31] Ibid. V, p. 157.

the union of the sexes there must be "a marriage of true minds as well as bodies," a fusion of souls as well as gratification of instincts. This Plato left out of consideration.

Another fact of which Plato was wholly unaware was that children cannot be successfully raised by wholesale, and that all his children would be foundlings. They would have lost that subtle sympathy between mother and child which "nurses and keepers" cannot give. The child feeds on mother love as surely as on milk. Plato seems to have been unduly influenced by what he had seen and heard of Sparta and applied it in a mistaken way to his ideal commonwealth. As Jowett says, "He probably observed that both the Spartan men and women were superior in form and strength to the other Greeks; and this superiority he was disposed to attribute to their laws and customs relating to marriage. He did not consider that the desire of a noble offspring was a passion among the Spartans, or that their physical superiority was to be attributed chiefly, not to their marriage customs, but to their temperance and training. He did not reflect that Sparta was great, not in consequence of the relaxation of morality, but in spite of it, by virtue of a political principle stronger far than existed in any other Grecian state. Least of all did he observe that Sparta did not really produce the finest specimens of the Greek race. The genius, the political inspiration of Athens, the love of liberty—all that has made Greece famous with posterity, was wanting among the Spartans. They had no Themistocles, or Pericles, or Æschylus, or Sophocles, or Socrates, or Plato." [32]

Plato's original ideas on the subject of scientific mating and state child culture, however, were not due to any morbid or materialistic motives. It was really the moral advantages of communism which appealed to him; the evils of the system, which later became known to him,[33] were not taken into consideration. Communism, he thought, would eliminate the motive of selfishness, and finally secure the solidarity of the state. With a thorough-going communism and a careful effort on the part of the state to prevent the indentification of children, by

[32] Ibid p lui

[33] It is worthy of note that Plato in Book V of his "Laws," written late in life, renounced the community of women and children.

the third or fourth generation all members of the ruling and fighting classes would be generally related to one another, and no member would be, or at least would not know that he was, particularly related to any other. This would be of advantage to the state for it would make for unity and similarity of purpose. All members would have so identified themselves with the whole, that whatever happened in any portion of the state would be felt by each member as happening to himself.

Whatever he did not succeed in recanting with respect to community of women and children is, however, fully compensated for in his theory of equality of the sexes,—a theory so advanced that it transcended his age by fully two milleniums. In this he shows a wonderful independence of mind. The Grecian woman of his day was in no way the equal of her husband; she was not the entertainer of his guests or the mistress of his house, but only his housekeeper and mother of his children, little removed from the status of a slave. Interest in political matters, and activity in behalf of public interests were strictly fields of male endeavor. There was a feeling that women were generally inferior and mentally incapable. But in secluding women and making them family drudges Plato felt that not only was the development of women stunted, but also the State lost the service of half of its numbers; so his ideal was very different. For him woman is but lesser man. There is no organic difference between men and women, but only the accidental one that men beget and women bear children. He makes this case analogous to that of the animals. There the sexes do not follow different pursuits, nor are they differently endowed.[34] Why then should we assume that such is the case with the sexes of mankind? Inherently woman is no less capable than man except that she is not as strong. Therefore Plato holds that, "There is not then, my friend, any office among the whole inhabitants of the city peculiar to the woman, considered as woman, nor to the man, considered as man; but the geniuses are indiscriminately diffused through both: the woman is naturally fitted for sharing in all offices, and so is

[34] "Republic," V, p. 146,—the example of the watchdogs.

the man; but in all the woman is weaker than the man." [35]
Hence the occupations of men and women are to be the same.
Women will even be permitted to rule the state equally with
the men, becoming magistrates and guardians.[36] But it is not
merely a granting of rights without the assumption of duties;
women will also be expected to train themselves as men do
and take part in the toils of war.[37] They are to lose as far
as possible the incidents of maternity and the characteristics
of the female sex. They must be freed from the bondage to
family and children if they are to be real citizens, interested
in the public welfare and loving not merely the family but the
great community. In this manner is woman raised to a higher
level of existence, and made the companion of man, sharing
with him his burdens and responsibilities. Plato brings not
sentiment, swayed by custom or feeling, but philosophy and
reason to bear on this ancient and yet modern question.
Neither the State nor any of its citizens can become strong or
approach perfection when half, and sometimes the most important half, of the population is in subjection. Hence he
would have all equals.[38]

Silver and gold are forbidden the inhabitants of the city,[39]
for they are to have at all times the divine gold and silver
of the gods in their souls. Money is the source of all evil
and corruption,[40] therefore there is none. Property is to be
held in common for when a man owns property he becomes a
hateful lord instead of the ally of his fellow citizens; he plots
and is plotted against, and is continually distracted lest something befall his substance.[41] So there will be neither buying
nor selling, owning nor borrowing, by any one, but all will enjoy
all according to fitness and need. Unlike more recent com-

[35] Ibid. V, p. 151.

[36] Ibid. V, pp. 152, 157

[37] Ibid. V, p 165

[38] Plato, however, writing at the time he did, did not recognize the
vital difference of nature and almost of kind between man and woman

[39] Ibid. III, p 107

[40] Ibid. III, p. 107,—"The money of the vulgar hath produced many
wicked deeds."

[41] Ibid. III, p 107.

munists, Plato would not have an equal division of material ⅄
goods for the sake of an equal diffusion of material happiness,
but an equal abnegation of material goods for the sake of ideal
happiness. Plato wanted life divested of economic motives, of
all crass desires of self-satisfaction, so that men could lead
a life of reason and be animated by a desire to attain the
welfare of the larger whole. Social solidarity rationally attained was his goal.

Plato, however, places his greatest hopes for the perfection ⅄
of humanity on <u>education</u>, and his scheme of communism is
merely to reënforce education and provide a suitable environment for it. It is to be an education continuing through life,
contemplating it in its entirety, and serving as a preparation
for another life when it begins anew. It is to be participated
in equally and without any discrimination by both sexes.
Plato feels that vice and diseases of the state are due chiefly
to ignorance and that the primary means of preventing them
is to provide education, which will take care of all the rest, for
he says, "Whilst good education and nurture are preserved, they
produce good geniuses; and good geniuses, partaking of such
education, produce still better than the former." [42]

The education which he proposes for his citizens is really
one which will fit them for the ideal life of the philosopher or
man of genius, interrupted only for a time, by practical duties;
it is really a life, not for the many but the few. Furthermore,
as we shall presently see, it is to be conducted by an intellectual
board of education, composed of the city's select few. The
third class is not included in this educational scheme at all,
it being reserved for the children of the rulers and warriors
of the ideal state, the ordinary ability of practical life being
regarded as sufficient for the purposes of the other class. The
education is to follow a regular schedule [43] which seemingly
would cast all citizens in the same mould, and yet it is one
of harmonious growth, for it seeks to unconsciously teach
temperance and endurance, and to develop body and mind in
equal proportion. From before birth to the second year the

[42] "Republic," IV, p 113.
[43] The schedule here adhered to is that derived from the "Republic" by
Ueberweg in his "History of Philosophy," Vol. I, p. 132.

body is to be cared for. From three to six narration of myths is to comprise the bulk of the training. According to Plato the aim of early education is to teach truth as a matter of principle. Therefore, the children are taught first simple truths concerning the gods. The current myths or fables, however, will not do, for there are many elements about them which tend to lead children astray, or terrify them, or render them effeminate or sensuous. Therefore, these must be purged and revised. From the religious truths they are to pass on to the simple moral truths, and insensibly to learn the lesson of good manners and good taste. Fables are also to be invented which will bring this about, and also contain the praises of the gods and noble men. From seven to ten they are to be trained in gymnastics, for not only is the citizen to have wisdom but endurance.

We are not to infer, however, that the physical education is to cease with the tenth year, for it is intended to be continued throughout life as a correlative part of the philosopher's life. In fact, care of the body is the assistant to philosophy [44] Gymnastics should be taught, not as an object, as if the students were to be trained athletes, but as a means of rendering them more fit for their duties. Furthermore, it is to be the same for both sexes, since physical strength and military prowess are equally essential to both in Plato's communistic state. Nor will any one laugh at the naked woman wrestling with the men in the Palæstra [45] for "the man who laughs at naked women, whilst performing the exercises for the sake of what is best, reaps the empty fruit of a ridiculous wisdom, and in no respect knows, as appears, at what he laughs, nor why he does it. For that ever was and will be deemed a noble saying, That what is most advantageous for the public is handsome, and what is hurtful is ugly." And besides the women will "put on virtue for clothes." [46] Besides fitness for life as warriors and rulers, the object of gymnastics is to render resort to the medical art unnecessary. Consequently the prime purpose of the physician is not to cure diseases but rather the establishing

[44] "Republic," IV, p. 202.
[45] Ibid. V, p. 147.
[46] Ibid. V, p. 153.

of a regimen of exercise and the supervision of such diet as will make diseases and ills impossible.[47]

From ten to thirteen the children are taught reading and writing; and from fourteen to sixteen poetry and music. The poetry permitted the youth must have passed the inspection of competent judges, for frequently "poets and orators speak amiss concerning the greatest affairs of men." [48] Epic and dramatic poetry, even Homer and Hesiod, should be banished for they arouse and lead astray the passions and give unworthy representations of the gods. It would not be fit to allow poetical stories to be told about the gods' injuring and fighting one another; nor would it be well to have the minds of the future defenders and rulers of the state poisoned by statements that evil as well as good is caused by the gods, nor is it advisable to have death and the kingdom of Hades represented as something frightful; nor would it be wholesome to introduce tales of heroes quarreling with the gods and being partial to filthy liars. All music which induces to effeminacy and idleness, illiberality and insolence, is to be forbidden and only those harmonies, "the vehement and the gentle, which in the most handsome manner imitate the voice . . . of the moderate and brave," [49] are to be permitted them, for thus will they be inspired to courage and perseverance. They must have "an understanding truly adorned with a beautiful and fine temper." [50] Only that is really art which consists in the imitation of the good. Plato breathes a note which it would be well for us of the present day to heed when he hints that art must be regulated and supervised, for he saw that art, in reflecting life, in turn reacting, directs human life. Art, for him, must be selective as well as imitative, it should select those moments or phases of life which tell most in exhibiting its proper trend and purpose. Barker tells us,[51] "Plato would have recognized a deep truth in the saying, "Let me write the ballads of a country, and I care not who writes the laws"; he would indeed have

[47] Ibid. III, pp 90–98.
[48] Ibid III, p. 76
[49] Ibid. III, p 85.
[50] Ibid. III, p 87.
[51] Op cit, p. 133.

extended its scope, and made it read, "Let me write the right ballads for a country, and nobody will need to write its laws."

From sixteen to eighteen they are to be taught the mathematical sciences. As already stated the highest endeavor of Plato's state is to be the contemplation and cognition of the Idea of Good,—an abstract principle. Therefore the great aim of education is the cultivation of the habit of abstraction. And this is to be acquired through the study of mathematical sciences, such as geometry and astronomy, for they, alone are capable of giving ideas of relation and arousing the dormant energies of thought,[52]—of leading men out of the cave into the light. The education of the youth was regulated by Plato in accordance with the principle of a gradual advance to the cognition of the "ideas" and the corresponding practical activity in the state, so that only the best-qualified persons could rise to the highest stations, while the rest were destined for inferior practical functions. To this end, after this first test of ability of dealing with abstractions the first selection is made.[53] Persons possessing an inferior capacity for science, but capable of bravery, remain warriors; the rest [54] go on, until the age of thirty, learning the sciences in a more exact and universal form than was possible in their earlier youthful years, apprehending them in their mutual relations as parts of the whole. Then comes the second selection. The less promising are assigned to practical public offices. The rest pursue, from the age of thirty to thirty-five "the art of reasoning with perseverance and application, and doing nothing else, but in way of counterpart exercising in all bodily exercises." [55] They then, until their fiftieth year, hold positions of authority, and "govern both in things relating to war, and such other magistracies as require youth, that they may not fall short of others in experience " [56] After this they finally attain to the highest degree in philosophy, the contemplation of the Idea of Good. At the same time for the sake of the city, they each take their

[52] "Republic," VII, pp. 235–247.
[53] Ibid VII, p. 245.
[54] Ibid. VII, p. 248.
[55] Ibid. VIII, p 251.
[56] Ibid VII, p 251.

turn as rulers and fill the highest offices of the state, being charged with the superintendence of the entire government. But most of the time during this last period of their lives is devoted to philosophical contemplation. Finally "after they have educated others in the same manner still, and left such as resemble themselves to be the guardians of the city, they depart to inhabit the islands of the blest." [57] This is the path which Plato's men and women follow in attaining the goal of perfection. It is the means by which philosophers really become rulers of cities.

This is the ultimate aim of all of Plato's utopianism. To make the nearest approach to the cognition of the Idea of Good is to achieve the greatest possible likeness to God.[58] To this the "Republic" is to lead men. But it is attained by a few who by means of it exalt idealism and philosophic pursuits and establish justice in the state. It is the attainment of the highest perfection possible by the few, that benefit may be reflected upon the others. Thus the aim of the educational process is, for Plato, not so much the general spread of intelligence as it is the discovery and development of the superior man,—an idea which was again revived in the nineteenth century and expressed in Carlyle's "hero," Schopenhauer's "genius," and Nietzsche's "superman." [59] The lesser individuals are supposed to discover their natural bent as the selective process takes place, and to be satisfied without a voice in the guidance of the state, for that, according to Plato, is a reward for demonstrated capacity and not a "natural right." The great mass of workers, never are thought to be fitted to undergo the educational elimination tests, are held incapable of a subtler happiness than the assurance that they are doing what they are fit to do, and are contributing to the support and development of the geniuses who will make them happy, and to the prosperity of the community. With each person in his place individual happiness will be greatest and the highest good will be manifest in the organized state.

[57] Ibid VII, p 252

[58] Ibid. X, p 339.

[59] Durant, W , "Philosophy and the Social Problem," New York, 1917, p 46.

In his conception of philosophers-as-rulers Plato saw, as we now occasionally see, that the best governor must not only have practical experience and knowledge and adequate executive ability, but must also have the ability to see the aspects of the state in the broad and large, must have the power of vision and coordination, and be possessed of a sober temperament which will keep free of all entanglement in the vagaries of the populace.

What Plato attempted to bring out in the "Republic," and what prophets and apostles of every age have stood for, was the reality and power of the truth. He desired to have his wise men search for and grasp the truth, and then have it become common to all, in that way making perfection out of imperfection, right out of wrong. He believed in the truth; that truth rules aright; that men need to be compassed about by the truth in their infancy so that after attaining maturity they are full of knowledge and purpose and fit to live the life which the truth dictates.

Plato concludes his work with the Vision of Er, or Erus,[60] as it is sometimes called, in which he establishes the doctrine of individual freedom of will and individual responsibilty. By means of a picturesque mingling of symbolism, mythology and astronomy, he teaches that although God weaves the web of life for man, yet it is woven in such a way that every man exercises choice of the ends of his life, and so conspiring with fate, becomes responsible for the success or failure of his individual test. During life man must be satisfied and happy with the place for which he is fitted and to which he has been assigned in the state; but every man, individually, is "the guardian of his life, and the accomplisher of what he hath chosen"[61] for "virtue is free, and as man honors or dishonors her, he will have more or less of her."[62] The responsibility is with the chooser; he may not have had the first choice, but he can do as he will with the last choice.

Plato's last words are: "Wherefore my counsel is that we

[60] "Republic," X, pp. 340-348.
[61] Ibid. X, p. 347.
[62] Loos, I A., "Studies in the 'Politics' of Aristotle and the 'Republic' of Plato," Iowa City, 1899, p. 291.

hold fast to the heavenly way and follow after justice and virtue always, considering that the soul is immortal and able to endure every sort of good and every sort of evil. Thus shall we live dear to one another and to the gods, both while remaining here, and when, like conquerors in the games, who go round to gather gifts, we receive our rewards." [63]

We shall hear echoings of these doctrines of Plato later. This idea of all individual interest subdued to the interest of the whole, this renunciation of family life and private property, this ethical education of the whole by the select few, left its powerful impression on succeeding ages. It found its partial historical realization in the sacerdotal state of the mediæval hierarchy in which the priests occupied the same position with reference to the laity as the philosopher occupied to the other classes in the "Republic." Many of its elements are copied or reflected in later utopias and communistic schemes, some of which will be treated in this study.

Before leaving Plato we may be led to ask, "Did he leave us absolutely without any hope of realizing such an ideal?" and we answer, "No!" for Plato held the idea that the conception of an ideal city has the power to transform and mold the life of him who beholds it, if upon contemplating it he regulates himself accordingly. [64] He demands that efforts be made to realize it here on earth, and he shows, as we have attempted to do, the conditions and means by which such a state could be made actual by adapting its particular institutions and methods to counteract the defects arising from the different characters and temperaments of men. Society for Plato was not an aimless, inactive, unwieldy mass or aggregate of individuals, but a self-conscious thing, capable of directing and controlling its own form and process by its own deliberate action. He has given us the conception of a better world so that seeing this world as ugly we may be enthused to strive and reshape it. Therefore he conceived of philosophy as being an instrument, not merely for the interpretation, but for the remolding of society. The "Republic" is not vague and fantastic, but full of hope and inspiration.

[63] Loos' translation of the last paragraph of the "Republic," Bk X
[64] "Republic," IX, p. 315

A few words comparing Plato with his predecessors, the Hebrew prophets, are in order here. The prophets, it will be remembered, were the exponents of righteousness and justice, and the portrayers of an ideal state wherein these attributes were to be common to all. Their greatness lay in their sensitiveness and soundness of conscience, and their skillful discrimination between right and wrong. But, with the exception of Ezekiel, they suggested no concrete methods of assisting or bringing into being their anticipated states. They were essentially preachers, and while they presented beautiful abstract ideals, and gave advice, they did not get very far with the principle of a transfigured humanity. Oral and transcendental methods of social reconstruction are seldom successful to any great degree, nor are reforms accomplished by hortatory means alone. Plato was greater at this point, for he perceived the rôle of institutions. He saw that social reconstruction must be given a definite objective, and that this objective can best be approached by carefully devised efforts. Hence, he proposed institutions with specific functions.[65] His system of systematic education is an example. While the prophets believed in the inculcation of ideas they made no mention of specific means of bringing the attention of the people, to these ideas, nor did they have any way of having the ideas constantly borne in upon the populace until they became mental habits. Plato, as we have just seen, made provision for this.

Plato, by his eugenics program, demonstrated the necessity of a sound physical basis for an ideal state. Happiness and the contemplation of the good were far more possible when the body was sound and healthy than when it was broken and decrepit. The rose may bloom in the desert, but not so well. Such ideas never entered the minds of the prophets. They gave free will to the reign of fancy, to the expression of abstract ends, but never a thought to a program of reform. As religionists they failed to see, what religionists of to-day are only beginning to see, namely, that the consummation of religious and ethical ideals also demands specific means of

[65] We find all the other secular utopians in substantial agreement with Plato in this regard.

dealing with folks as they are, and not with inspired beings seeking a vague and ill-defined objective, the product of spiritual efflorescence.

Plato also shows his greatness by refraining from advice or any other attempt to force his ideas upon the people. His was a straightforward exposition of principles and methods, and he left it to the reader to weigh their merits and accept what he would. Considering human resentment and individuality as undeniable facts, Plato's plan doubtless offered far greater possibilities of acceptance. Plato touched upon life as it is.

CHAPTER IV

THE EARLY MODERN UTOPIAS

1. The Events Antedating the Early Modern Utopians

' Following the appearance of Augustine's "City of God". there was a period of nearly a thousand years during which there was no instance of even the most meager and insignificant utopian literature. These thousand years composed a period, which, though it was fraught with great political upheavals and dynastic changes and though it marked the rise and extension of that stupendous organization, the hierarchically organized Church, yet was not an age conducive to new and various thought, or inventive effort along lines of social welfare. The mind of man was comparatively quiescent with respect to the necessity or possibility of human or social perfectibility. Society was asleep. Classes with their attendant evils, existed, and yet there was no consciousness of these evils. People saw the deficiencies of their age but there was no stimulus to excite them to an expression of their thoughts. Here and there some longed for a better day when humanity should have clothed itself in perfection, yet, fearful lest resentment be shown by a drowsy world, their longings were unspoken.

Toward the end of this period, however, we have the beginning of a series of events, which so tremendously shook the world, that after half a millenium, we are still within the throes of this mighty revolution. In fact, the most superficial observer must acknowledge that the forces then liberated initiated the ripples which have become the immense tidal waves now sweeping across the world.

The first of these great movements was the Crusades (1096–1273) which, while they were primarily religious in nature, were of profound significance for many other reasons. They were the first expression of that growing restlessness and adventurous spirit which has since led the Teutonic peoples to untold exploits of nature and mind. They were an incitement to the long list of maritime discoveries which came later, they contributed to enrich and develop the industrial life of Europe and start in motion some of those forces which produced problems of widespread importance later on; most of all, however, they served to give freedom to the mind and stirred the intellect and imagination of people. New nations, customs institutions and people gave a breadth of vision never before conceived.

Another factor of utmost importance was the appearance very early in the fourteenth century of "The Travels of Marco Polo,"—an account of the travels and events of one Marco Polo, a Venetian, who had made a trip to China, to the Court of Kublai Khan, where he sojourned for many years. He was at times sent on missions and also probably served for a while as governor of a province. These travels were only the beginning of a growing intercourse with Asia, which was to bring many revolutionary ideas and inventions to Europe. During this century, however, they drew attention to the size of the world, the broad expanse of civilization, the diverse social forms and institutions in far-away lands, and brought an unprecedented widening of the mental horizon.

Another of these momentous events was that terrible plague, the Black Death, which, after first appearing in southern Europe along the Mediterranean in 1347, swept north during the next two years, and through its pestilential ravages reduced the population of Europe by one-third or one-half according to authoritative estimates. This caused a frightful decimation of the ranks of the serfs, and in many cases resulted in the entire disappearance of some hereditary line. Labor was scarce and wages were forced up; in many sections serfs found themselves actually in control of vast estates; almost everywhere the landowners (feudal lords) came to recognize their utter dependence upon the laborers, a fact which the latter also saw for the first time; the lower classes, like a fledgling, were beginning to realize that they had wings. The Black Death precipitated the process of class-differentiation.

From that time on we perceive the gradual evolution of a class consciousness and the appearance of recognized class interests. Fresh classes were forming out of the dissolving feudal and manorial society with its domestic relationships and were beginning to affect social, industrial and political conditions. The cleavage between the land-holding capitalist and laboring classes was becoming apparent to all, and with this cleavage we have the beginning of that social unrest, the allaying of which has ever since busied social reformers and fostered ideals of a life in which the absence of this unrest and conflict is conspicuous. At the same time, throughout Europe, a great number of serious economic and social problems were developing, which, with the passing of time became extremely acute. Once the blanket of silence was lifted this discontent would find vent in angry discussion. What these problems were in England, where they were particularly accentuated, we shall presently see in our treatment of Thomas More.

Another event of tremendous influence in the creation of the early modern utopias was the threatening advance upon Europe at the beginning of the 15th Century of the Ottoman Turks, and its culmination in the fall of Constantinople in 1453. For a half century previous to this latter event Greek scholars had been migrating from the East to the West. These fugitives brought with them many valuable manuscripts of the ancient Greek classics and philosophers still unknown to Western scholars. They also brought with them the spirit of culture and learning, the desire for knowledge and the enthusiasm for independent efforts in human research. Western Europe was thus brought into contact with a mass of newly discovered knowledge with unsettling suddenness. There was a genuine new birth of intellect, a passion for extending the limits of human knowledge, and for employing man's capabilities to new and better advantage than of old. All the nations of Europe came under the domination of this mighty movement of Renaissance, and although national idiosyncrasy molded and colored its expression and development in each country, yet its broad outlines everywhere bore close resemblance in these ways: the enormous literary productivity; the yearning for adventure and novelty, the great intellectual restlessness and recklessness. All this application to the problems of philosophy and society differed little in broad outlines, however much they varied in detail; it was a universal spirit.

The outstanding aspect of the Renaissance was the manner in which it again called men's thoughts to the subject of reform. The Humanists, instead of devoting themselves to sophistical and useless disputing, took a practical turn toward the affairs of life, devoting themselves to the discussion of the spiritual, mental and social welfare of mankind. And among them Plato lived again. Their indebtedness to him was tremendous. Little had been heard of him through the Arabs, who cared little for his poetic method, but with the revival of learning he had become a force in Europe, a strong aid to the Reformers and Utopians, and his masterpiece the model for ideal commonwealths.

The spread of this new learning was greatly accelerated, through the introduction of paper and printing in Europe about 1450. These inventions introduced in the rough from Asia, were slowly improved upon, but as soon as they were perfected, their employment in turn spread with amazing rapidity under the stress of the prevailing stir of intellectual achievement. In fact they revolutionized the world of the scholar, by making his product accessible to practically every one. One writer has said "The invention [1] of printing was to the sixteenth century what the invention of steam locomotion was to the nineteenth." [2] It greatly contributed to the dissemination of the ideas, which the Renaissance had bred.

The most profoundly effective of this series of events, however, were those remarkable expeditions during the last decade of the fifteenth century and the additional knowledge of these new worlds brought back by the Spanish, English and Portuguese explorers of the following century. These discoveries and explorations unveiled new expanses of land and sea which reduced to insignificance the fragments of earth with which men had before been familiar. To the west, Columbus had

---

[1] We know now that it was an introduction.

[2] Lee, Sidney, "Great Englishmen of the Sixteenth Century," New York, 1901, p. 18.

brought to light for the first time a continent larger than the
whole known world; to the south Vasco da Gama had discovered
that Africa which was thought to be merely a narrow strip
along the Mediterranean Sea, proved to be indeed a gigantic
continent thrice the size of Europe, and extended far into the
southern seas. Contemporaneously there were also the revelations of Copernicus who first discovered the true dimensions
of the earth and its just place in the limitless firmament.
Such discoveries were far more than contributions to geography and cosmography; they tended to give men realization
of the narrowness of their former point of view and lifted
them to exalted altitudes. New continents inhabited by un-
heard and unthought of races, and new worlds in the vaulted
dome of the heavens, provided food for the imagination, the
like of which the world had never known before, and made
necessary a total reconstruction of thoughts and theories. But
this translation came rapidly; all branches of human endeavor
were eventually remodeled in the light of these new physical
revelations.

What the combined effect of the factors discussed above upon its age and generation was, can be imagined, but not readily
expressed. Men believed that a new universe had been born,
and that they were to produce a new method of life, purged
of the imperfections of the old. The intellectual stimulation
of a new culture and a new social philosophy coming into a
discontented world, which was then reënforced by the physical
revelation of new earthly and heavenly bodies, gave to men
the conception of a human perfectibility to occur in an
ideal world; and the prodigious feats of human beings gave
to them the assurance that such an achievement, such a victory over the forces of both animate and inanimate nature was
possible, especially with a good plan and model already at
their disposal. Men were fired to make the best of life on
earth. At the same time we perceive, not a revival, for none
was necessary, but a renewed attention to Christianity, and
an emphasis upon its purer phases which resulted in that other
tremendous upheaval of the times, the Protestant Reformation. The ecclesiastical hierarchy had permitted itself to
become so encrusted with great layers of superstition, cor-

ruption and temporal distractions that the reaction had become inevitable, just as soon as men began to see things with the clearer vision of the time. This reaction naturally tended to accentuate the aspects of primitive Christianity. We thus find a strange blending of the Greek and Christian culture, a subtle spirit underlying the motives of the day which came from both and yet was neither. This spirit evidenced itself in the literature of the time.

It was not strange that utopian literature should again spring up and thrive following events of this kind. Idealism, fantasy, metaphysical speculation, all permeated with the impulse of improving the corrupted civilization in which men were living, were finding their expression in schemes of human perfection, solutions to social and economic problems, the result of which were visions of perfect, but idealistic social communities. Distant lands of the sea were represented as being inhabited by people living under reformed systems of production, government, education and religion. We cannot expect these utopias to be the result of a quiet contemplation of facts, nor can we expect them in their entirety to offer practicable solutions of social distress, of any sort at all, for they were conceived of and produced during a time of upheaval, a period of transition, when the tumult of the world reflected itself in men's minds as fantastic dreaming and romantic fiction. And yet, he who will, can glean an abundance among the dry metaphysical, theological, or occult straw.

In spite of their fantastic nature, these utopias attempted to portray a land and a people released from the bonds of artificiality and scholastic formalism, from the thraldom of ignorance, superstition, degeneration and man-made tyrannies, and living their life without extreme or noticeable restrictions of law, and yet in reasonable harmony and order. The utopists desired a return to the natural, original condition of humanity. They were the vanguard of that train of later writers who felt that civilization could be redeemed only by stripping it of all vain conventionalities and returning to nature. They contended that this complete reversal or regeneration of life was only possible if it was based upon a rational view of the world. The life of reason alone offered such possibilities.

Rigid dogmatism and ingrown beliefs and superstitions must be cast aside in favor of a rational view resting upon the serious contemplation of historical social evolution in the past and unshackled development of human thought and human life in the present.

2. THE "UTOPIA" OF SIR THOMAS MORE

The first of the writers of this new era of speculation and learning with whom we are concerned was Sir Thomas More, the Humanist, who gave to the world in his "Utopia" a vision of a perfect communistic commonwealth. This has so far surpassed those of his contemporaries and later rivals, not only in vividness and daring but also in its depth and scientific contribution, that it has given its name to the whole class of literature and has become a word of common parlance. This book, written as it was in the days of More's early maturity was the beginning of a literature that played no small part in the social and scientific progress of the sixteenth and following centuries.

Thomas More was born in London in 1478 and died on the scaffold in 1535, a victim of the intolerance and despotism of his royal master Henry VIII. His life was a strangely inconsistent combination of idealism and reactionism. condemned in the concrete what he approved in the abstract. He did not believe that a work-a-day world with established institutions could be accommodated to ideal politics, where those institutions had never grown up. The young Humanist, who having lived through the discovery of America and having read the accounts of Amerigo Vespucci's voyages, who having breathed the intellectual atmosphere of Oxford at a time when Colet, Erasmus, Linacre and Grocyn were students and his close friends, and who expressed this spirit of expectation and intellectual freedom in the "Utopia," is only with difficulty not reconciled with Lord Chancellor More, the successsor of the Chancellor Wolsey. For More, the chancellor, never attempted to introduce into the country which he helped govern, the reforms which he had sketched as a younger man. And yet in the latter rôle he presents many of the same qualities that he made significant in the former for we know that his death in the Tower by beheading was due to his conviction for high treason as the result of his disagreement with the king on the Catholic question, and his refusal to take the degrading oath of supremacy.

Be this as it may, however, there is little dispute as to the high place More holds among the great scholars and statesmen of his time. His associates mentioned above, were among the ablest and most brilliant men of the Renaissance age. He was also the companion and adviser of the king at a time when the greatest minds not only in England, but of the Continent graced the English capital. His contemporaries in their writings [3] pay flattering compliments to the genius of the man. Lilly [4] goes so far as to say "More represented the highest perfection discernible among the men of the Renaissance. A true child of his age, feeling deeply its new aspirations, assimilating its highest culture, rejoicing in its fuller life, his whole being is yet penetrated by truths which are not of an age, but for all time."

The strongest evidence of his genius, however, is his "Utopia" written in the years 1515–1516, when More was about 38 years old. This work embodies the social, economic and political thought of a great scholar and a profound student of social affairs, written at a time when discontent was rife but when few were seriously theorizing on social problems. Revolutionary forces had been at work in the political, the intellectual and the religious world; but had not as yet concentrated themselves in any volcanic explosion. Here and there, however, there were a few people, capable of anticipating this social upheaval. It was to be a breaking away from scholastic formalism and an embracing of the free spirit of the Renaissance, with its progressive attitude. This work of genius, the "Utopia," under the form of an interesting narrative, full of subtle irony, keen criticism, tender humor, wise suggestions and brilliant flashes of wit, gives full expression to the deepest insight of the small scholarly group of which More was a member and breathes the aspirations of a new order in

---

[3] See Seebohm, Frederic, "The Oxford Reformers, John Colet, Erasmus, Thomas More," London, 1887, p. 25.
[4] "Renaissance Types," N. Y., 1901, p. 309.

trade, in politics, in social life and in religion, free from the
deficiencies which they had been wise enough to note in their
day.

The "Utopia" like all the other Utopias studied reflected the
spirit of its time, and this spirit depended upon the literary
models and environments. The Humanists beginning with
Thomas More combined the elements of both Greek and Christian culture and pictured a society ruled by neither the voluptuous ease of the one nor the austere asceticism of the other.
More's work was a curious yet fascinating blending of the
Christian and pagan which had come down from the Classical
age. The "Republic" of Plato is prominent in it. This ancient work, as we shall presently see, was the model on which
most later artificial and idealistic schemes were constructed.
It furnished not only the form of social control, but it also
determined the manner of exposition. Augustine's "City of
God" also influenced More very much in the writing of his
"Utopia." We are certain of this because More was well
acquainted with this work, having as a young man lectured
on it in Grocyn's Church. What is more, the social bearings
of the teachings of Jesus are discerned throughout the "Utopia."
But while the thread of Plato and Augustine run throughout
the "Utopia" it has much, however, that is original and unique
about it for the general notions of these worthy men differ
widely. As Guthrie says,[5] "Plato had a more general abstract end in view, he was seeking an explanation of abstract
justice; More was interested in the practical solution of actual
and present social problems and busied himself with plans to
alleviate existing unfortunate conditions." Augustine we know
had as his purpose the reconstruction and strengthening of a
great church. More's work appertained more specifically to
the concrete problems of his time.

The philosopher and practical statesman of early sixteenth
century England was forced to devote his energy to the examination of the causes of the formation of classes, the constantly
widening gap between rich and poor, the accumulating evils of
poverty, the decay of the Church and religion which were be-

[5] Guthrie, W. B., "Socialism before the French Revolution," N. Y., 1907,
p. 64.

coming more and more insistent. He devoted his ingenuity to devising means of preventing, counteracting or alleviating those evils. So More had a serious purpose in writing the "Utopia," although he chose to mask that purpose under a veil of humor. The book is an indictment of the society in which More found himself, and an aspiration after a fairer and juster ordering of the commonwealth. In it he displayed the power, of which we have a few examples in every age, of looking out of his environment and beyond his time and perceiving a better society. He realized that he was not in the best possible world and produced a scheme which he believed would allay the social unrest of this imperfect one.

We must first, however, briefly consider his commentary upon and indictment of the England of his own day and age. This indictment is the work of a keen, careful, and fearless observer with profound insight, and gives an unerring analysis of the causes of the prevailing evils. It is one of the earliest expressions in England of the consciousness of social wrong. This is to be found in the first book of the work which serves as a sort of frame work or setting for the second and was written after the second book had been completed.[6] Living not long after the War of the Roses, and in the days when the Catholic Church in England has been reduced in its power, he was indignant at the corruption of the clergy, at the luxury of the nobility and gentry, at the sufferings of the poor, at the calamities caused by war. The world seemed to be in process of dissolution and decay because of the many evils, hence he attacked those institutions from which social wrongs seemed to emanate.

He first speaks of the great number of thieves, and the frequency of capital punishment for theft and its ineffectiveness in stopping it. He shows in the first place, that hanging is neither just in itself nor good for the public, and secondly, that theft is great because there is for many no other way of earning a livelihood. "There are dreadful punishments enacted against thieves, but it were much better to make such good provisions by which every man might be put in a method

6 Introduction to Morley's Edition of the "Utopia"

how to live, and so be preserved from the fatal necessity of stealing and dying for it." [7] Half the thieves would be honest laborers if they had a chance. The maintenance or development of industries which provide employment would be an effective cure; but instead of seeking a cure, the authorities fall back on punishment. But the severity of the law instead of checking the minor misdemeanors converts the petty thief into a dangerous robber, who, having no worse penalty to fear for a graver offense, resorts to violence without hesitation, so that the system regularly manufactures the worst ruffianism.

The increase of pastures by means of the system of enclosures likewise contributed to the volume of thievery. The avaricious gentry and nobility and even "those holy men the abbots," [8] not contented with the old rents which their farms yielded, destroyed homes and towns and cultivated lands, thereby dispossessing owners as well as tenants, and enclosed the ground for pasturage that they might lodge their sheep in them and thereby increase their profits. These people, then, forced to dispose of their household goods for very small amounts, and finding no other work, had nothing else to do, but either to steal, and so be hanged, or go about and beg.[9] Furthermore, through this process of enclosing, not merely the common land was taken from the laborers, thus destroying a lucrative by-industry, but along with it came new methods of culture under which more land could be utilized with fewer hands. It served to displace labor, decrease wages and increase profits, thus increasing unemployment, misery and discontent. Because of these great numbers of idle and semi-lawless people, unnecessary multitudes of soldiers had to be kept. This in extreme cases results in seeking occasions for making war "that they may train up their soldiers in the art of cutting throats; or as Sallust observed, for keeping their hands in use, that they may not grow dull by too long an intermission." [10] This

[7] "Utopia"—Morley Edition of "Ideal Commonwealths," London, 1893, p. 61.
[8] Ibid. p. 64.
[9] Ibid. p. 64.
[10] Ibid. p. 63.

great army of idle soldiers again aroused the hatred of the
great mass of unemployed.

A further instability and disorganization of industry was
produced by engrossing and forestalling, prototypes of what we
now call "corners," and combination. The rich bought cheap
and sold again at high rates, and in holding the cattle or whatever the stock of goods was, this process resulted in much scarcity—all because of the accursed avarice of the few.

He absolutely discountenances the haughty display of luxury
among all ranks, for it throws in relief poverty and misery.
He objects to gambling and gaming, for those who lose, he
feels, must betake themselves to robbing for a living. The
debasing of coin for enrichment of the monarch, the pretense
of war that money may be raised by taxation though it shall
never be so spent, fines enacted on account of old and obsolete
laws revised for the purpose of extortion either in the form
of penalties for offenders or in payments for dispensations by
those who do not choose to observe them, all were forms of
outrages enacted by the privileged and ruling monarch which
were serving to make the lower classes less willing to submit
to the cruel and unjust government of the haughty king. Furthermore, it is not so becoming the dignity of a king to reign
over beggars as over rich and happy subjects. "For one man
to abound in wealth and pleasure, when all about him are
mourning and groaning, is to be a gaoler and not a king." [11]
The men of religion were a scandal to their profession, being
guilty of the same offenses which were condemned among the
laity. The church was by no means exempt from reproach.

More also protested against the institution of property, particularly as he saw it administered. The evils were many
"for when every man draws to himself all that he can compass,
by one title or another it must needs follow, that how plentiful
soever a nation may be, yet a few dividing the wealth of it
among themselves, the rest fall into indigence. . . . I am per-
suaded, that till property is taken away there can be no equitable or just distribution of things, nor can the world be happily
governed. for as long as that is maintained, the greatest and

[11] Ibid. p. 80.

the far best part of mankind will be still oppressed with a load of cares and anxieties. [12] The existence of money was an evil akin to property for it made possible as a form of property, the accumulation of wealth among a few and the alignment of men into hereditary, useless, protected groups.

Existing conditions which were inimical to human welfare were roundly scored whether in church, state, industry or society at large. Under the transparent garb of fiction, he bitterly satirized all abuses and arraigned all who were responsible for them. Draconian justice which punished all violators of the law was not what society should encourage but such a change in society as would stop crime at its source. The greater part of the guilt for the wrongdoing of the individual was due to the perverted arrangement of the whole.

The Utopianistic elements of the work are largely found in the second book in connection with his description of Utopia. In his portrayal of Utopia he follows out closely the characteristics of England, and Amaurot, the chief city, is London in nearly every detail. His purpose in presenting the ideal commonwealth was to contrast the habits and conditions of England as she was with England as she might be, if proper and equitable measures of social control were adopted and socially desirable institutions established. The life in Utopia is but England reversed. This contrast, however, is most often left to be drawn by the reader from his own knowledge of contemporary political and economic conditions or from his remembrance of the indictment made in the first book, hence the peculiar advantage of the choice by More of such a vehicle for the bold satire he employed and its exceptional value as a medium of presenting ideals and fundamental principles of social reform and ideals of human perfection.

More, did not, like Plato, start out first looking for the logical principles on which a state should be constructed and build it story by story; but imagined his ideal commonwealth already complete, giving us glimpses of a world in which men were actually living and moving and pursuing their business or their pleasure, thereby adding to the general vividness and

12 Ibid. 85, 86.

impression of the work. As we follow his plans for the re-constructed society we are keenly impressed with a sense of its possibility. We feel that they are the dream of a man full of the sense of power, confident of the intelligence and the ability of human nature, and deeply impressed with that meliorism in human affairs, possible if sufficient stimulus is given. "The masterful instinct of the Renaissance plays through the book and invigorates it. More has indeed no expectation of immediate change, but he sees, as Plato saw before him, an entire nation living under conditions of whole-some freedom; and so vivid is the picture that it works con-viction in his mind." [13] With happy ingenuity he made use of a suggestion from the records of the voyages of Amerigo Vespucci to locate his dream city in realms which some of the eminent traveler's company might have visited alone of Europeans. Thus, while the "Utopia" is fantastic, yet More describes it in such a way that unbelief completely vanishes at the outset and we are transported into a land which actually exists. It is the means by which Utopia is conducted, inhabited as it is by a perfected people, living with perfection-produc-ing institutions, that interest us.

In his Utopianism More was thinking primarily of how the State could be conducted to make for social welfare, and since the evils, as he saw them, were largely economic and industrial, the remedies he suggests are primarily those of eliminating industrial evils and the over-throw of harassing conventions. His is one of the first complete schemes for the reorganization of society.

The first basic principle in his Utopianistic scheme is the community of property.[14] Plato, it will be remembered, de-manded community of property and wives upon the part of his ruling classes as a renunciation of the natural impulses toward one's individual concerns, in order that they might devote themselves entirely to the general weal. More has in mind the abolition of class distinction and the equality of all citizens, before the law; consequently the abolition of private property and the establishment of common possession is the

---

[13] Scudder, V. D , "Social Ideals in English Letters," Boston, 1898, p. 76.
[14] "Utopia"—pp. 83–85

surest way of bringing about equality of claim and the abolition of crime. Going further than Plato, More would have
this equality in the division of material interests as the indispensable basis for making it possible to all citizens to enjoy in
like measure the best of everything—science, art, material
goods.

More's happy land is based, not upon desire, but upon the
disdain of desire. He would have complete detachment from
all our pre-occupation over mine and thine, for then
much of the occasion for theft, envy and ambition would be
banished and all could devote themselves to that which is best.
More says,[15] "In all places it is visible, that while people talk
of a commonwealth, every man seeks his own wealth; but there,
where no man has any property, all men zealously pursue the
good of the public: and, indeed, it is no wonder to see men act
so differently; for in other commonwealths, every man knows
that unless he provides for himself, how flourishing soever the
commonwealth may be, he must die of hunger; so that he sees
the necessity of preferring his own concerns to the public; but
in Utopia, where every man has a right to everything, they all
know that if care is taken to keep the public stores full, no
private man can want anything; for among them there is no
unequal distribution, so that no man is poor, none in necessity:
and though no man has anything, yet they are all rich; for what
can make a man so rich as to lead a serene and cheerful life,
free from anxieties; neither apprehending want himself, nor
vexed with the endless complaints of his wife?"

Consequently, due to this community of property, the Utopians have no use for money. In fact they prefer iron to gold
or silver, "for men can no more live without iron, than without
fire or water; but Nature has marked out no use for the other
metals so essential as not easily to be dispensed with."[16] The
folly of men enhanced the value of gold and silver, because of
their scarcity, hence their hoarding, and the social cleavages
arising out of their ownership. Therefore, the Utopians in
order to bring into ill-repute these metals, employed them for
their vessels of baser use, and in making chains for their slaves

15 Ibid. p. 162.
16 Ibid. p. 110.

—— ————, —— —— a badge of infamy. They even forced their criminals to wear gold rings for punishment. Gold ornaments were a mark of childhood and when grown they cast them away as they would dolls and puppets. With telling satire he renounces the exaggerated idea of the value of gold and silver and makes a plea for the consideration of goods of primary value. He shows that as money loses its value men's fears, solicitudes, cares, labors, and watchings would all perish [17] for there would then be no frauds, thefts, contentions, seditions, or treacheries arising out of the desire for this "root of all evil." Men would be able to devote themselves to something higher and better.

More also recognized that dress is frequently the cause of cleavages and dissension among people so his people were all dressed alike in simple clothing characterized by wearing qualities and garment purposes rather than for purposes of ostentatious display. Outward beauty and variety are almost wholly indifferent to More. Even the prince himself had no distinction, either of garments or of a crown, but was only known by a sheaf of corn carried before him; similarly the high priest was also identified because preceded by a person carrying a wax light.

Illustrating how completely the Utopians had become emancipated from the love of gold, jewels, and fine dresses, the visit of the ambassadors of a far distant land is related. Not knowing of the ill esteem of the Utopians for such marks of ostentation they came bedecked in garments of various colors, adorned with chains, earrings and gems, and the people of Utopia held them to be slaves. The story goes, "You might have seen the children, who were grown big enough to despise their playthings, and who had thrown away their jewels, call to their mothers, push them gently, and cry out, "See that great fool that wears pearls and gems, as if he were yet a child." While their mothers very innocently replied, "Hold your peace, this I believe is one of the ambassador's fools." [18]

The society More pictures for us is the most de-materialized that any dreamer ever conceived of. In costume, in social

[17] Ibid. p. 165.
[18] Ibid. p 112

forms and almost all the outward concerns where diversity and
elaboration naturally prevail, More would preserve a uniform
plainness of living. And this came at a time when England
was sumptuously aglow with color, exulting in the pride of
life.

Meals are taken in common, although no one is hindered in
taking food from the market-place. But few do this, "since
it is both ridiculous and foolish for any to give themselves the
trouble to make ready an ill dinner at home, when there is a
much more plentiful one made ready for him so near hand." [19]
The women sit at one side of the hall and the men at the other.
But More gives us to understand that, while this is an expression of sociality and economic efficiency, its purpose is primarily
cultural, for it was a means of inculcating morals in the young
and of spreading an appreciation of good things generally.
He naïvely states, [20] "There is a mixture of old and young,
who are so placed that as the young are set near others; so they
are mixed with the more ancient; which they say was appointed
on this account, that the gravity of the old people, and the reverence that is due them, might restrain the younger from all
indecent words and gestures." He further states in bringing
out the cultural advantage of their meals, [21] "Both dinner and
supper are begun with some lecture of morality that is read
to them; but it is so short, that it is not tedious nor uneasy to
them to hear it; from hence the old men take occasion to
entertain those about them with some useful and pleasant en-
largements; but they do not engross the whole discourse so
to themselves, during their meals, that the young may not put
in for a share; on the contrary, they engage them to talk, that
so they may in that free way of conversation find out the force
of every one's spirit, and observe his temper." They also have
music with their meals. In brief, More would have meal
time be a time when men grow culturally and ethically. This
is just one expression of that indirect and veiled utopianism
in which his work abounds.

The second basic principle in More's doctrine of utopianism

19 Ibid. p. 105.
20 Ibid. p. 106
21 Ibid. p. 106.

is that all political power should be vested in a single hand.
Largely because he was a humanist he introduced into his perfect social system a notion of autocracy. His pattern was the
absolute monarchs of the Tudor House, and he desired a strong
personal ruler at the head of his system. But there is something of a democratic element in it nevertheless for he advocated
that the Syphogrants, the representatives of the people, elect
the Prince, and that he existed and ruled only for the people.
Moreover the elected magistrates have neither class interests
nor personal interests to deflect them from their proper function
of selecting and voting with a single eye to the interests of the
whole people.

Legislation must also be carefully considered. "It is a fundamental rule of their government, that no conclusion can be
made in anything that relates to the public, till it has been first
debated several days in their council." [22]

To sustain the effectiveness of centralized rule More utilizes
the city-state as the most perfect form of organization, herein
following Plato. He did this doubtless because of certain
characteristic features of the city-state which fitted well into
his scheme. The city-state makes necessary a close and extensive control over the details of everyday life, which More
felt to be necessary. His city presented a condition of extreme physical order in construction of streets and buildings,
similar to the mechanical accuracy of social life.

More was not seeking a state of social equality; he made no
pretensions at liberty. What he desired, and more than this no
one of sane reason can demand, was a state of equal social opportunity. More recognized difference in rank, having his prince,
the graded rulers, the priests and men of learning as well as
the rank and file. But the procession from one office to another
was not determined by inheritance but by manifested gifts,
for all offices except that of Prince were open to ambitious,
competent and virtuous citizens. In this theory of equal opportunity More struck a note which is still sounding insistently.
for it still is ahead of all but the most advanced democracy
of our own day. As an ideal it offered the purest utopianism.

[22] Ibid. p. 95.

However, More, by his benevolent absolutism did not crush all spontaneity as he is sometimes accused of doing,[23] but allowed for much freedom of inclination and development. Each child, for example, was allowed to choose its own trade, after the common training of country life had been received.

A third principle of More's utopianism is a state-controlled family as the basis of social organization, primarily for the purpose of securing a strong and well-trained offspring. Here More departed from Plato and most communist writers who have held the family as the complement or bulwark of property. They held that the abandonment of property meant the destruction of the family. But More was satisfied with a supervised mating and family life. This supervision begins with the creation of the family. Marriage for him is one of the most sacred and important relationships and hence should be carefully regulated. It dare not be abused. The law of natural selection must be supplemented by statutory enactment. Hence the marriages are not consummated until the physical soundness of the contracting parties is assured; for how absurd it is for men to inform themselves as to the minutest details of the soundness of a horse when they buy it and yet marry a wife upon trust. Not that he places emphasis only on the physical qualities, but adds "even wise men consider the body as that which adds not a little to the mind; and it is certain there may be some such deformity covered with clothes as may totally alienate a man from his wife when it is too late to part with her." [24]

Families are limited to sixteen, and are governed by the father. "Wives serve their husbands, and children their parents, and always the younger serves the elder." [25] They allow neither polygamy nor divorces, except in the case of adultery, or insufferable perverseness; for in these cases the state dissolves the marriage, and grants the injured person leave to marry again; but the guilty are disreputable, and are never allowed the privilege of a second marriage. But he also states, "It frequently falls out that when a married couple

---

[23] See Guthrie, op. cit. pp. 128–130.
[24] "Utopia" p. 131–132.
[25] Ibid. p. 103.

do not well agree, they by mutual consent separate, and find out other persons with whom they hope they may live more happily." [26]   But this cannot be done without the consent of their Senate, "for they imagine that too great easiness in granting leave for new marriage would very much shake the kindness of married people." [27]   Sexual choice must be a reasoned process throughout.

A fourth outstanding chapter of utopianism is their educational system and their other methods of inculcating morality, culture and social worth.   Theirs is a universal education extending throughout life, and is intensely practical in content. They devote themselves to the exact sciences as arithmetic and geometry.   Inhabitants of the cities are sent by turns into the country so that they learn something about agriculture "and so commit no errors, which might otherwise be fatal, and bring them under a scarcity of corn." [28]   All however are permitted to select their own trade or vocation which they follow except while serving this apprenticeship on farms. [29]   In addition their children, and a great part of the nation, both men and women, are taught to spend those hours in which they are not obliged to work in reading: and this they do through the whole progress of their life." [30]   Those persons, who in childhood are discovered to have an extraordinary capacity and disposition for letters, are wholly excused from labor so that they can give themselves exclusively to their studies.

The pleasures of the dwellers in Utopia are both those of the body and the mind.   The pleasures of the mind lie in knowledge, and in that delight which the contemplation of truth carries with it; to which may be added joyful reflection on a well-spent life, and the assured hopes of a future happiness! [31]   The pleasures of the body permissible are those which conduce to health and allow us to live accordingly to nature. the most valuable are those which lie in the mind, the pleasures of the body being chiefly valuable as they contribute to those

26 Ibid. p. 132.
27 Ibid. p. 132.
28 Ibid p. 91.
29 Ibid p 96.
30 Ibid. p 114.
31 Ibid. p. 122.

of the mind. The Utopians, however, rejected the ascetic notion
that virtue consisted in crossing all natural desires, in ab-
stinence from natural pleasure, and stamping out the natural
instincts. Theirs was a wholesome satisfaction of the appetites. The purpose of all is happiness and it is an idea of
happiness which includes others. Theirs is a felicity which
postpones the immediate pleasure for the more remote, and
sacrifices lesser pleasure for the sake of the greater, spreading
all the felicity of the body politic over the individual. The
Utopians account it piety to prefer the public good to one's
private concerns. They hold that for a man to dispense with
his own advantage for the good of others, is a means of
securing one of the highest forms of pleasure for "the sense of
the good action, and the reflections that he makes on the love
and gratitude of those whom he has so obliged, gives the mind
more pleasure than the body could have found in that form
which it had restrained itself." [32] Pleasure is not appeasing
the body, but following the dictates of enlightened reason.
Their happiness then consists in all that is good and honest and
virtuous, which, in no way in time to come, will serve to harm
others—truly an exalted ideal.

As an encouragement to a wise and virtuous life in the interest of their fellows, they grant public honors. "They erect
statues to the memories of such worthy men as have deserved
well of their country, and set these in their market-place, both
to perpetuate the remembrance of their actions, and to be an
incitement to their posterity to follow their example." [33]

To make this widespread education and civic attainment
possible for every one More would have every one work but six
hours a day. Men are not to be wearied from early in the
morning till late in the evening, with continual work like
laboring and toiling beasts: for, this is worse than the miserable and wretched conditions of bondsmen.[34] Nor is this necessary. By making their building sound and of a permanent
character, and by the use of clothing durable rather than showy,
the labor of builders and of workers in cloth is greatly dimin-

[32] Ibid. p. 118.
[33] Ibid. p. 134.
[34] Ibid. p. 97.

ished. All luxuries are banished. Every one in Utopia
is expected to work. There is compulsory and almost universal labor. Women and the great body of the gentry and
clericals are put to useful labor. All are put to some essential
task and are taught some craft. The division of labor between men and women is based upon the fitness of the sex.
The women as the weaker sex, are put to the easier crafts,
such as work at wool or flax. Beggars are not tolerated
for there shall be no idlers in his society; no drones in the
hive, no leisure class whatever, neither beggars, nor begging
friars, nor hunting gentry. Thus if every one works the allotted time it will be enough to satisfy all the external needs of
the community. But what is to be done with the rest of the
day? All that time is to be devoted to the affairs of the
commonwealth, and the liberty and the development of the
mind, and to healthful recreation. He advocated the short day
that the laborer might be saved from debasing drudgery and be
given opportunity for culture and self-improvement.[35] And
Utopia offers these opportunities in abundance.

Furthermore, realizing that the mental and moral development of men depends to a considerable extent on their health
and the wholesomeness of their surroundings, this city was free
from the narrow, tortuous ill-paved streets and the low, dirty
and filthy houses of the horribly unsanitary London with which
he was familiar. In Utopia all was substantial and sanitary,
in every way conducive to the best physical and mental
health.[36] Thus because of this education and healthful life,
ignorance, the great cause of crime and misery, is banished.
The laws in Utopia are few, because it is against all right and
justice that men have imposed on them laws, which either
are in number more than can be read, or blinder or darker than
men may well understand.

Finally, the dwellers in Utopia detest war as a very brutal
thing. "They, in opposition to the sentiments of almost all
other nations, think that there is nothing more inglorious than
that glory that is gained by war." [37] More proposed that war

35 Ibid. p 97
36 Ibid. p 93
37 Ibid. p. 138.

should be carried on by assassinating the leaders of the enemy and if this fails by adopting any means of creating hatred and dissension among the enemy. As a last resort soldiers of a neighboring people are hired. The only wars Utopians willingly engage in are those of defense or protection of friends from aggressors. Even then they are magnanimous and humane in the treatment of their enemies, though they fight with magnificent courage and skill until they have won. Hunting also is counted as the lowest, the vilest and most abject sort of butchery.

The fifth broad, conspicuous utopianistic factor in More was the question of religious belief. In these matters he felt that toleration should prevail. The Utopians are largely permeated with a pure pantheism; for they "adore one eternal, invisible, infinite, and incomprehensible Deity; as a Being that is far above all our apprehensions, that is spread over the whole universe, not by His bulk, but by His power and virtue; Him they call the Father of All, and acknowledge that the beginnings, the increase, the progress, the vicissitudes, and the end of all things come only from Him; nor do they offer divine honors to any but to Him alone. And indeed, though they differ concerning other things, yet all agree in this, that they think there is one supreme Being that made and governs the world. [38] They differ, however, in the attitude which they take toward this Supreme Being, but this they felt to be in the interest of religion itself. For having arrived at their religion by reason and not by revelation, reason would soon determine which of the beliefs were false, and the native force of the true religion would break forth and shine bright.[39] They had faith that in the long run the innate force of truth would prevail, if not vetoed by resort to violence and tumult. There were no obstinate contentions and useless and enervating arguings among them as to which sect was best, which assist to disrupt friendships and create cliques, for every man was permitted to entertain his own belief, provided it was positive. but those who were atheists were not permitted to share in the administration of the State, for it was felt that such must despise all laws and customs, and were essentially men of base

[38] Ibid. p. 145.
[39] Ibid. p. 42.

and sordid minds.[40]   Yet beyond this they do not punish
atheists and unbelievers, "because they lay down this as a
maxim that man cannot make himself believe anything he
pleases; nor do they drive any to dissemble their thoughts by
threatenings, so that men are not tempted to lie or disguise
their opinions, which being a sort of fraud is abhorred by the
Utopians."[41]   Hence all religious views are tolerated which
are not manifestly anti-social.   Nowhere indeed has the great
doctrine of religious toleration been expounded with greater
force or fullness than in the "Utopia."   The bases of morality
are duly safeguarded, but otherwise every man in Utopia is
permitted to cherish, without let or hindrance, the religious
belief that is adapted to his idiosyncrasy.   Reason, the sole
test of beneficent rule, justifies no other provision.   Where no
religious views were aggressively expressed or repressed, no
strife of sects with their anti-social results were to be feared.

More's toleration extended to science also, something which is
not always seen even in the twentieth century.   One of the
most important and characteristic points of this utopianism is
its fearless faith in the laws of nature combined with a profound faith in religion.   The Utopians were filled with no
foolish misgivings lest science and religion might be found
to clash, for they saw that, if there is any truth in religion,
it will not conflict with Nature, for both are framed and fixed
by the same founder, and must be in harmony.   To shut their
eyes to facts, on the ground that they are opposed to Christianity, or any other belief, is to fight without the least chance
of success and with the greatest prospect of doing harm instead
of good.[42]   Therefore they regarded the pursuit of science
rather as a part of their religion than as in any way antagonistic to it.

This beautiful religious freedom finds a voice in the public
worship which is so conducted that each can participate readily
in the exercises and continue to conceive of God according
to his own thoughts and feelings, and yet so expressive of common brotherhood that all consider it an impiety to enter upon

40 Ibid p. 152
41 Ibid p 152
42 Seebohm, op. cit., p. 355.

it with a consciousness of anger or hatred toward any one; without having first purified their minds and reconciled their differences. The people, all clothed in white, congregate in their magnificent temples, the interiors of which are somewhat darkened and the air of which is scented with frankincense and other sweet spices, for purposes of quiet thought and worshipful devotion. We would like to hear their church music, for "all their music, both vocal and instrumental, is adapted to imitate and express the passions, and is so happily suited to every occasion, that whether the subject of the hymn be cheerful or formed to soothe or pacify the mind, or to express grief or remorse, the music takes the impression of whatever is represented, affects and kindles the passions and works the sentiments deep into the hearts of the hearers." [43] More four hundred years ago understood the utopianistic quality and office of music. They offer up prayers in a set form of words "and these are so composed, that whatsoever is pronounced by the whole assembly may be likewise applied to every man in particular to his own condition." [44] Theirs was a form of worship, which, while it unified, yet it permitted every man to satisfy his own spiritual needs in his own way. Those rites which were peculiar in each man's religion and which formed no part of the public faith, were observed by each privately and at home. Finally their religion was of such a nature that it commended social service as an expression of religion. [45] In religion the murmurings of the Reformation were beginning to be heard and the New Testament was beginning to be understood in its natural sense.

By these means More sought to make religion not a source of social divisions and castes, separated by the hard line of sectarian difference, but a tie of social unification and brotherhood—a true agency for individual perfection and social advancement. This may have been a dream, but it was one that we of the twentieth century are attempting to realize.

Thus we have seen that while More's Utopianism is not openly put forth as such, it is nevertheless present in profusion and

[43] "Utopia," p. 161.
[44] Ibid. p. 161.
[45] Ibid. p. 161.

detail. Beginning with those institutions which make men base he would vitally change them, or abolish them altogether, for superficial corrections meant nothing to him. He sought causes and dealt with fundamentals and, having discovered them, he utilized them as foundations for a structure of substantial social institutions and wholesome and effective ideals which were intended to educate - people unconsciously into perfection. His utopianism was the inevitable result of a broad rational reorganization. That he transcended his time by centuries cannot be denied. In fact much of his idealism is still held up, in other forms to be sure, as the height of social anticipation in the present century.

3. The Utopianism of Francis Bacon's "New Atlantis"

There was a paucity of Utopian literature for nearly a century following the appearance of More's "Utopia." This silence was broken in England by Francis Bacon, Baron of Verulam, with his ingenious fragment, the "New Atlantis." He never finished this work but enough remains to show what the nature of his thinking was, and illustrates the application of his best thought to social science.

Francis Bacon was born in 1561 at London, the son of Sir Nicholas Bacon, who was Lord Keeper of the Great Seal. Like More, he was intended for orders, but instead was educated as a lawyer. Unlike More, he attended Trinity College, instead of Oxford. He himself was one of More's successors as Lord Chancellor of England. His life was a peculiar combination of pusillanimity and grandeur. As a man in high office he stooped to the meanest of things and was guilty of all kinds of irregularities and unscrupulous actions in his dealings. He practiced deceit and dissimulation whenever it could be made to pay, passing at the same time as an honest and outspoken man. Similarly in his management of men he was a pitiable failure. But his unfortunate and two-faced political life came to an abrupt end in 1621, when after being accused of accepting bribes and committing other dishonesties, he admitted the charges, and was dismissed from his office of Lord Chancellor. He was sentenced to a fine of £40,000 and life imprisonment. but the King relieved him of punishment. Thus driven from London in disgrace he retired to his own country home at St. Albans.[46] Here he devoted the rest of his life to literature, philosophical speculation and science.[47] In the achievements he accomplished in his retirement, he showed himself to be truly great; few have been greater. The "New Atlantis" was a product of this final period of retribution and contemplation having been written in 1622.[48] It is thus the product of an old man, written at the end of his life, while the "Utopia" was written by a younger man, before he had undergone the strains and disillusionings of high public life. He died in 1626, at the age of sixty-five years.

Bacon doubtless stands next to Shakespeare, his contemporary, in the empire of human intellect of sixteenth century England. In mind Bacon was a typical product of the European Renaissance. His intellectual interests embraced every topic of the time, and his writings touched almost every subject of study. He was at once historian, essayist, legal writer, logician, philosophical speculator, and writer on almost every known branch of science, and to each he brought the same eager curiosity and efficient insight.

The "New Atlantis" was a great by-product of Bacon's studies in connection with the preparation of his "Novum Organum," which embodied his scientific methods. He received the vision of a "New Atlantis," a land of freedom and justice, in which were established institutions and principles which would carry into effect the system treated in "Novum Organum." While Thomas More was a representative of the Humanistic Period of the Renaissance with its emphasis on pantheism and recognition of equal social rights for all reasoning men, Bacon was a representative of the Natural Science period when thinkers had come to believe that man's ultimate regeneration and perfectibility depended primarily not on reform of laws of property or on social revolution, but on the progress of science and the regulation of human life by the scientific spirit. "Bacon's 'New Atlantis' proclaimed with almost romantic enthusiasm that scientific method alone was

46 Lee, Sidney, op. cit., p. 235
47 Fowler, I, "Bacon," N. Y., 1881, pp 23–24.
48 Cushman, H. E., "History of Philosophy," II, Boston, 1911, p. 41

the ladder by which man was to ascend to perfect living." [49]
Its new program to attain Utopia was the rebuilding of society
in the light of knowledge and discovery. Bacon shared and
expressed the confidence of his time that wonderful things
were to be revealed; and that nothing was impossible to man
provided he hit upon the right key to nature's secrets.
Just as every age that feels itself upon the threshold of a new
world epoch writes Utopias, so Bacon wrote the "New Atlantis,"
giving expression in it to his optimism about the future of a
distinctly secular science. Through experimental science men
gained dominion over things, "for nature is only governed by
obeying her." Or in the words of Durant,[50] "I accept it (i. e.,
nature), says Bacon, but only as raw material. We will listen
to nature, but only that we may learn what language she under-
stands. We stoop to conquer." He was convinced that the
possession of exceptional intellectual power properly applied,
would revolutionize man's relation with nature and reveal to
him her hidden secrets.

While Bacon's utopianism centers about the influence of
science and knowledge, there are a few other elements which
first demand our attention. From the spirit of the work we
gather that the end of government is the welfare of the people.[51] The King should rule by virtue of his ability and his
disposition to rule for the commonwealth. The state should
be to a large extent self-sufficient, echoing the mercantilistic
doctrines current at his time. Foreign influence must be carefully watched lest the inhabitants of the state be corrupted.

The family is for him the unit of society and upon it is built
the whole social fabric and he consequently glorified its office.
Its importance is emphasized by special ceremonies. One of
these is the Feast of the Family which is instituted and paid
for by the State, and celebrated in honor of him whose family
counts at least thirty living members above three years of age.
The head of the family from thenceforth wears a medal pre-

[49] Lee, op. cit., p. 252.
[50] Durant, W , "Philosophy and the Social Problem," N Y, 1917, pp
76-77.
[51] "New Atlantis"—In "Ideal Commonwealths," pp. 188-189.
[52] Guthrie, op. cit., p 185.

sented by the king. The feast is largely religious in character consisting partly of invocation hymns, prayer and benediction. It is also made an occasion for settling all petty disputes between members, to impress lessons of morality, piety, patriotism and obedience. It emphasizes three strong points from the social point of view. First, the principle of family unity is dwelt upon. It shall not be a family which breaks up for lack of cohesion or proper authority. At the ceremony one of the sons is chosen who shall henceforth live with the father in the latter's house, and so hold the family together by taking the father's place in case of his death. Second, the idea of raising a large family is emphasized, for no man is so honored throughout the state as such a "family-father." The world had not yet been disturbed by a doctrine of diminishing returns and a Malthusian theory of population. Third, unlike the conditions in all earlier secular utopias, there were no common tables, except for pupils in the boarding schools. The family met daily around its private board thereby tightening the family tie.[53]

In his discussion of the marriage relation, Bacon indulges in bitter satire on the social ethics of his age. He accuses them of making marriage merely a remedy for unlawful concupiscence. Marriage in Europe was "but a very bargain, wherein is sought alliance or portion, or reputation with some desire (almost indifferent) of issue." [54] Nor did marriage seem to change matters for the better so much among men. "The haunting of those dissolute places, or resort to courtezans, are no more punished in married men than in bachelors. And the depraved custom of change, and the delight in meretricious embracements (where sin is turned into art) maketh marriage a dull thing, and a kind of imposition or tax." [55]

Bacon would have marriage be the faithful nuptial union of one man and one woman, chaste and clean for "their usual saying is that whosoever is unchaste cannot reverence himself"; [56] the purpose of marriage being to supply a strong in-

[53] For discussion see pp.192–194.
[54] "New Atlantis," p. 198.
[55] Ibid. p 198.
[56] Ibid. p. 199.

telligent offspring to the State. Any union threatening social welfare was forbidden or frowned upon by social disfavor. Bacon objected to More's method of examining and selecting partners, "where the married couple are permitted before they contract, to see one another naked." Bacon said, "This they dislike, for they think it a scorn to give a refusal after so familiar knowledge; but because of hidden defects in men and women's bodies, they have a more civil way; for they have near every town a couple of pools (which they call Adam and Eve's pools), where it is permitted to one of the friends of the man, and another of the friends of the woman, to see them severally bathe naked." [57] Thus, in a rude way did More and Bacon grope after the eugenic ideal.

The utopianistic element of greatest value and that factor of the "New Atlantis" which has been primarily responsible for its fame, is the picture drawn and the description given of a great "college called Salomon's Home, a self-perpetuating group of learned and capable men endowed and working together for the common end of being— "the noblest foundation that ever was upon the earth, and the lantern of this kingdom," —the end of the attainment of knowledge by experiment, research and travel, the enriching of the world's store of information by the process of investigating into nature and the ways of men, and discovering the truths and principles which make for progress and happiness. Bacon sought to describe an imaginary college, which should be instituted for the purpose of interpreting nature, and of producing great and marvelous works for the benefit of men. Bacon has the governor of Salomon's House describe its functions as follows: "The end of our foundation is the knowledge of causes and secret motions of things and the enlarging of the bounds of human empire, to the effecting of all things possible." [58] Here we find the personal conviction and ideals of Bacon, the Renaissance scholar. He saw an ideal of comfort for human life, made possible through the systematic use of the knowledge and control of nature through science. He and his contemporaries felt that all social injuries would be healed by raising human society, by

[57] Ibid pp. 199–200
[58] Ibid. p. 202.

means of the scientific advancement of external civilization, beyond all cares and all the needs which vex it. What transformations were possible when invention, research and experiment became intelligently exercised arts! This reaction toward natural ethics was perfectly understandable, since it came at a time when the authoritarian sanctions of supernatural religion were becoming impotent and falling into the discard. Men felt that only by speculation and research could the evils of society be overcome. For them, to use the words of Turgenev, "Nature is not a temple, but a workshop," the raw material out of which Utopians were constructed.

Of course, there is much that is fantastic about Bacon's imaginings. There are caves sunk 600 fathoms deep in which "refrigerations and conservations of bodies" are effected, and new metals artificially contrived.[59] There are towers half a mile high used for purposes of meteorological observation.[60] By means of unsuspected chemical discoveries, by special changes as baths and air cures diseases are banished and life prolonged.[61] New flowers and fruits are brought into being in the orchards to add to the welfare of man. "And many of them we so order, as that they become of medicinal use." [62] Vivisection is practiced on beasts and birds so that opportunities may be at hand to test the effects of poison and new operations in surgery, and to widen the knowledge of physiology.[63] There is an establishment where tricks that deceive the senses like feats of juggling, or spiritualistic manifestations, or ghostly apparitions, are practiced to the highest perfection and then explained to serious students who go out into the world, and by their instruction prevent the simple-minded from being deceived by quacks and imposters.[64] They make divinations of diseases, plagues, earthquakes, temperature and divers other things, and give counsel as to what the people shall do for the prevention and remedy of them. And in short, the whole

59 Ibid. pp. 202, 203.
60 Ibid. p 203.
61 Ibid. p. 204.
62 Ibid. p 205.
63 Ibid. p. 205
64 Ibid. p. 210
65 Ibid. p. 213

purpose of the college itself directed toward improving the material state of society.

The House of Salomon is conducted by a great hierarchy of fellows, or endowed students, the real aristocracy of the island. These make experiments, devise philosophic inventions, conduct researches, and do anything to aid in the truly philanthropic welfare of the race. A number of these fellows are sent abroad every twelve years to study the affairs, improvements and sciences of other countries, remaining there until relieved by the next twelve, when they return home bringing back books, patterns and instruments and ideas of all kinds to make available the information they have collected. Bacon as one of the inhabitants says, "Thus you see we maintain a trade, not for gold, silver or jewels, nor for silks, nor for spices, nor any other commodity of matter; but only for God's first creature, which was light; to have light, I say, of the growth of all parts of the world."[66] This illuminating sentence sets forth the spirit and the high purpose of the writer. Generally the inventors of great things were to be honored by having statues erected to their honor in the House, and a liberal and honorable reward was given them.

Bacon's society was established, not upon a communism of wealth; but upon a communism of knowledge, and it was a communism which meant the largest possible participation of all members in the benefits of society.[67] And yet it was a communism something like that of Plato wherein the virtue flowed from the philosophic few to the untutored many.

In the "New Atlantis" Bacon illustrated the possibility of the influence of the social will consciously ordering social progress. Any people or any nation, by putting aside a substantial part of its material resources to the equipment of scientific work, research, exploration, and philosophic speculation could direct its progress as it wished. Ignorance, dark, prejudiced ignorance was the source of social evils, and human suffering. Society's hope lay in the reorganization for social purposes of the processes of discovery and interpretation of nature. Having discovered the truth, men would be free. Moreover Bacon

[66] Ibid p. 191.
[67] Guthrie.—op. cit., pp. 16, 17.

felt that this was a progressive process; men shall always become free. Quoting Lee,[88] "He refused to believe that any
limits were set beyond which human intellect when clarified
and purified could not penetrate. He argued that, however
far we may think we have advanced in knowledge or science,
there is always more beyond, and that the tracts lying beyond
'our present gaze will in due course of time come within the
range of a purified intellectual vision. There were no bounds
to what human thought might accomplish. To other children
of the Renaissance the same sanguine faith had come, but none
gave such emphatic voice to it as Bacon."

Another utopianistic truth stands out as we read the "New
Atlantis" and that is that there is nothing that we may not do,
if we but will it strong enough; but it must be a willing of
means as well as ends. Tenacity of purpose supported by a
careful organization of the arts and sciences and tempered by
a superb patience will make all things possible.

There is one thing, however, which Bacon and the men of
his time did not realize as clearly as we now do, and that is
that science and knowledge unaided cannot solve our social
problems. During the last four centuries we have invented
and invented, only to widen the hiatus between classes. The
scientist must also be a social philosopher and view his own
work as part of the universal whole, and seek to make his work
redound to human welfare and social progress in general.
Science for science's sake must become anathema. The results
of a humanized science are fittingly described by Durant: [69]
"Before it can be of real service to life, science must be enlightened by some consideration and fitting together of human
ends: without philosophy as its eye-piece, science is but the
traditional child who has taken apart the traditional watch,
with none but the traditional results."

4. CAMPANELLA AND HIS "CITY OF THE SUN"

Campanella, a contemporary of Bacon, wrote his "City of
the Sun" the same year (1623) that Bacon wrote his "New
Atlantis." He was an Italian, born in Stillo in Calabria in

[88] Op. cit , p. 249.
[69] Op. cit , pp. 83, 84.

1568, and died in 1639. Like More and Bacon he was intended for the church and unlike them continued his education until he became at last a Dominican frair. He was however at once monk, philosopher, university professor, [70] communist, and revolutionist. Early in life he evidenced a free and eager appetite for knowledge which eventually led him to become one of the best known philosophers of his time. He combined in an interesting manner a knowledge of practical affairs with a subtle philosophic insight and a keen metaphysical sense.

As we take up the study of Thomas Campanella, our scenes shift from the north of Europe to southern Europe, from England to Italy, from a section where the Renaissance immediately started theorizing along philosophical and social lines, to an environment which had been almost solely culturally and artistically colored by the New Learning. Yet it was not at all surprising that during the preceding period the South should also have been affected by social discontent and anti-social theories, especially since the capitalistic régime showed itself there quite early; yet the strength of the sentiment of social disorder was not insistent enough to lead to upheaval. This was doubtless due to the disastrous failures of the attempts at social reform in Northern Europe. The ferment of the Reformation had set things topsy-turvy and, as always, a reaction had set in. Radical agitators were stamped as enemies of state, church and civilization itself. This conclusion seemed justified by the history of Lollardy, the Hussite Movement in Bohemia and kindred uprisings. But with the opening of the seventeenth century the interest in social and political questions again flamed forth and could not be put down. And these questions together with those of a religious and economic nature and the typical questions of the Renaissance served to bring forth the most brilliant contributions from a select group of men. For at this time Italy knew, besides the philosopher Campanella, Bruno, the predecessor of Galileo, Telesius, Bodin, Cardamus, Patritius, Grotius, the political philosopher, and Paracelsus, the founder of medical science. [71] But of this learned group Campanella was the most idealistic, and the most

[70] Having taught at the Universities of Pisa and Padua.
[71] Guthrie op cit., p 137.

positively a social reformer. He had, however, sound judgment on political affairs even though his time thought him radical. What would now be called his radicalism led him to participate in the Calabrian conspiracy against the Spanish rule. Furthermore, it led the Spanish Inquisition to attack him. He was accused of books he had not written and of opinions he did not hold, he was seven times put to the question and suffered, with firmness of mind, the most cruel tortures; and what is more, he suffered imprisonment and martyrdom for twenty-seven years. It was during this incarceration that he wrote his political and social ideal, "The City of the Sun."

Released at last from his prison, Campanella went to Rome where he was defended by Pope Urban VIII against continued violence of attack. But he was compelled at last to leave Rome, and made his escape as a servant in the livery of the French ambassador. In Paris Richelieu became Campanella's friend, the King of France gave him a pension of 3000 livres, the Sorbonne vouched for the orthodoxy of his writings. He died in Paris at the age of seventy-one in the Convent of the Dominicans.[72]

Priest, as he was, Campanella was enamored of no conventional modes of thought or philosophies nor was he fooled by the politics of his day. Campanella once said: "I was born to combat three great evils, Tyranny, Sophistry and Hypocrisy." [73] He lent all of his massive intellectual powers to the new age in which he lived—an era just following the age of discovery and the influence of the Renaissance and the liberation of the human mind which they implied. Campanella first doubting these, denied the ancient dogmas and embraced the inductive philosophy. For him knowledge gained by sense perception was the only real knowledge, but for him it was to serve as a means of ushering in the dawn of a new age of social regeneration. In the "City of the Sun" we have the most clearcut expression of both his philosophy and his radicalism in social reform.

In discussing the utopianism of Campanella we will find

---

[72]. Kautsky, K. "Vorlaufer des Sozialismus," Vol. II, Stuttgart, 1895, pp 477, 478
[73] Quoted by Kautsky, op. cit., p. 478.

many resemblances to that found in the "Republic" of Plato
and the "Utopia" of More, showing how ideals persist and
bridge centuries.

The organization of the "City of the Sun" was on the city-
state principle, the type of structure most familiar to Campanella.   To him as to most Italians, including Machiavelli, the
problem of civilization had always been a municipal problem.
Similarly Campanella was devoted to a centralized form of
government, along with most of the reformers of his time,
who believed in a hierarchy of personal control.   Like Machiavelli, he believed in the "prince" and idealized his type, giving
him a place of commanding prominence.   But it was an absolutism for the purpose of better conducting the social welfare.
The great ruler among the inhabitants of the "City of the Sun"
was the priest Hoh or Metaphysicus who was head of all temporal and spiritual matters, and was the supreme authority.[74]
He was assisted by three princes of equal power—Power, Wisdom and Love,—who each had his separate and distinct
administrative duties.   "Metaphysic then with these three rulers
manage all the matters, and even by himself alone nothing is
done; all business is discharged by the four together, but in
whatever Metaphysic inclines to the rest are sure to agree." [75]

The government, however, was entirely elective, for as in
Plato, these and other officials and rulers were selected on the
basis of an eligible list limited to those whose training in
the arts and sciences made them most competent to rule.   The
governing body of the city-state was drawn from neither an aristocracy of wealth nor one of birth, but from an aristocracy of
education, into whose hands he would put the control of society.
Furthermore the teachers of the arts and sciences chose the
rulers of the different departments into which the government
was divided.   Campanella had no fear that education unfitted
men for practical duties and political authority, but did condemn the hereditary principle of selections.   In speaking of
the selection of Metaphysicus, Campanella said: "We indeed,
are more certain that such a very learned man has the knowl-

[74] Campanella's "City of the Sun" in Morley's "Ideal Commonwealths," p.
221
[75] Ibid. pp. 224–225.

edge of governing, than you who place ignorant persons in authority and consider them suitable merely because they have sprung from rulers or have been chosen by a powerful faction." [76]   The more any one knew the more power he ought to have in the state, in order to rule well and improve by his knowledge the material condition of his people.   Furthermore, if any one was particularly proficient in some particular line of knowledge he was utilized as a ruler for that purpose. Speaking of the magistrates, he says, "They are elected to duties of that kind, each one to that duty for excellence in which he is known from boyhood to be most suitable." [77]   The trained mind was for him the best mind to place at the head of the State, and we have some idea of the extent of the training demanded when we read: "No one attains to the dignity of Hoh except him who knows the histories of the nations, and their customs and sacrifices and laws, and their form of government, whether a republic or a monarchy.   He must also know the names of the lawgivers and the inventors in science, and the laws and the history of the earth and the heavenly bodies. They think it also necesary that he should understand all the mechanical arts, the physical sciences, astrology, and mathematics." [78]   Surely an enlightened ruler!

In spite of all that is whimsical and impossible about this scheme, the thought nevertheless asserts itself in Campanella's "City of the Sun," even more than in More's "Utopia," that the state should be an artificial product of human insight for the removal of social injuries. Neither writer desired to set up a mere creation of fancy, any more than did Plato; for they all believed in the possibility though they all doubted the probability, of realizing "the best political constitution by rational reflection upon an order of social relations that was in accordance with the best knowledge of nature." [79]

The proper bearing of the educational system was an utopianistic measure of equal importance with that of the state.   Education is a function of the state.   Since most people for the

[76] Ibid. p 229.
[77] Ibid. p. 226.
[78] Ibid. p. 228
[79] Windelband, W., "History of Philosophy," N. Y., 1896, p. 430.

most part educate their children badly,[80] the children at the beginning of their third year are committed to the care of the state, and are taught at first, not out of books, but by objects visually presented. Upon the seven walls of the City [81] were found presented all items of knowledge essential in a well-rounded life, and presented in such a way that they could be learned "without toil and as if for pleasure." [82] There were found mathematical figures and explanations of them, drawings of the earth, and tablets discussing the customs, laws, origins and inhabitants of the different parts, paintings and specimens of minerals and metals, medicines for diseases, descriptions of meteorological phenomena, the views and discussion of the various parts of the human body, the various fauna and flora of the earth, pictures of inventors in science and law, and of renowned heroes in peace and war. Education of the youth by the visualization process was thus suggested, the nature of it being such that children would unconsciously and without irksomeness acquire a knowledge of the great and essential things of life. Thus did Campanella anticipate present day pedagogy by three hundred years.

Both sexes are instructed together in all the arts by "men approved beyond all others." They are also led to exercise themselves with gymnastics, running, quoits, and other games, "by means of which all their muscles are strengthened alike." They are also taught practical things such as shoemaking, cooking, metal-working, carpentry, painting, etc.[83] When the children are seven years of age the teachers begin to discern "the bent of the genius of each one," [84] and the children are then taken to series of lectures on science which explain essentials. Then having found their particular specialty, they make themselves adept at it. The effort is made to train each so as to make him the most useful. "The men who are weak in intellect are sent to farms" [85] where they are put at tasks

[80] "City of the Sun," p. 236.
[81] Ibid pp 221–224.
[82] Ibid p 224
[83] Ibid. p 227.
[84] Ibid p 227.
[85] Ibid. p. 234.

requiring brawn mainly. But they do not believe in narrow specialization for "they consider him the more noble and renowned who has dedicated himself to the study of the most arts and knows how to practice them wisely." [86] Both men and women are trained in warlike pursuits also. Campanella, like Bacon, demanded that natural science be given a prominent part in the life of his Utopians, even making it part of his educational system. Here also Campanella was centuries ahead of practice.

Another utopianistic measure of the greatest importance is his means of securing social unity. Campanella, like More and Plato before him, saw the necessity of this if society was to be perfected. His theory of social unity is very similar to that of Plato. For him the permanence of social peace and the happiness of the individual depended upon the abandonment of private property and the family. To him property was the prime disturbing element and a fruitful source of discord, a permanent destroyer of that solidarity among men essential to progress. In the "City of the Sun" all things are common. "Arts and honors and pleasures are common, and are held in such a manner that no one can appropriate anything to himself." [87] "For private property is acquired and improved for the reason that each one of us by himself has his own home and wife and children." [88] Hence Campanella would also have community of wives and children, for self-love springs from family and "when we have taken away self-love there remains only love for the state," [89] and this was the end. Campanella defends the principle of community of women by showing that it was advocated in the writings of the apostolic fathers, in Clement, Plato and Socrates. [90] Thus, Campanella, like Plato, considered the family as an obstacle to the perfect devotion of the citizen to the state. With the banishing of the family no man would be led to "raise a son to riches and dignities," [91] nor would he have any stimulus to effort or

[86] Ibid p 228.
[87] Ibid p 225.
[88] Ibid p 225.
[89] Ibid p. 225.
[90] Ibid p. 238.
[91] Ibid. p. 225.

sacrifice, or source of pride except the state. Campanella was doubtless encouraged in accepting these views of Plato's by "the recent history of Italy which furnished an example as Guelph and Ghibelline struggled for mastery, and great families with their unbridled ambitions undermined, even destroyed, the unity, and threatened the very existence of the Italian State." [92]   When asked as to the success of this plan Campanella has one of the visitors reply, "I declare to you that they burn with so great a love for their fatherland, as I could scarcely have believed possible." [93]   There are no social classes in this commonwealth, for "with them all the rich and poor make up the community; they are rich because they want nothing, poor because they possess nothing; and consequently they are not slaves to circumstances, but circumstances serve them." [94]

The inhabitants of the "City of the Sun" lived in common dwellings and dormitories and ate in public dining halls where, during meals, "as in the refectories of the monks, there is no noise" [95]   The occupations were divided up and adapted as far as possible to inclination and capacity, thus freeing labor of much of its pain and sacrifices. "This," says Guthrie, [96] "was a part of his scheme for maintaining the efficiency of labor when the strong motive of individual gain had been removed.   But because all, both men and women except the indigent, work, "it only falls to each one to work for about four hours every day. . . . The remaining hours are spent in learning joyously, in debating, in reading, in reciting, in writing, in walking, in exercising the mind and body and with play." [97]   More, it will be remembered, had a working day of six hours, made possible in the same way and for the same purposes.   Unlike More and Plato, they had no slaves, for since all worked they needed none.   Furthermore, when people have slaves then they have great leisure classes given over to

[92] Guthrie, op. cit, p 178
[93] "City of the Sun," p 225.
[94] Ibid. p. 238.
[95] Ibid p. 232.
[96] Op cit., p 181.
[97] "City of the Sun," p 238

"idleness, avarice, ill-health, lasciviousness, usury and other vices." [98]

Insofar as they have lame, blind or other physical defectives they are also given tasks suitable to them, lest they degenerate or become public charges.[99] "No physical defect renders a man incapable of being serviceable except the decrepitude of old age," [100] and these indigent aged were cared for by the state.

Since all labor is honorable and since all work no class distinctions can arise. Idleness alone is condemned. Labor thus becomes a part of civic duty; in fact, "the occupations which require the most labor, such as working in metals and buildings, are the most praiseworthy amongst them." [101] Here is presented a new type of prestige,—a prestige built upon labor, an aristocracy of labor. Campanella saw that the social drones, be they beggars or princes, were carried by the laboring masses, and explained the hardships of labor. Hence he would have all members of society share in its toils and sacrifices, thus freeing the laborers from their long hours and degrading toil. Furthermore, by having each work according to adaptability and capacity he avoided irksomeness and dissatisfaction of work done without happiness, and made for industrial efficiency.

Insofar as Campanella considered women as well as men in his distribution of tasks, he recognized the equality of the sexes. He simply held that "the occupations entailing less labor belonged to the women." [102] Again "all sedentary and stationary pursuits are practiced by women, such as weaving, spinning, sewing, cutting the hair, shaving, dispensing medicines and making all kinds of garments." [103]

In addition, there is no money, "for gold and silver is reckoned of little value among them except as material for their vessels and ornaments, which are common to all." [104] Because

98 Ibid. p. 237.
99 Ibid p. 239.
100 Ibid. p. 239
101 Ibid. p 246
102 Ibid. p 247
103 Ibid. p 231.
104 Ibid. p 235.

of this state of communism with its well-developed social sense
and lack of temptations, and because of few laws [105] there are
no crimes.[106] While this communism is crude in places, yet
it is of a rather noble type, for it means a participation of all
the members of the community in all the benefits of the community, material and spiritual.

Furthermore, the union of the sexes was controlled for the
purpose of serving the interests of the state. That the state
may be of a high standard physically and intellectually, that it
may be able to defend itself against possible attack, that the
race may continue to be powerful, Campanella would have the
magistrates mate men and women, considering physical and
temperamental characteristics, so that a stalwart offspring be
assured. He has the visitor say, "Indeed they laugh at us who
exhibit a studious care for our breed of horses and dogs, but
neglect the breeding of human beings." [107] "Moreover, the
race is managed (among them) for the good of the commonwealth and not of private individuals. . . . For they say that
children are bred for the preservation of the species and not
for individual pleasure, as St. Thomas also asserts. Therefore
the breeding of children has reference to the commonwealth
and not to the individuals, except insofar as they are constit-
uents of the commonwealth." [108]

Here the artificiality of Campanella's view of society made
itself most apparent. Men and women were to have no choice
as to their companionship; emotions and natural affections
were to be ruled out, desire and impulse were to be thwarted,
while the whole matter was placed in the hands of the magistrates, and "they distribute male and female breeders of the
best natures according to philosophical rules." [109] If a love
should spring up between a man and a woman not acceptable as
breeders "the two are allowed to converse and joke together
and to give one another garlands of flowers or leaves, and

[105] "They have but few laws, and these short and plain, and written
upon a flat table, and hanging to the doors of the temple, that is between the columns," Ibid p 256
[106] Ibid. pp 226–227
[107] Ibid. p. 224
[108] Ibid pp 235, 236.
[109] Ibid p 236.

to make verses. But if the race is endangered, by no means is further union between them permitted." [110] But in general "they know in their love nothing other than feelings of friendship." Thus did the celibate monk purpose to improve the race physically by substituting the ideal of fitness for capricious fancy, and who can say that he had not caught the eugenics ideal? Here also we have another expression of the idea that society can never be a success until the social will completely dominates the individual will. He would destroy all those institutions that foster selfishness and egoism.

In his ideals of health and cleanliness Campanella set a standard sadly at variance with those of his age. The food is prepared under the direction of medical officers who "tell the cooks what repasts shall be prepared on each day, and what food for the old, what food for the young and what for the sick." [111] "They are very skilled in making dishes and they temper their richness with acids, so that they never vomit. They do not drink ice-cold drinks nor artificial hot drinks, as the Chinese do" [112] The people maintain scrupulous cleanliness with regard to their clothing, as also in the workshops, kitchens, pantries, barns, storehouses, refectories and baths. They have special conduits by means of which water is made accessible at all places. Proper exercise is taken by all. He especially advocates it for the women, so that they may be fit as mothers.[113] They consider most diseases to be due to lack of exercise, hence "by frugality and exercise, they remove every humour and spasm,[114] for by the sweat of exercise they diffuse the poisonous vapor which corrupts the blood and the marrow." [115] For fevers they have special remedies. Any one with only the slightest ideas of the ideals of personal cleanliness, the sanitary standards, and the state of the medical profession in mediæval Italy will appreciate how far Campanella transcended his age in this regard. "They do not use dung and filth for manuring

[110] Ibid. p 237.
[111] Ibid. p. 232
[112] Ibid. pp. 252, 253.
[113] Ibid. p. 236.
[114] Ibid. p 251.
[115] Ibid. p. 252.

the fields, thinking that the fruit contracts something of their rottenness, and when eaten gives a short and poor subsistence, as women who are beautiful with rouge and from want of exercise bring forth feeble offspring." [116]   "They know also a secret for renovating life after about the seventieth year, and for ridding it of affliction, and this they do by a pleasing and indeed wonderful art." [117]   "And the length of their lives is generally one hundred years, but often they reach two hundred." [118]   "They do not bury dead bodies, but burn them, so that a plague may not arise from them." [119]

We also find a strange parodox in Campanella's life, even as we did in the lives of More and Bacon. As an orthodox monk the religion which he would have the inhabitants of the "City of the Sun" embrace was one not at variance with that which he represented. For them God was their only Father, from whom they received all things, and whom they worship in Trinity, but a trinity of Power, Wisdom and Love.[120]   They greatly admired the life of the apostles, and they used the short prayer which Jesus Christ taught men in their worship. It is the duty of the chief magistrate to pardon sins. They believe in the immortality of the soul [121] and another life.[122] They also believe in prayer, having among them a practice of perpetual prayer. And yet Campanella was a free thinker and a worshiper of the stars, placing astrology above religion. On the walls of the temple representations of the stars are to be seen; and verses describing their size, course and secret influences are added.[123]   Trees are planted by gardeners, cattle are bred by their caretakers, even men and women are allowed to mate, only when certain heavenly bodies are in conjunction. Inventions and scientific discoveries are made, calamities are averted, all things are done under the influence of the heavens. In fact, all changes, material and social, are attributed to the

. [116] Ibid p. 248
[117] Ibid. p. 253.
[118] Ibid p 250.
[119] Ibid. p 260.
[120] Ibid. p 263.
[121] Ibid. pp. 240-262.
[122] Ibid p 263
[123] Ibid p. 222.

stars. Particular stress is laid throughout on the general cosmography as an aid in understanding the control of human affairs. Even the priests, we would understand, take their orders from the stars rather than from God.[124] Their festivities come at times when the sun enters the four cardinal points of the heavens, and not on the Catholic holidays. Their prayers are made to the four horizontal corners of the world. "They believe that the true oracle of Jesus Christ is by the signs in the sun, in the moon and in the stars."[125]

While most of Campanella's utopianism is only a modification of his predecessors', it is important in that it was the first comprehensive scheme of social reform suggested in Italy since the vigorous pronouncements of Savonarola more than a century before in Florence. It was an evidence that, while most philosophers were engaged in scholastic disputes, and while statesmen were struggling for the spoils of office and indulging in basest intrigue, here again a voice, that of a Calabrian monk, was lifting itself up in protest and at the same time announcing a new scheme of social reorganization in which public welfare and social expediency were the sole criteria. That he was effective is evidenced by the fact that among all the Italian states oppressed by Spanish rulers and exploited by despotic powers, Calabria alone arose in revolt and demanded a new social and political organization.[126]

5. HARRINGTON'S "OCEANA" [127]

In taking up Harrington's "Oceana," England again becomes our background, and this time it is an England in revolt. Charles I, who by means of his Star Chamber, his High Commission Court and other high-handed and despotic measures had made the Petition of Right a mockery, and the rule of himself and his clique a travesty upon England's political institutions, had just been disposed of. Cromwell and his pro-

[124] Ibid. p. 258.
[125] Ibid. p. 261.
[126] Kautsky, "Die Vor läüfer des Sozialismus," II, p. 472
[127] Throughout this work the references to "Oceana" cited will be to the reprint in John Toland's "The Oceana and other works of James Harrington," London, 1737.

tectorate, was then in power.   While nominally a republic with
a constitutional government, his rule was a dictatorship under a
military usurper, whose claim to title was simply that of the
sword.   Therefore, unlike the conditions surrounding the other
early modern utopians, the national chafing at this time was primarily political, and not economic or social.   It was a time
when questions that related to political constitutions, political
liberties, and balance of power were much in the air and demanding some sort of an answer.

Harrington, at this time, came forward with a solution, for
the presentation of which he used the utopian form as a vehicle
of expression.   This political Utopia "Oceana," appeared in
1656.   James Harrington was born in 1611, five years before the death of Shakespeare, and several years after the birth
of John Milton, the son of Sir Sapcotes Harrington of Exton
in Rutlandshire.   As a child he distinguished himself by a
studious and sedate spirit.   In 1629 he entered Trinity College, Oxford, as gentleman commoner, and became the pupil
of that master logician, Dr. Chillingworth.   While at the university he prepared himself for foreign travel by the study of
modern languages, but before going abroad, and while still under
age, his father died and he succeeded to his patrimony.   His
travels abroad were such as to peculiarly fit him as a construc-
tor of an ideal constitution, for they gave him an intimate
insight into the various forms of government.   Toland, his
enthusiastic biographer, tells us,[128] "He was often heard to
say, that, before he left England, he knew no more of Monarchy,
Anarchy, Aristocracy, Democracy, Oligarchy, or the like, than
as hard words whereof he learned the signification in his
Dictionary."   But after his return he was able to speak of
them more intimately and with greater conviction.   In Holland he experienced the aftermath of those struggles for religious and civil liberty which had taken place there during
Queen Elizabeth's reign.   He also served in the regiment of
Lord Craven, and afterward in that of Sir Robert Stone, was
much at The Hague and became familiar with the Court

[128] In his "Life" in "The Oceana and other Works of James Harrington,"
London, 1737, p xiv

of the Prince of Orange, serving for a time as manager of his English affairs.[129] From Holland, Harrington passed through Flanders, into France, and thence to Italy. Of all places in Italy, Venice pleased Harrington best. He was deeply interested in the Venetian form of government and he observed well and read much, for many of the suggestions there received bore fruit in his "Oceana." "The Netherlands and Venice alike captivated his imagination and roused his enthusiasm, but in a rather different way. In the Netherlands he had seen what a people can do. In Venice he was shown what institutions can achieve. The former turned his interests in the direction of politics; the latter made him believe in political science. With his strong faith in the people and his belief in institutions his mind was moving in the direction of republicanism."[130] Upon his return to England he kept himself as far as possible from the life of the Court and gave himself over to domestic pursuits and thorough study, chiefly of the history of political institutions. We hear of him involved in the Court troubles of 1646, when the Parliament Commissioners, having the king in their custody, desired Harrington to wait upon his majesty as a person known to him and connected with no party or faction. Republican though he was, he accompanied the king on the scaffold. With the downfall of the Commonwealth and the restoration of Charles II, Harrington lived in a retired manner, not taking sides in any political feuds. However, to have been a republican was then a crime. He was committed to the Tower of London in 1661, as having been engaged in treasonable practices. Here he was long imprisoned without any real cause, subjected to inquisitorial examinations without his tormenters finding anything against him except the theories in his writings. His health suffered under his confinement. Finally after being taken with the scurvy and having become insane, he was liberated through the efforts of his family, by his gracious majesty Charles II. He never regained health, but still occupied himself much with his pen. He married in these last days of his shattered life. He died at Westminster in

[129] Toland, op. cit, p xiv.
[130] Smith, H. F. R., "Harrington and his Oceana," Cambridge, 1914, p. 5.

1677, at the age of sixty-six, and was buried in St. Margaret's Church, by the grave of Sir Walter Raleigh.

Harrington lived at a time when a most heroic effort was being made to put political institutions to the supreme test and when found defective, create new ones. Puritanism was in the air. It was not merely an effort to restore purity to religion, but also a protest against all authority, sparing no institution in the state which could not give account of itself. "It proposed," says Dwight,[131] "after destroying what was antiquated and useless, to set up not merely a new spiritual, but also political kingdom, in which both the state and church were to be reëstablished and brought into official relations, which it was fondly hoped would be harmonious as well as permanent. To accomplish this great result, everything must undergo revision. Nothing could be regarded as settled." As in all times of stress and crisis many great men were brought to the fore. The best thoughts of Thomas Hobbes, Oliver Cromwell and John Milton, besides those of James Harrington, had lately been put in print, and were agitating the minds of their contemporaries at this time.

The "Oceana" stands alone in the field of Utopian literature. Although in the form of an ideal state, it is the work of a different type from the others discussed. It was not written to express a great social philosopher's theories as was the "Republic," nor was it written as a satire on its time as was the "Utopia" nor was it written to give expression to one's deep longings and theories as were the "New Atlantis" or the "City of the Sun"; it was written to solve the needs of its country at a very critical time in its history, and its author, in order to insure its publication, resorted to the picturesque and gave it the form of what he called a "political romance."

The book was written during the days of Cromwell. "The scene is laid in England, which appears as Oceana. The hero of the story is Cromwell who under the pseudonym of Olphaus Megaletor is depicted as being troubled in the night by pondering over what a single man, Lycurgus, was able to do for Sparta.

---

[131] Dwight, T W., "Harrington and his Influence upon American Political Institutions and Political Thought," Pol. Sc. Quart., II, p. 2.

Fired by this example, he calls together a number of political scientists, and together they produce a new constitution. Cromwell is given a post not unlike that of protector, and institutes the new order. He waits till the wheels are running smoothly, and finally retires into private life, leaving England the most prosperous and contented republic in the world. The book stripped of its allegorical trappings is little more than a magnified written constitution. Without having the poetical atmosphere of the legendary Utopia, it goes into details which a constitutional document does not presume to include, but it never leaves the political standpoint or wanders off into impossible suggestions that could not be realized in practice. It is a definite proposal for solving the difficulties in which England had become entangled since the abolition of monarchy, and one which its author hoped Cromwell might be induced to consider." [132]

And yet Harrington was very much a child of the Renaissance, for the classical learning with which he was saturated is very perceptible throughout the "Oceana." Although much of it is Jewish, Venetian or English, much more of it is Greek and Roman. He looked much to the constitution of Sparta, Athens and Rome; but there was another constitution, made for an imaginary colony in Crete to which he also turned for inspiration, namely Plato's second-best republic, "The Laws," which are also a practical sort of Utopia bearing similar resemblance to an elaborated written constitution. Hence since Harrington discovered his "Oceana" in the "archives of ancient Prudence" [133] and not in "phansy," we must judge it by its political thought and not by its art or fantasy. It is doubtless because people have searched for the exotic and spectacular in mediaeval literature, that must account for the fact that the "Oceana" has not become widely known.

The Utopianism of Harrington is mainly a political Utopianism, and it has as its purpose the setting up of political ideals which would bring political order out of chaos, and the arrival at certain social and economic principles necessary in con-

[132] Smith, op. cit., p 13.
[133] Oceana, p. 179.

nection with these. His whole Utopianism centers about the
idea of the sovereignty of the people. He cries out, "This free-
born nation, distributing her annual Magistracys and Honors
. . . is herself King People " [134] He recognizes, without
any fuss or feathers, the ability of the people to work out their
own political salvation. He has faith in the commonwealth
and in democratic principles. What is more, he has faith,
that proper political ideals and suggestions of superior political
institutions will be embraced and put into effect, and having
been put into effect will be administered in the common interest.
The essence of his Utopianism then is a perfected political
government; having this, the people will become perfect.

Important among this class of utopianistic measures was the
emphasis upon definite written laws This supremacy of laws
and not of men was basic. He says,[135] in defining government,
"It should be the Empire of Laws, and not of Men." Men
with their fickleness, uncertainty and individuality upset the
most careful calculations, listing whither the wind bloweth; but
laws written in black and white and not subject to accident,
are the true foundation upon which to build. This idea was
quite prevalent among the thinking few of the time; they placed
their hopes for a future devoid of disputes and uncertainties
upon some sort of a Greater Charter, which should be unalter-
able. What is more, they wanted few laws.[136] Thus laws
are the basis of political liberty, for they alone make the fact
of the existence of freedom tangible. But it is not *from* the
laws that liberty is obtained, but *by* the laws.

His second great utopianistic measure was the creation of
proper "balance of property." This balance of property is
explained in the dictum, "As is the proportion or balance of
Dominion or Property in Land such is the nature of the Empire," [137] a proposition which since has met with general
acceptation. This dominion of property counted, whether real
or personal, lands, money, or goods.[138] Where land is in the

[134] Ibid. p. 100.
[135] Ibid p 37.
[136] "The best rule as to your laws in general, is that they be few." Ibid.
p 60
[137] Ibid p 39
[138] Ibid. p. 39.

hands of one, there is a monarchy; where it is owned by the few, there is an aristocracy; where it is controlled by the people generally you have a commonwealth. Of these forms of property land is the most important for upon it political power is usually based. This balance of land is termed by him an "Agrarian balance." [139] Harrington desired a democracy, hence he felt that the ownership of land should be much divided, for in this way would an equilibrium of political power be effected. He says,[140] in speaking of the orders necessary to establish a commonwealth: "An equal Agrarian is a perpetual Law establishing and preserving the balance of Dominion by such a distribution, that no one Man or number of Men, within the compass of the Few or Aristocracy, can come to overpower the whole People by their possessions in Lands." This is the foundation of commonwealth. History gives us many examples of the political importance of the possession of land and later students of political science have come to see the wisdom and truth of this theory of Harrington.[141] It has been recognized from the time when Joseph made his investments in property before the Egyptian famine. Among other instances the institution of the Jubilee among the Jews, the reforms of Lycurgus and Solon, the work of the Gracchi, of Julius Caesar and the later Roman Emperors, as well as the whole feudal system depended on the practical recognition of this fact.

His contribution lies in his being the first to consciously recognize it as a fact substantiated by numerous instances, and stating it definitely as a theory. This theory is chiefly important from the utopianistic point of view because it recognizes the vital relationship between property and social stabil-

[139] Ibid p. 40
[140] Ibid. p. 54.
[141] Smith, op. cit., pp. 23, 24, quoting other writers on this point states that Bonar, in his Philosophy of Political Economy (p 90) ascribes the importance of "Oceana" to its "new principle that the economical element in a state will determine its government." Cornwall Lewis in "A Treatise on Politics" (II, p. 46) includes among the general true propositions of politics "that the seat of power in any state is dependent on the preponderance of property." Thorold Rogers in "The Economic Interpretation of History" (p 163) counts it "a common-place in practical politics that they who own the land of a country make its laws."

ity. Harrington was one of the first writers to give economic matters the prominence they merit in connection with government and politics. In his epitome of the commonwealth at the end [142] he maintains that the balance should be so struck "that the Power can never swerve out of the hands of the Many."

The desired division of land had however been taking place for some time in England.[143] The great feudal estates were splitting up and political power consequently was becoming more and more diffused. But monarchical institutions had become incapable of caring for these new conditions. He saw that the coincidence of property and power could be effected in two ways: either by changing the government to suit the changed balance of property, or by changing the balance of property to make possible the old form of government. He himself, in view of the multitudes of other changes, was of the opinion that it was both better and easier to change the form of government than to revert to old economic conditions. This without a doubt accounts for his uncompromising republicanism. Therefore his endeavor was to formulate proposals which should establish and ensure a republican form of government.[144]

Harrington advocated the utilization of four contrivances for the purpose of keeping government pure and healthy, and to prevent that shifting of power which results in upheaval. They were the secret ballot, indirect election, rotation of offices, and a two-chamber legislative system in which the functions of debating and voting were kept separate. These were contrivances for creating a democracy, but a democracy with checks. To be sure, like devices were to be found in the cities of Italy, especially Venice, in Germany, Switzerland and the Netherlands, in church institutions, in private clubs, etc., but Harrington's audacity lay in his proposal to extend them to a nation and weave them into its constitution.

The secret ballot was directed against the two separate evils of disorder and bribery into which electors fell, which it was

---

[142] "Oceana," p 204

[143] Ibid. p 73.

[144] For further references on his "Agrarian" balance see, Ibid pp. 54, 57, 61 and 63.

intended to correct.[145] He says,[146] "The election or suffrage of the People is most free, where it is made or given in such a manner, that it can neither oblige nor disoblige another; nor through fear of an Enemy, or boastfulness towards a Friend, impair a Man's liberty." [147]

A second device utilized chiefly to prevent the disorder and corruption by which electors were beset was indirect election of officials. The disorder and corruption prevalent in parliamentary elections of his day forced the idea upon his mind that some reform was necessary here. He proposed to divide the country into fifty tribes approximately equal with twenty hundreds in each tribe and ten parishes in each hundred.[148] The elections were to be in two stages, the first stage was the election of one-fifth of the total voting strength of each parish to act as a sort of electoral college for the whole tribe.[149] The second stage, enacted at the chief city of each tribe at which the delegates assembled, was the election of the actual representatives for the national parliament.[150] He desired an intermediary element of somewhat more enlightened minds representative of the people, to be sure, to carry on the important and responsible task of selecting the governing officials. Harrington felt at all times that the true ideal of democracy was not attained when the people took the government into their own hands but that their sovereign power lay in their electing representatives who conducted government for them.

The other two devices, rotation, and Harrington's peculiar form of double-chamber government, were directed against the temptations to which elected persons are exposed. He was a firm adherent of the principle of rotation or alternation in office for "prolongation of Magistracy, destroys the life or natural motion of a Commonwealth." [151] The purpose of rotation was to secure continuity yet prevent the risk of oppression attendant on long tenure of power. It was achieved by annual election for triennial terms, thus having a new set of officers

145 Ibid p 120
146 Ibid p 54.
147 For details see Ibid. pp. 113 ff.
148 Ibid. pp. 84 ff.
149 Ibid pp. 89, 90.
150 Ibid pp 92-99.
151 Ibid. p 54

entering office and an old set retiring each year, "having at once Blossoms, Fruit half-ripe and others dropping off in full maturity." [152]

The fourth device was a two-chamber parliament in which the functions of law-making, debate and voting were kept separate. The senate was to consist of 300 members who were to be more or less wealthy and representatives of the aristocracy of intellectual and moral worth.[153]   Harrington had the idea that there was a natural aristocracy of this type, and he therefore would have these act as guides for the people.   Their functions were to discuss, debate, give advice and enlighten the people. Their decrees were never laws, until they had been submitted to and approved by the Prerogative Tribe or Senate, made up of 1050 members representing the people.   These were truly the legislative body for they accepted or rejected in turn all these proposed measures.   After listening to the arguments on both sides of the question, presented to them by specially selected senators, they voted upon the proposals presented without debate.   Thus "whatsoever upon debate of the Senate is proposed to the People and resolved by them, is enacted by the authority of the Fathers, and by the power of the People, which concurring, make a law." [154]   In this Harrington was reflecting the political philosophy of his time.   England was then in a transitional stage, in which control was gradually passing from the aristocracy to the commons.   This was the intermediate stage, for in it the assembly was without power to initiate legislation, it still being a stage where the people simply had the right to give their approval or disapproval to the proposals of their rulers, whether elected or not.   The next step was the acquisition of that positive power which enabled them to also initiate legislation.   Utopian as he was, Harrington did not go that far though he may have been restrained by practical motives.

The utopianistic measure of somewhat different nature from those discussed above was his particular theory of religious toleration.   His principle was not an absolute liberty of con-

[152] Ibid p 140
[153] Ibid. p. 47.
[154] Ibid. p 48; see also pp. 121-131

science with no national, church, or state interference with
religion of any kind whatsoever, or an unlimited toleration
around an established church, but a limited toleration around
an established church.[155]   Harrington was no extremist, but
he recognized the existence of dissent and was willing to grant
liberty of private conscience.   After granting liberty of private conscience, he felt that this must then be accompanied by
liberty of National Conscience, and this was the basis of
his national religion, for he says:[157]   "A commonwealth is
nothing else but the National Conscience, and if the conviction
of a man's private Conscience produces his private religion,
the conviction of the national Conscience must produce a national Religion."

But this national religion was broad in its scope and admitted
differences of opinion.   All parties he insisted should be equally
protected in their peaceful professions, and equally capable of all
elections, magistracies, and preferments in the commonwealth.
In fact, his council of Religion was to "suffer no coercive Power
in the matter of Religion to be exercised in this Nation." [158]
He did, however, bar Jews and Catholics.   These principles of
toleration emphasized by Harrington made it a complement of
his democracy with checks,—the first time this combination
had been suggested.   These ideas of Harrington stand in
marked contrast to the bitter and intolerant legislation of the
early years of Charles II's reign when deviation from the
established religion by Protestant non-conformists as well as
others, was visited by deprivation of important civil rights
as well as severe punishment.

To insure the continuance of his form of government and the
preservation of society in general Harrington advocated general education.   His argument is one to which we of the present
day can subscribe.   He says,[159] "A man is a Spirit raised by
the Magic Nature: if he does not stand safe, and so that she
may set him to some good and useful work, he spits fire, and

[155] Ibid. pp. 58–127.
[156] Ibid p 58.
[157] Ibid. p 58.
[158] Ibid p. 127
[159] Ibid pp 171, 172

blows up Castles: for where there is life, there most be motion
or work; and the work of idleness is mischief but the work of
industry is health.   To set Men to this, the Commonwealth
must begin betimes with them, or it will be too late: and the
means whereby she sets them to it, is Education, the plastic
art of Government."   Thus education was to prevent disorder,
preserve society from decay, dispel ignorance, and supply a
constant stream of new men for the government.   Education
was most important, for it would teach the great bulk of the
people a proper sense of values and give them. a proper insight
into matters of importance.   He says, "There is not any reason
why your Grandees, your wise men of this Age, that laugh
out and openly at a Commonwealth as the most ridiculous thing,
do not appear to be, as in this regard they are, mere Idiots,
but that the People have not eyes." [160]

But he did not believe that the education of a man's children
should be wholly committed or trusted to himself.[161]   He proposed the institution of compulsory free schools under government inspection, where people with more than one son were
compelled under threat of punishment to send their sons, the
education being "gratis" for those who could not afford to pay
for it.   With his usual moderation, however, he left the education of only sons to the discretion of their parents and gave
all parents the liberty of choosing the schools to which they
sent their children.   This rule was to continue until the age
of fifteen.   After that the child should be made an apprentice
to some trade or be sent to a law-school or university.[162]   The
commonwealth still had an interest in him, for he must not
stay beyond the age of eighteen unless he was fitting himself
for some profession, the object being to prevent a person from
occupying himself with aimless study.   This is a remarkable
instance of an early plan for free and compulsory education.
He also recognized the advantage of public discussion as an
educational measure and hence would have "The Tuesday lectures or orations to the people," [163] the purpose of which was

[160] Ibid p. 160.
[161] Ibid p. 172.
[162] Ibid pp 177, 178.
[163] Ibid. pp 157-160.

to disseminate knowledge to the general populace on matters of national import and assist in producing public opinion.

This educational scheme of Harrington's has, however, one weakness which the other early modern utopians would not have permitted, namely, that he made no allusion whatever to the education of girls. But women played an extraordinarily small part in the revolutionary movement in England, and since classical enthusiasts could find very few examples of women who had played great parts in ancient history, Harrington assigned them no important rôles in his Utopia.

In summary, Harrington's was a typically Utopian mind although intensely practical withal. Eagerly, he projected it beyond the existing horizon, discerning that which might be if adequate provisions were made. Undertaking the work historically, and with an element of audacity uppermost, he developed on large scale, national lines, ideas and institutions which had long been in effect on a small scale, in both private and ecclesiastical organizations and the municipalities of the Continent. Thus Harrington gave a sudden tremendous stimulation to the growth of national forms of democracy which previously had been merely slowly evolving. In fact, his ideas can be traced in many of the newly devised American political institutions.[164]

Harrington's utopianism was almost exclusively political in nature, but it was a utopianism which sought not only perfection in government, but though this was chiefly implied in the "Oceana," an unavoidable improvement of society. Good ideals of government carried into effect, make possible a wholesome body politic. The essence of this good government which he sought was a democracy obtained and perpetuated by such laws or orders or institutions as would give the upper hand in all cases to common rights or interests. In all his suggestions the interest of the commonwealth is the specific object in view. To that everything must bend.[165] The checks and balances which he advocated were merely to give stability to this new political structure.

[164] This will be discussed in the last part of this work.
[165] Ibid. p. 194.

6.   SUMMARY OF THE EARLY MODERN UTOPIANS

We have not discussed all of the early modern utopians but we have discussed the most important, and in them we run the whole gamut of utopianistic elements of the period   We have discussed the best and most representative, those which most truly mirror the social idealism of their age.[166]   For these utopians were the social theorists of their age, contemplating the past happiness of the race, chiefly through the medium of the Classics and looking ahead and seeking future perfection, in order that the evils of the present might be eradicated.   As true children of the Renaissance they were not afraid to depart from conventional paths.   Theirs was an airy liberation from the toils of the humdrum; they permitted their fancy to fly to new heights and attained new levels of thought, and yet, because each was writing for some purpose other than to merely give expression to fantastic imaginings, they were thoroughly serious and practical.

Being children of the Renaissance they were imbued with a love of knowledge and a profound admiration for the newly discovered truths of science.   They felt that the common attainment of knowledge means the largest possible participation of all members of society in its joys and benefits.   This is the main note in Bacon's exposition and is by no means absent in

[166] The sixteenth and seventeenth centuries were the richest in speculative treatises of an Utopian nature of any period in history.   Among other works of this age the following are significant.   Hall, Joseph, "Mundus et Alter Idem," (1607); Puteanus, Erycius, "Comus" (1608); Andreæ Johann Valenti, "Christianopolis" (1620), Eliot, Sir John, "Monarchy of Man" (1622), Barclay, John, "Argenis" (about 1630), Erythracus, Jani Nicii, "Eudemiæ" (1637); Godwin, Bishop Francis, "The Man in the Moon" (1638); Bidermannus, Jacobus, "Utopia" (1640), Milton, John, or Gott, Samuel, "Nova Solyma, the Ideal City, or Jerusalem Regained" (1648); Hobees, Thomas, "Leviathan" (1651); Sadler, John, "Olbia, the New Island" (1660); Filmer, Robert, "Patriarcha" (1680); Swift, Jonathan, "Gulliver's Travels" (1726).   For a most excellent and complete bibliography on French, German, English, Italian, Spanish, Scandinavian, and Russian Utopias see Schomann, Emilie, "Französische Utopisten und ihr Frauenideal," Berlin, 1911.   A more limited bibliography, but more descriptive, in English, is found at the conclusion of the second volume of the Rev. Walter Begley's edition of "Nova Solyma," New York, 1902.

'the others. Hence one of their oustanding utopianistic measures was education which was stressed by them without exception.   They believed that the mind must be exercised and the
proper habits formed if perfection, after being attained, was
to be maintained.   They had a new vision of education as a
great agency for social solidarity, a great opportunity ladder,
by which the lower classes were to attain heights formerly held
by the privileged few, a great inculcator of a socialized ethic.
It has only dawned upon a few of us to-day, as it had already
appeared to these writers three centuries ago, that education was
utopianism par excellence; through it and by it alone can
social idealism and brotherhood be instilled into the commonalty.

All recognized the necessity of unity in the state although
the means and the objects they had in mind differed.   Three
hundred years back they had caught the significance of the
principle of social solidarity.   With them it differed in application, however.   More, Bacon and Campanella felt that this
unity could be best maintained by making the state supreme
at the cost of the individual; Harrington went to the other
extreme in making the liberty and power of the individual the
first condition of a stable and happy state, but it was power
which was grouped and its elements balanced.

Nor did they all agree on the question of private property
and privately owned land.   We have observed Harrington's
radical departure from the land theory of the others, who had
advocated an absolute abandonment of private property, especially in land.   They saw the permanence of society, the disappearance of selfishness, the happiness of the individual, to be
possible only through the abolition of private property.   For
them it was a prime disturbing element, and a fruitful source
of discord.   Harrington, on the other hand, favored a careful
preservation of private property, especially land, for he thought
it absolutely essential to the permanence of society and the
protection of the individual.   For him its properly distributed
ownership meant social and political equilibrium.

While More and Campanella were seeking an abolition of
class distinctions, as such, and an approximate social equality,

Harrington, eminently more practical, saw that classes could not be so readily abolished, and therefore attempted to establish a working means of maintaining equilibrium between them.

All recognized the necessity of having political power centered in a single person, chosen for the post because of demonstrated fitness, but guided and assisted by a representative body. Here also wisdom was evidenced which present day thinking substantiates. Our democracy is more impressed than ever with the necessity of having political power vested in a single hand, carefully selected by the people, and checked by a body representing popular opinion.

With the exception of Harrington, all expressed ideas which to-day would be called eugenic. They recognized the physical basis of social perfection. A contented, happy, intelligent race must be physically fit, and to be physically fit, it must be born of physically fit parents and raised under sanitary and wholesome environmental conditions.

Furthermore, they saw that attention must be paid to industrial and economic conditions in a scheme of social betterment. Unsupervised, individualistic industry meant deterioration, unrest and anti-social conditions. Regulated, they served as instruments of social construction. And so we might go on, but it is unnecessary. Suffice it to say, the early modern Utopians were men ahead of their time; they were prophets of an order, which, in many instances, is just coming into action. The utopianistic measures they suggested are those being used to-day, for the same purpose—the remaking of society in conformity with the progressive ideal.

CHAPTER V

THE UTOPIAN SOCIALISTS

1. INTRODUCTION

The doctrines of the Utopian Socialists were, in some cases, a continuation of the spirit that brought on the French Revolution, and in others a form of rational reaction against the excesses of the great upheaval. But regardless of whether they were a continuation or reaction, they were products of these same great social forces,—forces which had been accumulating for a century and a half; forces which were economic, political and philosophical in character. Since the Utopian Socialists are all French, with but one exception, we will briefly trace these forces as they unfolded themselves in France.

The seeds of the French Revolution were sown in the days of Louis XIV. Whether or not he was responsible for the expression "L'Etat c'est moi" we do not know, but his seventy-two year reign made concrete the idea of autocracy and absolutism which it voiced. And, even though his reign aroused but little active expression of opposition, it hid that leaven which works but slowly at first. His insatiable ambition led him to carry on unceasing wars of conquest which drained the land of men, checked its productiveness, and necessitated an unprecedented burden of taxes. His brilliant court at Versailles, with its dazzling extravagance and its enormous coterie of nobility and clergy increased taxes and decreased commerce. His country approached bankruptcy, his peasant subjects were miserable and starving, and discontent was everywhere rife. Furthermore, Louis discredited absolute monarchy by shameful misuse of his unlimited power. The vast mass of misery and suffering due to his practice of the horrid irritating doctrine that "the many are made for the use of one," did

181

much to prepare the way for the gigantic catastrophe, the French Revolution. Finally, during the reign of Louis XIV art was encouraged, especially polite literature, but solely so that it might serve as a blanket to smother political and philosophical propaganda. Here was volcanic matter which must break forth sometime.

The reign of Louis XV seethed with the struggle of social forces. Vigorous onslaughts were being made upon the House of Bourbon and its supremacy was passing away, for with the shameless misrule of the corrupt Duke of Orleans and the mistress-controlled Louis XV how could it be otherwise? Materially and militarily France continued on the down grade. It was a period in which the lone citizen was striving to gain his rights under the institutions that had so long repressed him, but to no avail. The French Enlightenment was coming into power and with its new individualism was beginning to sweep away the church with its superstition and the state with its profligacy and tyranny. While the Enlightenment at first was purely intellectual, [1] it gradually developed into a mighty emotional and social movement largely due to the work of Rousseau. Voltaire had never aimed at a social revolution. His objective was to reinstate the understanding and to emancipate the individual by self-culture and freedom of thought.[2] He was not historian enough to see that he could not revolutionize intellectual France without pulling down the social structure. He was dealing with impotent material. But Rousseau perceived how absurd the intellectual Enlightenment was amid the distressing social state of France. He turned against both the existing order and the self-appointed intellectual reformers, and insisted on condemning the entire reigning order, for it was artificial, degraded and tyrannical beyond cure. He desired to sweep all of so-called civilization away, level inequalities, and get back to nature. Private property was based on plunder. The growth of communities but widened the gulf between the strong, the rich and the hopeless. To bring back

[1] Under Voltaire, Montesquieu and the Encyclopædists, among them Diderot, D'Holbach, D'Alembert, and Helvetius.
[2] Cushman, H E, "History of Philosophy," Boston, 1911, Vol. II, p 213

justice and peace these institutions had to be destroyed; and their works had to perish, also. As mankind was originally things were held in common, and envy and violence were absent. Restore the Golden Age by returning to nature.

In an age tired of oppression and corruption, Rousseau, with his majestic language of compassion and sympathy, struck a responsive chord. His philosophy started a world-wide agitation, the conspicuous aspects of which were an enthusiasm for nature, an exaltation of man, and a contempt for the age and for the society then existing. People welcomed the presentiment of impending change.

The hauteur of Louis XVI made political readjustment impossible, there was no thought of revision of institutions. The American Revolution introducing a state newborn of republican simplicity made that impossible. By revolution only were the rights of man to be recovered it was proclaimed. This liberty which the French people had helped the American colonists to receive, they were impatient to see France herself enjoy.

So, events rushed to a climax in the French Revolution. Its mighty movements swept across France upheaving, changing, and sweeping away that which had been objectionable. Institutions crumbled, power was transferred to other groups, new ideas came into ascendency; absolutism was crushed and liberty was sought, the calendar was changed, reason was enthroned, but the idyllic state had not been and could not be ushered in. [Men had been made equals before the law, .but their natures had not been changed, nor had the principles of individual ownership been touched. When the agitation had ceased, and men could take an account of what had been accomplished, they saw that the essential causes of social inequality had not entirely been corrected by the political reforms. So far as the general bearing of its results were concerned, the world's future was likely to resemble the world's past. It was also now apparent, that the Industrial Revolution which had been going on before and during the political and social revolution was showing its effects in France. It directed attention increasingly to the disturbing changes in economic structure, unemployment due to the invention of machines, and as a result the re-alignment of groups on the labor and capitalist basis; an awakened class consciousness; also, the newly acquired *laissez faire* philosophy, which resulted in the established and economically powerful classes entrenching themselves still deeper at the cost of the great masses. It created a new feeling of hopelessness. Many who had hoped for some kind of perfect state on earth were discouraged by such failures. Their exaltation turned into indifference or bitterness. But the fruits of the Revolution were not wholly of this unfortunate nature. It struck off a world of ideas, it showed the transitory character of the existing order, it had produced a picture of a simple state free from conventional wrongs which had not entirely faded, it inspired some by its failure to seek other means of social reconstruction. What is most important for our purpose, there came a fresh era of Social Utopias produced by the so-called Utopian Socialists. [3]

The Utopian Socialists did not produce romantic descriptions of Utopias, such as Isaiah, or John, or Plato, or More gave; but they nevertheless merit a place among idealists of this class because their age, and in some cases succeeding ages, considered the ideal schemes they offered as preposterous and incapable of attainment. For them, their ideal society was the result of conscious and arbitrary construction, to be superimposed on all. And yet, this idea was not as arbitrary as we would suppose, for at that time, society was conceived as the outcome of a contract made in remote ages which might be unmade or altered at the will of its individual members at any time. They were Utopians inasmuch as in their imaginations the future world was separated from the present by an unfathomable abyss. Because the people of their day were not habituated to an idea of development in history, they took but little interest in these schemes. Their writings were replete with what we have called utopianism, and it is the most outstanding of these elements that we desire to delineate. They

---

[3] In this work we are considering the Utopian Socialists not from the political and economic point of view as forerunners of scientific socialism, but from the sociological viewpoint as promulgators of theories of social reform

mapped out principles by which perfection was to be attained and perpetuated.

The Utopian Socialists and their immediate followers were all men in deadly earnest. While they were dreamers, possessed by vague, intangible, but wonderfully broad-horizoned ideals of humanity's perfection, they were sincere in the extreme, and were resolved to make the dreaming come true, to preach the new gospel to all the world and give reasons for it until all men should accept. As Skelton says, "One and all, the leaders of this school were men of contagious enthusiasm and unbounded self-confidence, well content to suffer neglect and obloquy to-day, to be hailed savior of society to-morrow." [4]

Most of the Utopian Socialists entertained the hope of a future ideal state which was really based upon past ages. Though their panaceas varied from the most rigid state control to the most implicit reliance upon voluntary coöperation, and though their utopianisms varied from free play of the passions to highest rationality, each believed salvation to lie in the perfect social order of Nature, one which man had corrupted and must now rediscover. Man was inherently good and nature was good, but man by his evil conventions and hampering regulations and vicious institutions had contaminated this natural goodness, and now all was wrong. Their schemes of ideal societies and utopian states were justified by the dogma of primitive goodness. Man, they considered perfect, or at least perfectible, if the evils of conventional society were removed; in a state of nature he would be happy and benevolent, and with proper social environment might be kept so.[5] It was just a question of discovering this natural state. When society was so organized that Nature's forces had free play then social

---

[4] "Socialism. a Critical Analysis," Boston, 1911. p. 12.

[5] Molinari—"The Society of Tomorrow," pp. 207-208 in paraphrasing this idea writes: "We can prove that a society truly free—a society relieved from all restrictions, all barriers, unique as will be such a society in all the course of history—will be exempt from most of the ills, as we suffer them to-day. We can prove that the organization of such a society will be the most just, the best, and the most favorable to the production and distribution of wealth, that is attainable by mortal man."

perfection would naturally come about. But the parting of the ways came with the specific deductions from these general assumptions, hence the varying methods of organization proposed.

2. MORELLY

Independent of Rousseau, another writer was tremendously influential in inspiring utopian socialism, for his theories are reflected in almost every one of the schemes of the Utopian Socialists. In fact we must regard him, if not the founder, at least as the most conspicuous forerunner of the Utopian Socialists I refer to the Abbé Morelly, whose theories have been admirably presented for American use by Professor Guthrie. [6] Morelly is one of the unknown writers. Data of his life history are extremely rare and the records of uncertain value on essential points. Judging from the opening of his literary activity he was born about 1720, thus being a contemporary of Rousseau, Voltaire and the Encyclopædists. Very little can be learned of his nature or the events of his life except insofar as they can be gathered from his writings. His fundamental principles are found in his "Code de la Nature" [7] which does not appear to have been due to the influence of Rousseau, but rather to general ideas of the kind "in the air." [8]

While his writings on society appear in the form of fiction to escape the severe censorship of the press then prevalent in France, yet it is possible to cull from these writings the utopianistic elements of value to us. Of the writers of his time he was the one who saw most clearly the need of a new system to replace the old; he alone was truly constructive, for he actually outlined a new social structure which he thought would meet the needs should ancient society be overthrown. While the others deserve merit as critics and analysts and destroyers, he alone deserves the name of utopianist at this early period.

As a prelude to his social analysis he undertook a study of the human soul. [9] Dealing with the human passions, this study

[6] "Socialism before the French Revolution," pp 195 ff.

[7] About 1755

[8] Graham, W., "Socialism, New and Old," N. Y., 1891, p 65.

[9] "L'Essai sur le cœur humain," Paris, 1745

contained some of the ideas further elaborated in the extensive system of Fourier. Man for him was a physical and sentient organism, whose sole end or *summum bonum* was pleasure. Just as in the physical world the power of gravitation is dominant, so in the moral world, the place of gravitation is supplied by that of self-love based on the passions. He considered none of the human passions as wrong or harmful; all were to be developed and in this way a more perfect socialization was to be attained. He denied that man had any natural tendency toward evil, or any spirit of jealousy or disorder. Men naturally recognized the claims of others and had moral rectitude. It was socialized egoism and enlightened self-love which characterized man truly and was to be the controlling power and lead to highest social action. Man, as Morelly saw him, was of good qualities, capable of improvement and destined by the laws of his being to be more completely socialized.

Therefore, Morelly claimed that evil arose from secondary and not from primary causes, in the maladjustment of social forces as indicated particularly by the environment. It could thus be eradicated and society redeemed if those institutions whereby the social instincts were perverted were destroyed. Here he foreshadowed Owen.

The present state of inequality and its accompanying human misery he saw to be due to the institution of private property, [10] for it was the inroads of the latter upon the communism originally reigning among men that was the foundation and source of all evil and chaos in society. He insisted with Babeuf and some of his successors upon the abandonment of private property and the adoption of common ownership of all wealth, and the equal enjoyment of the good things of life by all alike; because then, he thought, all social problems would be solved. This communism would transfer the control of property from the individuals to the community conceived of as a unit, and property rights would be socialized. There was to be no private ownership of productive goods; only those things for immediate use could be held privately. [11]

[10] For a brief discussion of this also see Bax, Ernest B., "The Last Episode of the French Revolution," Boston, 1911, pp. 77, 78.

[11] "Code de la Nature," p. 152, discussed by Guthrie, op. cit., p. 263.

Industry was to be publicly controlled and every person was to become a public servant and do real work, for there was no provision for a leisure class either at the top or at the bottom. In fact he originated the phrase later used by Saint-Simon and several others: "Each is to labor according to his ability and share according to his needs." [12] This was the basis of his social reconstruction. Moreover, Morelly, like Fourier, had the idea that it was not labor that men avoid, but the unpleasantness of it. Make labor attractive and idleness repulsive and unpopular, and the problem was solved. More and the other Early Modern Utopians before him, and Fourier and Owen after him, demanded a free and compulsory system of education, the purpose of which was instruction along lines at once fitted to further the individual interests and the common welfare. He also laid emphasis on the importance of training in the industrial arts, and, since all must labor in his society, none were exempt from this technical training.

As regards marriage, Morelly insisted that every citizen who attained to man's estate should be compelled to marry, and to that end he would have "festivals of marriage" where men could get them wives, provided the girls accepted. Celibacy was only allowed after the fortieth year was attained.

Thus did Morelly break with the past, ignore traditions and prejudices and proceed to suggest plans for a new social structure, which served as a foundation for the Utopian Socialists.

3   BABEUF

In the last period of the French Revolution we note a character who might be termed the first of the Utopian Socialists. He was distinguished as a critic of the institution of civilized society, and as a painter of an ideal society. However, he was greater as a political revolutionist and insurrectionist, and devoted most of his later years to these dangerous activities. In the last analysis his name is remembered largely because of his conspiracy to inaugurate violently his communistic state, in which economic equality was to be maintained by the side of political equality.

---

[12] Code, pp. 153–154; in Guthrie, p. 266.

François Noel Babeuf was born in St. Quentin, in the Department of the Aisne, in 1764, of an apparently good family. At the age of sixteen he was left alone, and from then on his whole life was stormy and wild. As a comparatively young man he became involved in the Revolution, playing a very conspicuous part in the Society of the Pantheon and the Secret Directory and in several projected insurrections. ⟨He was so virulent in his abuse of authority and so radical in his activities that in 1797 he was guillotined.[13]

Babeuf never presented his utopianistic ideas in organized form; they must be collected here and there from his "Tribun du Peuple," the protest paper of the Society of the Pantheon of which Babeuf was editor, from his "Manifesto of Equals" and the work of his contemporary and fellow conspirator Buonarrote.[14] Since they are largely a repetition of Morelly we will not dwell upon them here but briefly outline only the most important elements.[15]

He was a pure communist advocating a highly centralized system, the theories he maintained having come largely from the "Code de la Nature." It may be added that these ideas of Morelly's supplied the groundwork for the definite communistic principles of Babeuf's "Society of the Equals." He did, however, expressly stress equality more than did Morelly. He stated, "The aim of society is the happiness of all, and happiness consists in equality." He emphasized again and again that this equality should be perfect and absolute, for he had the idea of Rousseau that social organization is based upon a mutual compact. Each member entering this compact was equal with every other. In this primitive society there was absolute equality of wealth and of individual opportunity. Inequality arose with early civilization, and afterward it came to be fixed and established in the civil law. Babeuf would return to this

[13] For an extensive account of Babeuf's life, activities, and theories see the excellent work of Ernest Belfort Bax on "The Last Episode of the French Revolution," Boston, 1911.

[14] "Histoire de la Conspiration pour l'Egalite, dite de Baboeuf," 2 vols., Brussels, 1828.

[15] For a brief but excellent statement of the general principles of Babeuf see the chapter on "Babeuf" in Ely, R. T., "French & German Socialism in Modern Times," New York, 1883.

natural state. The object of society was to defend this equality.[16]

This ideal social organization demanded community of
goods and of station. He says, "Nature has given to every
man an equal right to the enjoyment of all goods." [17] Private
property was considered the enemy of justice and order, and
he hoped to see disorder, misrule and idleness destroyed when
communism became dominant. Only then would the social
question be permanently solved. He and his followers also advocated that every one has the right to lodging, food, clothes,
washing, warming, lighting, and medical attendance. In brief,
he aimed to secure as the aim and end of his system absolute
mechanical equality in both quantity and kind of goods, and in
their use and distribution.

Babeuf also advocated that (all labor must be organized on a
national basis and be regulated by law, and he gave a fairly
detailed plan of the organization of France for production.
As with Morelly, none were exempt and none were to be over-
burdened. The feeble were not to be idle, but were to be relieved from heavy labor, the stronger members enduring the
heavier hardships. However, not all kinds of labor was considered useful. (Literature and art, in particular were regarded with disfavor. The exercise of political right was
dependent upon the usefulness of the citizens' labor.

Babeuf further held that society must always be troubled
by dissensions so long as disproportion exists between-the resources of the different social classes. He says, ("In a true
society there ought to be neither rich nor poor." [18] All social
distinctions save those of age and sex [19] were pernicious and
unnatural. Since all have the same needs and the same natural
powers, all should enjoy the same opportunities for culture and
the same natural support. Hence he would have equilibrium
between classes as regards wealth, thus removing one of the

[16] See paragraph 2 of his official statement of the general aims of the
Insurrectionary Committee in Bax, op cit., p 114.

[17] Bax, op. cit , paragraph 1.

[18] Bax, op. cit., paragraph 7, p. 115.

[19] "Manifesto of Equals."

primal factors now disturbing the safety and stability of society. All differences, even of dress, were to be abolished.

Unlike the spirit of most of the other utopians, education was restricted to the acquirement of elementary branches of knowledge, and of those practical in a material sense. His was a leveling down to a stupid self-satisfied mediocrity. In his writings we find little of the exalted imaginings and the brilliant ideals of the other utopians. His schemes breathed the crass materialism and the stultifying equality of the Revolution. Beset on all sides by tumult and warring factions, the mind was not permitted to soar independently to the heights later attained by successive Utopian Socialists.

4. SAINT-SIMON

In Saint-Simon we have a man who reacted in an entirely different way to his time than had Babeuf. Although he had been a participant in the American Revolution and had passed through the French Revolution he had not become impregnated with the idea of equality which produced the reactionary and retrogressive spirit characterizing Babeuf. Saint-Simon was without doubt a man of genius and insight,—a bold and original thinker and reformer who succeeded in elevating himself above the common thought of his period.

Count Henry de Saint-Simon was born at Paris in 1760. He was a member of a family of the nobility which traced its origin to Charlemagne and which had long been famous in the history of France. At the age of sixteen he already gave indications of exceptional ideas, if not of exceptional ability. Upon learning that he had been disinherited by his uncle, the Duke of Saint-Simon, because of a quarrel between the Duke and his father, he remarked, "I have lost the titles and the fortune of the Duke of Saint-Simon, but I have inherited his passion for glory." [20] He studiously nursed this passion for glory by demanding that his servant remind him of the grand destiny before him every morning when he woke by calling the words: "Arise Monsieur Le Comte, you have grand

[20] Quoted by Ely—"French & German Socialism," p 54

deeds to perform." [21]   At the age of 17 he went to America
to assist in the War of the Revolution.   That his sojourn there
was of great importance in shaping his later life and giving it
direction is shown by extracts from his "Letters" written late
in life about his experiences in America.   In one of them
quoted by Professor Ely, he says: "My vocation was not that
of a soldier; I was drawn towards a very different, indeed I
may say, diametrically opposite kind of activity.   The life
purpose which I set before me was to study the movements of
the human mind, in order that I might then labor for the perfection of civilization.   From that time forward I devoted my-
self to this work without reserve; to it I consecrated my whole
life."

Returning to France he contemplated several great scientific and engineering undertakings, but received no encouragement.   His followers later took up some of these and completed them.   He also became interested in the political events
about him, and sided with the people, in spite of his training
and family traditions.   In fact, losing faith in aristocracy, he
renounced his title of Comte and became president of his Commune.   But he suffered, nevertheless, because of his nobility,
being imprisoned for nearly a year.

From then on his life is a strange combination of poverty
and suffering, exalted and inspired writing and the leadership
of a brilliant coterie of admirers and disciples in his great
social schemes.   It is worthy of note in passing that one of the
most famous of these disciples was Auguste Comte, who developed in exhaustive and systematic form in his epochal "Philosophic Positive" the fundamental ideas of his master.   Saint-
Simon died in the year 1825, just after he had finished his
greatest work, the "Nouveau Christianisme."

While Saint-Simon realized that the nations about him were
in a chaotic muddle of social mismanagement, he did not hold,
as did Babeuf, that revolution was a means of social regeneration.   It was destructive and consumed the good with the
evil.   Saint-Simon wanted a constructive and gradual reorganization of society, and he, and his school of disciples after

21 Ibid. p. 54.

him, (undertook to convert public opinion to their ideas by spoken and printed word and by deed. (They were not destroyers of that which was, but crusaders for that which might be. And their chief instrument in bringing about this reorganization was knowledge and industry. (Feudalism, theological dogmas and beliefs were inadequate in the new age. Men must resort to new means. Having discovered and utilized these means the golden age of humanity would be approached, and the perfection of the social order be assured. It is the discussion of these means which will introduce us to Saint-Simon's Utopianism. Since his scheme in general is rather widely known, we will devote ourselves only to the exposition of those ideas of his which directly bear a relation to our study. His greatest utopianistic agency is his hierarchy of talent or capacity and his other means, which is a complement of the first, is social religion. These will occupy us in the remainder of this discussion.

If Saint-Simon based his conception of an hierarchy of talent upon any older one, it was that of Campanella, to which it bears a striking similarity. The rule of Metaphysicus and the three princes together with the magistrates, all carefully selected as the result of demonstrated superiority, could well have served as a model for that great interdependent graded organization which Saint-Simon proposed. But whether Saint-Simon was familiar with Campanella's conception we do not know. At any rate his view was a reaction from the ideas of communism and mechanical equality of the French Revolution, and also a rejection of the feudal and ecclesiastical situation before the Revolution. He had no confidence in hereditary or institutional control or in all-embracing mediocrity as a means of conducting society. His faith rested with the genius, and not the military genius, but the scientist, the savant, and the industrial chief. This faith represented a sharp departure from the thought of his time and really showed his ability to detach himself and strike out along new unconventional paths. He saw that the day of the feudal noble, the military leader, even of the priest in the old sense, was gone. A state organized with war as a normal trade was not to be thought of; for industry was henceforth to be the main business. [The true aim of man in society henceforth was the production of things useful to life—"the exploitation of the globe by association,"] as he expressed it in more general and grandiloquent terms.

Saint-Simon started out in "L'Organisateur" (1819) with a tripartite plan of social control,[22] half practical and half utopian, vaguely akin to Campanella's triad of Power, Wisdom and Love. Saint-Simon proposed three chambers, one of Invention, one of Examination, and a third called the Executive Chamber. The members of the first and second were to consist of engineers, savants, men of letters, artists; they were to be paid by the all-embracing state, but were to be merely consultative bodies. The members of the third were to be the great industrial leaders, capitalists, and bankers. To these last he gave the executive power, and the control of taxation and expenditure; and by so doing he gave them real temporal power. But he wished their edicts checked up as much as possible by submitting their messages to the superior scientific light of the other chambers. To the savants, supplemented by literary men and artists, was virtually left the spiritual power. In the "System Industrial" (1821) a change was made. The savants and men of letters were disestablished. The spiritual power was withdrawn from them, and especially from the savants, on the express ground that such power would quickly corrupt the scientific body. The temporal power was left with the industrial or capitalist class; and the power withdrawn from the savants was to be handed over to positive philosophers. (Thus his idea of Government was a body of scientists conducting the business of society in the most scientific way.

Therefore, when Saint-Simon left out the aristocracy of blood and rank from his plans, he did not call upon absolute democracy to lead the way. Instead he invented a new aristocracy of experts. This conception of the world under rule of eminently fit officials is Saint-Simon's greatest contribution. He could not imagine a society in which all were equals any

[22] Discussed by Graham, W, "Socialism New and Old," 1891, N. Y., pp. 74 ff

more than he could conceive of a workshop where all were masters. Work to be well done and society to be well administered must be work by experts whom we must raise to power. Saint-Simon had that unshakable confidence in personal capacity for leadership which so often exists in those whose ancestors have been ex-officio leaders for generations. He, like Carlyle after him, was obsessed by the value of the great man. When he proposed marriage to Madame de Staël he said, "Madame, you are the most remarkable woman in the world, as I am the most remarkable man; and doubtless our child will be still more wonderful!" His friends and followers were all large-caliber men, later noted as great engineers, industrial chiefs, and scientists, aristocrats of spirit and talent; practical examples of the theory of salvation from above.

In this great hierarchy positions were to be assigned according to capacity, again reflecting the idea of the Early Modern Utopians. The capacities of children were to be detected and they were then to be trained and equipped for those occupations for which they seemed best fitted. (He aimed to open all careers to talent, and to prevent any man of promise from being hopelessly handicapped in life's race by the barriers of either political or economic privilege. Therefore, he demanded a state ownership of the land, capital, and all instruments of labor. The right of succession to property with the unfair advantage which it gave in life had to be abolished in order to do away with any artificial interference with the success of merit. But there was to be no communal sharing of the wealth produced. Since the capacity of workers was unequal, they were to have proportionate rewards. "Every man shall be appointed as his power befits, and paid in proportion to his labor." Reward was to be according to capacity. There could be presumably almost as many gradations in society as at present but their basis would be personal, and the result of energy, intellect, skill and moral qualities and not inherited rank or property. Furthermore, a whole sex could not be excluded. Women, he felt, were still in the servitude of religious, political and civil inferiority. Saint-Simon would abolish this servitude, and make the wife the equal of her husband. Women

were to enjoy the same possibilities of achievement in the state
as the men.[23]

This then was the fundamental utopianism of Saint-Simon.
He believed in the natural inequality of men, and regarded
this inequality as the very basis of association, as the indispensable condition of social order. By recognizing this truth,
the greatest men would rise to the top and society would be
conducted by the very best men of its age, and the greatest
good for the greatest number would prevail. All efforts to perfect humanity had to proceed from this as a starting point.
It was progress and perfection achieved by the expert. The
knowledge of the few was used for the benefit of all; the weak
were guided by the strong. Saint-Simon said on his death-
bed: "All my life is comprised in this thought; to guarantee to all men the freest development of their faculties." [24]
If this could be done, then social perfection would be attained,
for this was true equality.

His second great utopianistic element was social religion
which really was to serve as a sort of complement to the first.
In order to secure the solidarity and enthusiasm essential for
the smooth working of the "reward according to merit" principle the centripetal force of religion was to be employed. It
was necessary to inspire the chiefs of the hierarchy to the
height of their great task, and to give to the rank and file a
sense of the justice of their position. His was an attempt to
discover an authority which would rule the inner life of man
as well as his external acts.

It had to be a new morality, resting on a new basis. He
wanted his hierarchical society permeated by moral and religious ideals; but they had to be appropriate to the new state of
things and to the new "positive" state of knowledge. In modern phraseology, they had to pass the social efficiency test.
And in seeking this inner governor he hit upon a principle of
Christianity, of great ethical and humanitarian value, which
caused the social question to become the essence of religion.
Saint-Simon said, "In the New Christianity, all morality will

[23] Ely, op. cit., p. 71.
[24] Quoted, Ibid. p. 61.

be derived immediately from this principle; men ought to regard each other as brothers.   This principle which belongs to
primitive Christianity, will receive a glorification, and in its
new form will read: (Religion must aid society in its chief
purpose, which is the most rapid improvement in the lot of the
poor." [25]   In his "Nouveau Christianisme" (1825) he gave a
slightly revised version in speaking of the duty of all classes
above the lowest, when he said that ["all should labor for the
development, material, moral, and intellectual, of the class the
most numerous and the poorest." [26]   This was the starting
point of Saint-Simon's disciples, and led to the formation of a
Saint-Simonian sect with a priesthood.   While it may have
been conceived with a purely utilitarian or perhaps even
pragmatic purpose in mind, in effect, it nevertheless was truly
religious in character, for it recognized the spiritual power and
the moral effectiveness of the principles of fraternity and mutual love, and as such was the most sublime utopianism.

5.   Fourier

While the failure of the French Revolution led Saint-Simon
to repudiate mechanical equality with its tendency toward
mediocrity, and caused him to observe society and study its
history and development, finally discovering his great principle
of the hierarchy or aristocracy of talent as the greatest utopianistic means, another Frenchman at the same time, was seeking
in the recesses of his own consciousness for a new social science,
whose sociological laws when recognized and put into effect,
would do away with the poverty and vice and other calamities
of the human race, and make possible the construction of an
ideal and perfect society.   The object of this other man was to
discover the laws which govern society.   In this he may be
called the pathfinder for later sociologists and especially modern
psychological sociologists.

This other man was Charles Fourier.   He was born in 1772
in Besançon of an ordinary family of the middle class, his
father being a cloth merchant.   As a boy he showed consider-

[25] Ibid pp. 65, 66.
[26] Quoted by Graham, op cit., p. 78.

able precocity, taking prizes for excellence in French and Latin
at the age of eleven years.   He was also passionately fond of
music and flowers and showed remarkable mechanical ability.
Upon the death of his father he inherited about one hundred
thousand francs, which he invested in foreign trade, and lost
in the siege of Lyons in 1793, during the Reign of Terror,
when his bales of cotton were used to form barricades and his
provisions to feed the soldiers.   Later he was imprisoned.
Upon his release he joined the army where he showed great
aptitude.   Early in life he became impressed with the fact
that the present organization of society was a disastrous failure and should be condemned as such.   About him he saw
lying, deceit, wastefulness, discord, maladjustment.   So he
early set to work to build up a social scheme which should promote truth, honesty, economy of resources and the development
of our natural propensities.[27] / He died in 1837.

Fourier's Utopianism is largely an outgrowth of his great
discovery.[28]   Newton had discovered and Leibnitz had revealed
and explained the law of attraction in the material universe.
Fourier, however, had discovered that there were three additional movements, the social, animal and organic, in turn in
which this powerful law of attraction held sway.   (He discovered
that there was unity in the system of movement for the material
world and for the spiritual.   In these latter three spheres it
was spoken of as the "law of passionate attraction," and it was
a great fundamental principle which governed the whole domain
of human activity and learning.

It rested upon the emotions or "passions" which were the
mainspring of human action.   "The passions," he says, "which
we have thought hostile to concord, tend only to concord, to
the social unity from which we thought them so far removed."
(He recognized no injurious passions or impulses.   It is a
fundamental principle with him that the misery and discord

27 For a more complete biography see Ely, "French & German Socialism
in Modern Times," pp. 82–84.

28 Fourier's chief works are: "La Théorie des Quatre Mouvements et
des Destinées Générales" (1808); "Traité de l'Association Domestique
Agricole au Attraction Industrielle." or as it was later called, "La Théorie
le l'Unité Universelle" (1822); "Nouveau Monde Industriel et Sociétaire"
(1829).

of the social world came from checking and thwarting natural
passions, impulses and instincts. Nature, and here he echoes
Rousseau, intended them all to be gratified. If they were
bound in and restrained they were but straining, chained tigers;
given free play, they made for social harmony and happiness.
Instead of repressing the passions he would increase their in-
tensity and their control of the individual by keeping them
in a constant state of tension. Giving this a more social expression it seemed to him that men were by nature inclined to do
right if their wishes were given free play; they only did what
was wrong and harmful because they were restrained by the
rules of a stupid, archaic system called civilization. Civilization must be adapted to the passions for they are the unalter-
able steady element, while the social forms are changeable and
transitory; the social order should be such as to afford the
possibility of directing these passions to the advantage, and
not to the detriment of society. By unbridling the human passions, Fourier believed that he had succeeded in solving the
problem of the greatest happiness for all.

These passions, which should be further cultivated, rather
than repressed, because they are in consonance with nature,
he classifies in the following way.[29] There are twelve in all
divided into three classes. The first class tend to "luxe" or
"luxisme" or luxury, and are the five appetites of the senses
which exercise more or less sovereignty over the individual,—
taste, touch, sight, smell, hearing. These are sensual in the
original sense of the word, or sensitive. The second class are
"the four simple appetites of the soul," tending to form affective groups, viz., the group of amity or friendship; the group
of love; that of paternity or family; and the group of ambition or corporation. The third class of passions were discovered by Fourier and were revealed by him under the collective name of "distributive passions," and formed the "Seri-
ism" or desire series. They were the "cabaliste" passion or
the desire for intrigue, planning and contriving, the purpose
of which was to excite emulation between groups; the "papil-

[29] See Ely, op. cit , pp 91, 92; Warren, F. M., "Ten Frenchmen of the
Nineteenth Century," New York, 1904, p. 55.

lone" or butterfly passion, which was the need in man of variety, change of scene, novelty, which stimulates the senses and also the soul; and finally the "composit" passion or the desire for union which is also a state of exhilaration derived from interplay of several pleasures of the senses and the soul enjoyed simultaneously. (All twelve passions unite together into one mighty all-controlling impulse called "Uniteisme" or "harmonism" which is the tendency of the individual to harmonize his happiness with the happiness of all that surrounds him and all the human race; it is a passion unknown to civilization. These will establish a limitless philanthropy, a universal good will. But in order to establish them there will be necessary graduated offices for the five senses, entire liberty for the four affective groups, and distributive justice for the "distributive passions." To repeat, Fourier argued that all the passions should be given free rein. Any other course was contrary to nature. (By allowing them free reign they would give rise to higher forms of passion, create new ones, and eventually lead to the perfect state of harmony and happiness,— social perfection attained.

The great master passion "Uniteisme" meant for Fourier that all men were naturally inclined to club together in social groups and work together for mutual good, instead of fighting with one another under the system of competition.(But in order to permit this to work itself out effectually the existing artificial social environment would first have to be condemned and abolished. The environment would have to be helpful. Therefore Fourier provided such an ideal environment and called it a phalange or phalanx,—an environment in which the passions, having perfectly free play, would combine harmoniously, operate to society's benefit and justify this ideal environment. (This social organization or social unit he made the framework of human society.

Each phalanx or phalange was a combination of a suitable number of individuals, occupying buildings know as phalansteries and inhabiting land a square league or so in extent. This area was to be worked in agriculture and industry, by the united efforts of the whole community, acting under the direction of managers chosen by the people. Each community was housed in a great central building known as the phalanstery, containing the workshops and the living apartments wherein the economies of consumption in common gave comforts and luxuries unknown in the scattered households of existing society. The proper number of persons in a phalanx again depended upon the twelve passions of man. These could be combined in eight hundred and twenty different ways in as many individuals, and no possible combination ought to be unrepresented among the workers of any phalanx, or there would be a lack of harmony. Four hundred persons were mentioned as a possible but und sirable minimum, eighteen hundred to two thousand members were recommended; [30] a large number would produce discord But even these eighteen hundred to two thousand could not be thrown together helter-skelter and promiscuously; they had to be ordered intelligently in series of from seven to nine harmonious individuals having similar tastes; the series then combined into groups of twenty-four to thirty-two each, and the groups combined into the phalange or phalanx. While Fourier was not anxious for a State at all, he foresaw a time when the phalanges of the world would be federated under a rather visionary Great Chief of the Phalanges, who was to live at Constantinople. Taylor remarks concerning this: "As there were no railways or telegraphs then in view, he probably thought such a far-away monarch would be fairly safe, from the point of view of liberty." [31]

In the phalange each person's particular place lay with the individual himself who was free to choose his occupation or his several occupations, for variety of work was especially recommended by Fourier; then he must attach himself to one of the elementary groups of seven to nine workers which formed the unit of industrial organization. Like Campanella, he hoped to adapt employment to the inclination and capacity of the laborer. Furthermore, he remembered that work should always be a source of pleasure. He saw that in existing so-

[30] For similar description see Ely, op. cit , p. 93.

[31] Taylor, G. R. S., "Leaders of Socialism Past, and Present," London, 1908, p. 39.

ciety work was made repellent rather than attractive, so that the best energies were held up rather than utilized. There was no attempt to fit capacity to task, no opportunity given the young to discover in what direction their talent lay and to train themselves for that work.[32] In his phalanges, the moment labor became fatiguing and lost its stimulus, the series or group stopped working and its members entered a new group where they set at the new task with renewed energy. What in his time was termed laziness, was at bottom nothing but aversion to monotonous work. The "papillone" passion must be appeased. In the phalange, no work would be monotonous, for all would do what they wanted, and all would quicken the energy of their exertions as each attempted to distinguish himself. Each would be drawn to work by his natural propensities. (Emulation, self-love, and other motives, compatible with self-interest, would spur each on.[33] Production would thus increase, because labor would become dignified and attractive as soon as men could do what they liked and work with whom they liked. Present day employment managers could profitably read Fourier. It may be asked, how the unpleasant work would be done, and Fourier would reply that a certain mutual adaptation continuously existed as to where men would exert their labor powers and the nature of the requirements of the community. Production would be kept at the maximum because of the "cabaliste" passion which would lead each group to attempt to surpass every other.

Fourier favored, in the main, a complicated system of payment in proportion to services rendered. The share of each series in the communal dividend varied directly with its importance in fostering harmony and inversely with the pleasant-

[32] Skelton, op. cit., p. 67.

[33] In criticism of this Skelton says· "Fourier, it is true, has put his finger on a weak spot in modern industry by his indictment of the monotony of toil, but the solution is to be found, it is being found, in the better fitting of capacity to task which universal education makes possible, in the improvement of the working environment, and in the opportunity shorter hours afford of utilizing leisure at one's will, rather than in the organized dilettantism, the perpetual kindergarten playing at work, the lack of adequate training and discipline implied in his phalanx a dream" Op cit, p 84

ness of the work. This share was again divided into twelve parts; of these five were to be allotted to a labor fund, which was distributed on the principle that more was paid for hard or unpleasant work than for pleasant work; three parts were to go to "talent" which was judged by the rank to which an individual had been elected by his fellow-workers, the remaining four parts were to be paid as interest on the capital advanced by private people to the community for Fourier permits both private property and interest within the limits of associative use. To have vetoed this would have been to thwart one of the strongest passions, and Fourier was too passionate a protector of free will to do this.

In strict conformity with his doctrines of the sovereignty of passion and attraction, he developed a thorough-going system of free love. For him the phalanx was substituted for the family on the one hand, and the state on the other as the unit of organization. To both he assigned a very minor rôle.[34] In fact, the marriage bond was entirely at will. The woman of the future was to be emancipated, and assigned a high rank in society, assured of economic support due to her equal participation in the activities of the phalanx, she was left free to choose permanent marriage, or promiscuous intercourse. Friendship would be free, paternity free, ambition free; all ties of marriage and family would be voluntary, for true attraction did not belong to compulsion or restraint.

It was these doctrines which swept through France to America and resulted in many attempts to set them up in practice. Fourier's plan was a recognition of the fact that social organization must group itself around the requirements of industrial life, and still further that industrial life must be subject to the desires of the individual human mind. It was a theory by which personal freedom was to suffer no restraint. Fourier thought that his theory of the passions combined with his principle of association was going to change the lot of the

[34] See discussion in Skelton, op. cit, p. 79, and Taylor, op. cit., p. 38.
[35] For accounts of Fourierism in America, see Commons and Associates —"History of Labor in the U. S, Pt. IV, Chapter 2, and "Documentary History of American Industrial Society," edited by John R. Commons, Vol. VII.

human race by satisfying the basic desires common to most men, and alluring them on to perfection by the seductions of profit and pleasures.

While this appears to be a most delectable bit of "Schwärmerei" and while it is fantastic almost to the point of being ridiculous at times, there is much that is substantial about it, much that we are only now coming to realize in its full importance. Fourier had something of the realist about him. (He realized that to improve men we must begin with them as they are; and they are essentially selfish and self-seeking. They are such because of their equipment of instincts and the motivating forces derived from these, none of which can be transformed by newly devised intellectual elements. Would that some of our present day social reformers, especially those of the philosophical habit of mind, might recognize this fact! The only quarrel we have with Fourier is that he went too far, and in the end bordered on the positively anti-social.

6. CABET

Another Utopian Socialist, and his utopianism also we will consider only in its most fundamental points, was Etienne Cabet. Here was one, who, imitating Morelly and Babeuf, pushed the demand for equality further and sought to counteract the principle of the inheritance of ability. He represented a sort of reaction to the principle of gradation according to ability, stressed so much by Saint-Simon and Fourier. When asked whether he made no distinction for ability, intelligence or genius, he replied: "No; are they not merely gifts of Nature? Would it be just to punish in any way him whom fortune has meanly endowed? Should not reason and society redress the inequality produced by blind chance? Is not the man whose superior ability makes him more useful fully recompensed by the satisfaction he derives from it?" [36]

Etienne Cabet, the son of a cooper, was born in Dijon, France, in 1788. He received a good education, including a university training, became a lawyer, and practiced first in his native city, then in Paris. He took a leading part in the

[36] "Voyage en Icarie," p 102.

Revolution of 1830, as a member of the "Committee of Insurrection." For this he was practically banished to Corsica, where he was made Attorney-General. Here again he took part in radical anti-administration activities against Louis Phillipe, and was removed from office, and condemned to two years' imprisonment. He escaped, however, and took up his residence in London where he fell under the influence of Owen's preaching and became a convert to his views. During this time of exile he also became acquainted with the "Utopia" of Sir Thomas More and was fascinated by it. The idea of writing a similar work of fiction, to propagate his own ideas of communism impressed itself upon his mind and he wrote a "roman philosophique et social" entitled "Voyage to Icaria," which was published soon after his return to Paris in 1839. In this Cabet follows closely the method of More, and describes "Icaria" as a Promised Land, an Eden, an Elysium, a new terrestrial Paradise." [37] While it is not our purpose to discuss the mechanical and physical details of his communism and of his perfect island of Icaria, we will say that he had cared for these externals of life in all their minutiae. Government, division of land, nature of houses, dress, etc., are all delineated in the light of his two great regnant principles, those of absolute equality of all, and brotherhood of man. It is these ideals which demand our attention in this work.[38]

In many respects Cabet represented a modernized and Christianized Babœuvianism. Both desired to destroy the social system and base a new era on the natural rights of every individual; on the right of freedom, equality, brotherhood; and on a national basis erect a system of communism; and through a democratization of political life to effect a reconstruction of economic life.[39] But while Babeuf appealed to an ascetic, queer type with his mediocrity-breeding communism, Cabet's

[37] For more extensive account of the facts just cited see Ely, op. cit., pp. 39–40, and Spargo, J , "Socialism," N Y., 1906, pp. 50, 51.

[38] The best account of Cabet's "Voyage en Ecarie" is that of Lux, H , "Etienne Cabet und der Ikarische Kommunismus," Stuttgart, 1894. See particularly pp 111–160

[39] Muckle, F. "Die Geschichte der Sozialistischen Ideen im 19ten Jahrhundert," Vol. I, p. 146.

utopianism was full of a spirit of optimism and elevation that included all in its scope of interests. Babeuf's communism was depressing; Cabet's was inspiring.

The principle of absolute equality was the fundamental law of the social structure. The community had to take all possible measures to stifle at birth every inequality. All trades and professions were on a par; the shoemaker was considered just as highly as the physician. As was indicated above in a quotation, no special privileges were given to genius or talent, for genius was a gift of nature and those who had not received this gift should not be penalized. Each citizen received from the State all articles he consumed; to all alike homes and furniture were assigned; clothing of the same design and quality made in large quantities was delivered to all; they were fed in social boarding houses. Theirs was a community and equality of goods and work, of duties and rights, of burdens and benefits and enjoyments. All was to represent a national social organization with its equality, effected by means of the conscious will of man; all was to be reasonable and contribute to the common welfare.

But to maintain this absolute reasoned equality the State was demanded, and its control was all-inclusive. This is best illustrated in their control of the press, in the educational system and their religion. The state was sole printer, and of course, "the state prints none but good books"; so infallible was its censorship that it even burned all the ancient books which were considered dangerous or useless, differing, however, from Omar's burning of the library of Alexandria in that it was acting in humanity's interest instead of against it: "We light our fires to burn wicked books, while the brigands and fanatics lit theirs to burn innocent heretics." [40] Each commune, each province and the State as a whole, were permitted to publish but a single paper, a commercial, a provincial and a national one. Editors, who were elected by the people, were not to be guided by personal tastes and opinions concerning current events, for as Cabet has one of his characters say, "In order to root out this evil we decided that the paper shall

[40] "Voyage en Icarie," p. 127.

bear the character of simple records, noting facts without any critical review on the part of the journalists." [41]

Education was also a very important function of the state, and Cabet regarded it as his fundamental utopianistic measure. It was to be a far-reaching training—physical, intellectual, ethical, industrial and civic. The parents were responsible for the training of the children up to the age of five, after which they attended the national schools, where they were taught by teachers selected with great care, for the Icarians said: "The teachers train the Nation." By the time the young people had attained maturity they were supposed to be fit producers, citizens, and husbands and wives. Effort was made throughout to teach each sex the highest regard for the other, hence they were taught together.

Cabet felt that society could not be held together, reinvigorated and reorganized by mere reasoning and science, but required also the force and life which faith and religion alone can impart. Hence he would provide an official state religion. This was supposed to be an expression of the religious spirit of all the people and its fundamental principles on the basis of this inclusiveness were prepared by a council of priests, professors, philosophers, moralists, and other scholars. The emphasis was placed on the honoring of God, and the inculcation of morals. It was in fact an attempt to approximate the communism of early Christianity which emphasized the principles of brother love, equality, freedom, association and communal ownership.

Of these, the greatest from the point of view of efficient equality was the spirit of brotherhood with which he desired to have the entire people permeated. This was the very basis of the whole system. Here he introduced an element unexpressed by other Utopian Socialists. When the Icarians were asked "What is your science?" they replied, "Brotherhood." "What is your principle?" "Brotherhood." "What is your teaching?" "Brotherhood." "What is your theory?" "Brotherhood." [42] It was an ideal which was going to work out so

[41] Quoted by Tugan-Baranowsky, op cit., p. 14.
[42] Quoted by Muckle, op cit., p 148; also by Ely, op. cit., p 50

perfectly that there would be no crime, no police, no jails, no poorhouses in Icaria. Every man would be his brother's keeper.

Cabet's theories, like those of Fourier, found wide acceptance and efforts were made to carry them into effect, but like most abortive social schemes they failed partly because they were impractical and partly because perfect human beings were scarce.[43]

7. Blanc

Louis Blanc published his great work, the "Organization du Travail," in 1839, the same year that Cabet published his "Voyage en Icarie." But this work of Blanc's was wholly different from that of his contemporary. While Cabet was outlining a Utopia, Blanc was giving the details of a contemplated economic organization making for social perfection and indicating the agencies for actually bringing it into effect.

Louis Blanc, journalist, author, politician, and socialist, was born in Madrid, Spain, October 28th, 1813.[44] His father was at the time General Inspector of Finance under Joseph Bonaparte. They soon left Spain, however, for Corsica, his mother's native land, where he passed his early years. He studied at the college of Rodez and went to Paris about 1830 to continue his studies. Since the revolution had ruined his father, Louis lived in narrow circumstances. He earned his keep by copying, teaching and literary hack work. He eventually became newspaper editor, contributor to periodicals, and founder of the "Revue du Progrès" in which his "Organization du Travail" appeared, before being published in book form. Later Blanc became famous as an author of two famous historical works.[45] He was prominent in the Revolution of 1848, being a member of the Provisional Government in February 1848. The meas-

[43] For an account of the American Icarian attempts see Ely, op. cit., pp. 40 ff; and Shaw, Albert, "Icaria, A Study in Communistic History," N. Y., 1884.

[44] Ely, op cit., p 109

[45] "Histoire de Dix Ans—1830–40," in 16 volumes published 1844; and "Histoire de la Revolution Française" in 12 volumes, published in the years 1847–62

ures he sponsored met, however, with little success as we shall presently see. Adverse political movements caused him to flee in May to Belgium, and thence to England, where he lived until the overthrow of Napoleon III in 1870. Upon his return he was elected to the National Assembly where he took his place on the Left. However, his activities here were far from radical, being almost conservative at times. His life was frank, generous and clean, and full of purpose and sincerity to the end. Ely says, "He continued to advocate quietly his doctrines in behalf of oppressed humanity, and had so gained in public estimation that upon his death, on the 6th of December, 1882, in Cannes, France, the Chamber of Deputies voted him the honor of a state funeral." [46]

Louis Blanc's cry for the organization of labor was secured from Saint-Simon; in fact, he was debtor, also, to Saint-Simon for the name of his famous work and many of his reform ideas, particularly his general ideas of the organization of labor by the state. Like his predecessor he saw in economic anarchy the chief evil of his time, and consequently agreed that a social science must be created which would, on the basis of facts, lay down what was to be done to create a harmonious social existence. But unlike Saint-Simon and Fourier, he was not merely a social reformer, for he tried to give practical effect to the programs of social reform his predecessors had discussed. He sought to use not revolutionary sentiment, or religious fervor, or self-interest, or brotherly love, or public opinion, as had his predecessors, but the political machinery of society, as a means to his ideal end of a regenerated social life. He happily combined the reformer and politician. Louis Blanc thus occupied much the same position relative to Utopian Socialism that Savonarola did to the ethico-religious utopians. He sought to set up in working order the ideals of his cult, by use of political power, and, like Savonarola, he was overthrown by reactionary forces and his beautiful scheme fell about his own head. Blanc was the intermediate step between utopian socialism and Marxian socialism with its political and evolutionary aspects. He suggested the political remedies; Marx

[46] Ely, op. cit., pp. 114, 115.

introduced the Hegelian principle. He was utopian because he thought that the impossible at the time could become possible, that his scheme could become reality.

For Blanc as for nearly all socially minded thinkers, the purpose of human existence was happiness. Any acceptable, any tolerable organization of society must make this possible for every single human being. But according to his analysis, present-day society did not permit this for it was one where competition, individualism and *laissez faire* reigned supreme. The result was want and misery, rendering the fulfillment of the destiny of man impossible. This had to be corrected by a new organization of labor, which abandoning individualism, private property, and private competition,—the fundamentals of existing society,—adopted fraternity as its controlling principle.[47] For the fundamental reason why these maladjustments persisted was because social institutions did not provide the certainty of being able to live by one's own labor. The propertyless proletariat could not free themselves from the economic servitude in which they found themselves because they had no tools nor were they assured of means of work. In other words there was no socially recognized "droit au travail." Thus Blanc's Utopianism.

The first step was the contriving of means of guaranteeing to every one the certainty of finding work. This was a duty of the state to be accomplished by the erection of social workshops,—"ateliers sociaux,"—farms for agriculturists, factories for workmen, shops for tradesman, "destined to replace gradually and without shock individual 'ateliers.'[48] Blanc was well aware of the importance of the rôle the state could play in the reconstruction of the existing economic fabric if its powers were properly utilized. He considered it the state's function to found these "ateliers sociaux," pass laws for their government, watch over the administration of these laws, for the profit of all. But he expected it to be a democratically organized state, and one which, as it created and protected social workshops, and as economic classes consequently dis-

47 See Ely, op. cit., 117.
48 "Organisation du Travail," pp. 13, 14, 17, 18, 199.

appeared, would itself disappear. The state for him was a
necessary evil, but an evil which in the course of time brought
about its own disappearance.

For the present, however, the state was to mobilize in its
hands all those branches of industry which, by their very
nature, admitted or required centralization. Hence he agitated
for the buying by the state of the railways, canals, mines, the
great industries, the banks and insurance companies. Furthermore, as temporary remedies there were to be state loans of
money, or state guarantee of private loans, to groups of workmen, whereby they could establish workshops of their own.
Thus the state would assist in many ways in having individualistic and capitalistic enterprises with all their evils gradually
superceded by enterprises of labor associations and coöperative
unions, under the control of the state. Presently all separately
organized associations producing the same commodities would
be assimilated, and brought together in one politico-economic
organism, administered from the center. Competition would
then have disappeared and all industries would stand in mutual
relationship to one another. Economic, and through it, social
solidarity, would then be attained. Here we had a sort of
primitive guild socialism anticipated where each branch of
production lay in the hands of organized workmen loosely controlled by the state and utilizing the agencies of production
supplied by the state. Each industry was regarded in the market as a separate undertaking and distributed among its members, after deduction of the portion due the state, the net proceeds. Here we note a gradual transition from the existing
environment to the ideal state, rather a more hopeful and more
feasible program than that of Babeuf or Fourier for example.

Blanc recognized that there would be a social hierarchy just
as Saint-Simon had. Faculties, powers, abilities were of infinite variety, but they were all to be used to full capacity and
for the good of others and insofar as this was done rank was
granted in society Blanc, however, opposed Saint-Simon's
idea of reward proportional to works. This, he said, was selfish and hard, and would condemn the weak and feeble to
extinction. He demanded that each person render service

in proportion to his strength of body and mind, but receive in
proportion to his needs; insofar as the means of society would
admit it.   No such thing as equality existed and if it did it
would be unnatural and unjust.   Blanc said: "Equality, then,
is only proportionality, and it exists in a true manner only when
each one in accordance with the law written in some shape in
his organization by God himself produces according to his
faculties and consumes according to his wants." [49]   This was
the formula for distributive justice.

Thus Blanc's Utopia was an ideal economic organization
which he thought would bring perfection; and his utopianistic
agency was an efficient and kindly state, working for the
salvation of humanity.   That it was a dream which appealed to
many, we know.   As early as 1846 the French workers demanded that Blanc's workshops be established, and this clamor
became so insistent that on February 28, 1848, the provisional
government passed a decree ordering the establishment of
national workshops in France; the further measure of April
27th, extended them to the French colonies.   As a matter of
fact they were only founded in Paris and its neighborhood.[50]
The real purpose of the government in doing this, however,
was not to satisfy the demands of the workers, but to discredit
Blanc and his theories.   Émile Thomas, one of Louis Blanc's
worst enemies, was made director of the Paris workshop and
was informed by M. Marie, the Minister of Public Works, that
"it was the well-formed intention of the government to try this
experiment of the commission of government for laborers; that
in itself it could not fail to have good results, because it would
demonstrate to the laborers the emptiness and falseness of these
inapplicable theories and cause them to perceive the disastrous
consequences flowing therefrom for themselves, and would so
discredit Louis Blanc in their eyes that he should forever cease
to be a danger." [51]   That Thomas succeeded in running them
into the ground we know.   After attracting the riff-raff of half
of France to Paris and paying them for idleness, the entire

[49] "Organisation du Travail," p 72
[50] Menger, A "The Right to the whole Produce of Labor," London,
1899, p 21
[51] Lorenz von Stein, "Soziale Bewegung." iii, p. 292.

scheme collapsed. The plan may have been faulty in itself; France surely was not ready for it at the time; but under the management which instituted it any scheme however perfect and timely would have failed. Blanc stood repudiated, but to-day he is the idol of the French workmen.

8. OWEN

England, no less than France, was swayed by the philosophy of the eighteenth century, but the English temperament and English economic conditions were such that the social reform movements did not take the same form of Utopias. The Latin temperament with its fiery and imaginative character expressed its protest against an existing order in the form of more or less unrealizable schemes. The phlegmatic Anglo-Saxon was different, and yet the economic conditions probably are more responsible for the lack of Utopias in England. The Industrial Revolution had advanced further and become more far-reaching in character in England than on the Continent. While the introduction of new mechanical inventions had enormously increased the productive powers of England, they brought with them terrible poverty and hardship. The machine came to be everything and the human being next to nothing. Agriculture was suffering, small manufacturers, unable to compete with the big machine producers, were forced to the wall, and became wage-workers in competition with others of an already far too numerous wage class, and this compounding of misery added greatly to the woe of the time. But perhaps the worst of all the results of the new régime was the destruction of the personal relations which had hitherto existed between the employers and their workers. Now only a hard, cold, cash *nexus* remained. Housing conditions became frightful, child and woman labor was augmented with disastrous results, unemployment was on the increase, *laissez-faire* both in industry and in personal relations was pitiless and in undisputed sway. Mammonism was in its strength and humanitarianism almost unknown.

This state of affairs left no room for vain imaginings and whimsical anticipations. It was a challenge to the hard-headed

English social reformer to devise immediate solutions of problems, progressively growing worse. The social history of England during the first half of the nineteenth century is an account of one such movement after another. One of the reformers of this period, however, beginning with hard, cold reality, gradually approached in his thinking that which his time called the "utopian."

This man was Robert Owen. He was born in 1771 of Welsh artisan descent. He began life as an apprentice in a cotton factory, but, being indomitable in his purpose to rise, soon set himself up as a master spinner. His rise was extremely rapid and at the age of thirty he found himself co-proprietor and director of the New Lanark Mills. Riding on the crest of the commercial maelstrom he made a fortune and won fame as one of the greatest captains of industry of his time. He also made a name for himself at New Lanark by his technical improvements and his model dwellings for his workmen. It was here that his ideas on education also took shape. In fact, his reforms and social experiments were so unusual and knowledge of them so widespread that pilgrimages, even participated in by various members of royalty, to his plant became common. Distinguished men from all parts of the world visited the place and with a unanimity that is a rare tribute to Owen's skill and sincerity praised it highly. His other practical achievements were by no means insignificant. He was primarily instrumental in bringing about the first labor legislation, the Factory Acts, in England in 1819. He directly inspired the great coöperative movement, for the Rochdale pioneers were the result of the success of New Lanark; he was one of the pioneers of trade unionism, presiding at the first organized congress of labor unions as far back as 1834. Essentially a Utopian, he was nevertheless very much of a practical reformer, and shrewd man of business. He numbered among his friends some of England's greatest men, at least from the social and economic point of view, among them being, Malthus, James Mill, Ricardo and Godwin. He died in 1857 at the advanced age of eighty-seven.

It is mostly the theoretical in Owen, the Utopian, that we are concerned with, and since he did not write a work analogous to the romance of Thomas More, for example, we must seek his theories and ideas in the formidable array of pamphlets, manifestos, lectures, debates, books and philosophical treatises which he left us.[52]

Owen's fundamental postulate was that the object of human society was to increase the happiness of each individual to the greatest extent practicable, that is consistent with the greatest happiness of the whole. This conception of maximum happiness, the aim of this Utopianism, he received from his friend Jeremy Benthan, who for a time was associated with him in business. Owen states:

"The primary and necessary object of all existence is to be happy. . . . But happiness cannot be obtained individually; it is useless to expect isolated happiness; all must partake of it, or the few can never enjoy it; man can, therefore, have but one real and genuine interest, which is, to make all of his race as peaceful in character and happy in feeling as the original organization or nature of each will admit. When all shall be cordially engaged in promoting the happiness of all around them to this extent, then will they have entered upon the real business of life—then will they be occupied in promoting to the greatest limit, their own individual happiness, which has been made permanently to consist in the happiness of the race; and the only contest among men then will be, who shall the most succeed in extending happiness to his fellows."[53]

This desire for happiness was for him both the aim and the religion of society. He says, "Herein will consist true religion, and the pure and genuine adoration of all that is great, good, beautiful, and magnificent throughout the universe."[54] The whole duty of man is to be happy himself, and to make his fellow beings happy. In the millenium to come "to produce happiness will be the only religion of man; the worship of God will consist in the practice of useful industry; in the acquisition of

[52] His chief works are "A New View of Society or Essays on the Principle of the Formation of the Human Character," 1813 ff.; "Book of the New Moral World," 1826–44; "The Life of Robert Owen, written by Himself," 1857.

[53] "The Book of the New Moral World," Pt. IV, p. 54.

[54] Ibid.

knowledge; in uniformily speaking the language of truth; and in the expression of the joyous feelings which a life in accordance with nature and truth is sure to produce."[55] Owen thus expressed his social ideal in the form of a practical social religion, which was not to be a religion of temples and forms and ceremonies, but "daily undeviating practice in thought, word and action of charity, benevolence, and kindness to every human being." When this was attained then the "New Moral World"—the golden age—would be with us. It was this program in its details which won for him the title of Utopian.

A man's ability to become fit for this new world depended, however, entirely upon his environment. Man's whole life and character were determined for him by circumstances. Podmore, on the flyleaf of his great work on Owen,[56] gives this quotation: "It is of all truths the most important that the character of man is formed for him and not by him." This is the gist of his famous theory of environment,—a theory which almost became an obsession. It was an etiological principle resting upon the subordination and adaptation of man to his environment. It was based upon the environment of Morelly and the denial of the doctrine of innate ideas as maintained by Helvetius.

Owen's was a deterministic conception resulting in the absolute denial of individual responsibility. "The character of man is, without a single exception, always formed for him, . . . it may be and is chiefly created by his predecessors; . . . they give him or may give him, his ideas and habits, which are the powers that govern and direct his conduct. Man, therefore, never did, nor is it possible, he ever can form his own character "[57] There was no such thing as "original depravity" or moral responsibility. Podmore feels that Owen practically ignored what Christianity calls "original sin" and modern science knows as "inherited tendencies."[58] Hence as a utopianist, his whole system of reform was based upon the proposition that with proper social and industrial environment people

[55] Ibid Pt II, p 33
[56] Podmore, Frank, "Robert Owen," 2 vols , N Y., 1917.
[57] "A New View of Society," 4th ed , pp. 83.
[58] Podmore op. cit., II, P 648

would generally be good and do good. "Any general character, from the best to the worst, from the most ignorant to the most enlightened, may be given to any community, even to the world at large, by the application of proper means; which means are to a great extent at the command and under the control of those who have influence in the affairs of men." [59] For our purpose, it is important to note that Owen thought environment was directly under human control. Therefore, the necessary thing for society to do was to establish a right physical, moral and social environment, and thereby impress upon humanity, which was admittedly in woefully bad straits, proper standards of conduct. This Owen optimistically believed could be done by suitable training and proper social and economic organization. Man was essentially a healthy animal in body and mind, and he was fundamentally good; what was necessary for his proper development was a fitting environment. All wrong, all crime and suffering, all maladjustment proceeded from circumstances created by the perversity of man in the past. Abolish these evil conditions and man would rise to his full stature and perfection.

He suggested several measures which should be adopted if human society were to be reconstructed. The first was a national scheme of education, in which he saw a fit instrument for gradually perfecting the social state, for knowledge was the most potent agency. In his address at the formal opening of the New Lanark School building on January 1, 1816, Owen said, "I know that society may be formed so as to exist without crime, without poverty, with health greatly improved, with little, if any, misery and with intelligence and happiness increased a hundred-fold; and no obstacle whatsoever intervenes at this moment, *except ignorance,* to prevent such a state of society from becoming universal." [60] By education the inhabitants of any community could be trained to live perfectly. Thus education was to be universal and compulsory, and no child in the whole Empire was to be excluded from its benefits;

[59] "Autobiography," Vol. I, p. 226, from his "Essays on the Principle of the Formation of Human Character."
[60] Podmore, op. cit., I, p. 130

it was to be unsectarian and real teaching, and not merely the teaching by rote of the beggarly elements. It was to begin with the imparting of the principles of fraternity and industry to individuals in the plastic stages of infancy and childhood and then mold the life of each community in conformity with the welfare of the whole. "The child, who from infancy has been rationally instructed in these principles, will readily discover and trace whence the opinions and habits of his associates have arisen, and *why* they possess them. At the same age he will have acquired reason sufficient to exhibit to him the irrationality of being angry with an individual for possessing qualities which, as a passive being during the formation of those qualities, he had not the means of preventing." [61]   He will thus be moved to pity, not to anger, for those less fortunate in their upbringing than himself. A child so educated will be filled with a spirit of universal tolerance and good will; he will constantly desire to do good to all men, even to those who hold themselves his enemies. "Thus shortly, directly, and certainly may mankind be taught the essence, and to attain the ultimate object of all former moral and religious instruction." [62]

But the remodeling of social institutions did not necessarily have to wait until the education of the rising generation on rational principles had been completed. There was much else that an enlightened and resolute government could do at once to improve the circumstances which hindered and oppressed men and women whose time for education was past. He advocated the establishment of a Labor Bureau "for the purpose of obtaining regular and accurate information relative to the value of and demand for labor over the United Kingdom," [63] for "it ought to be a primary duty of any government that sincerely interests itself in the well-being of its subjects to provide perpetual employment of real national utility in which all who apply may be immediately occupied." [64]

[61] "Autobiography," Vol. I, p 273
[62] Ibid. p 273
[63] "Essays on the Principle of the Formation of Human Character," p 324
[64] Ibid. p 329

These two, National Education and National Employment,
were the principal and urgent measures necessary to his plan
but among the minor reforms he advocated, the abolition of
State Lotteries, the regulation of the drink traffic in the
interests of the nation, the reform and ultimate suppression of
the Poor Laws, and the purging of the Church of theological
dogmas and the founding of universal charity, had a significant place.[65]

But he also proposed a Utopia. In 1817 the disorganization of industry which followed the sudden end of the great
European wars at the battle of Waterloo, set Owen in search
of a remedy for unemployment and misery; and he propounded
his scheme of "villages of unity and coöperation," in which
the unemployed were to be collected together into self-support-
ing communities, where they would coöperate for their mutual
benefit. This principle began to grow on him and eventually he gave up his work at New Lanark to preach his ideal
of a coöperative world. He saw the world made up of villages,
rid of the capitalist and free from that private property which
was completely incompatible with social well-being, producing
solely for the collective good. It was when he passed on to
suggest the method by which this communistic world was to be
inaugurated that he ceased to be scientific and became a Utopian. Briefly stated, he recommended that the Trade Unions
turn themselves into productive societies; or that colonies of
workers should be formed on the coöperative principle. These
colonies or villages of coöperation with a population varying
from 500 to 2000 souls, were then to furnish the favorable
environment desired. Compared to the fine-spun dreams of
Fourier, Owen's was coarse and crude. The members were
to be engaged in both agriculture and manufacturing; they were
to be housed in great quadrangles located in the midst of each
colony, containing the common dormitories, common kitchen
and dining rooms, common schools, library, reading rooms,
guest rooms, etc. The spaces within the quadrangle were to
be planted with trees and laid out as gardens and playgrounds.
Other gardens surrounded the quadrangle on the outside, and

[65] Podmore, op cit, I, p. 118

beyond these were the stables, laundries, manufactories and farm buildings.[66] All were to work at suitable tasks according to their ability, except that children were to attend school the first few years of life, and only gradually take part in manual labor, working as half-timers at first. These voluntary communities were to form a great federation of tens of thousands of villages, covering the civilized world and making the ancient state superfluous. It would be a different world occupying the place of the capitalistic system with its poverty and misery, its injustice and inequality, its falsehood and deception; and all were to be united in brotherly coöperative effort.[67] Owen actually carried on utopian experiments at Orbiston and Motherwell in Scotland, and at New Harmony in Indiana. But they, like all previous isolated paradises, failed, simply because society is an organic unity, and must be reformed as a whole. A subtle osmosis takes place between such ideal spots and the world at large which from the first condemns them to failure

Such in skeletal form were the utopianistic measures of Robert Owen. While he passed in his day as both captain of industry and reformer, he actually was greater; he was a prophet who saw far off the vision of a thankful race living in an environment where happiness was the rule. He was a prophet of the tradition of Rousseau and preached the gospel of the essential goodness of human nature. And "if the New Jerusalem which he saw found its embodiment in a rather ridiculous quadrangle, it must be remembered that his vision was limited as Owen himself would have reminded us in any other case than his own—by his nature, his personal experience, his environment, the whole circumstances of the time." [68] His utopianism was effective as that of few has been; he had a most beneficent effect on the social progress of his country. Engels says of Owen, "Every social movement, every real advance in

[66] See Podmore, op cit., I, pp. 218, 219

[67] Podmore states: "The glittering vision of a whole planet partitioned out into quadrangular paradises, each with its sufficiency of well-cultivated acres, was always before his eyes; and the millenium seemed never further off than harvest is from seed time." II, p. 462.

[68] Podmore, II, p 646.

England on behalf of workers links itself on to the name of Robert Owen." [69] A great man withal. Adin Ballou, the founder of Hopedale, in 1845, gave the following rather eulogistic description of Owen, which is an excellent summary of his characteristics: "Robert Owen is a remarkable character. In years nearly seventy-five; in knowledge and experience superabundant; in benevolence of heart transcendental; in honesty without disguise; in philanthropy unlimited; in religion a sceptic; in theology a Pantheist; in metaphysics a necessarian circumstantialist; in morals a universal excusionist; in general conduct a philosophic non-resistant; in socialism a Communist; in hope a terrestrial elysianist; in practical business a methodist; in deportment an unequivocal gentleman." [70]

9. CONCLUSION

What is our conclusion to be concerning the Utopian Socialists?

Unlike many modern social reformers or revolutionists, not one of them was representative directly of that proletariat which others wished to benefit. They were great socially-minded editors, journalists, politicians, scientists, business men, —men who felt the "Weltdrang" and gave it individual expression, but in pretty much the same language. Furthermore, their intention was not to free a particular class to begin with, but all humanity at once. Like the French philosophers, they desired to bring the kingdom of reason and eternal justice, and while the fundamentals of their various perfect states were essentially the same they differed as widely in method and atmosphere as did their creators.

One and all they turned from the spectacle of disorder and misery, which their day presented, to the contemplation of the ideal commonwealth that was to be, "certain of the possibility of realizing a social organization which would universalize wealth, happiness, and harmony, unify mankind and elevate them to the highest degree of power, beauty, splendor and

[69] "Socialism, Utopian and Scientific," London, 1892, p. 25.
[70] Quoted by Noyes, "History of American Socialism," pp. 88, 89.

glory . . . calm the suffering of the peoples, deliver the unfortunate from the anguish of hunger and misery and the fortunate from their egotism, and bring about a marriage upon earth between work and pleasure, between riches and kindly feeling, between virtue and happiness." [71] But no two of these visions of Eden agreed in detail. Yet, as has been said, they were similar in spirit and fundamentals.

Fundamental was their belief that God, or Nature, had ordained all things to serve the happiness of mankind. From Morelly's belief that Nature had aimed at the promotion of general happiness to this declaration of Fourier half a century later we find the idea constantly expressed: "God has done well all that he has done; . . . His providence would be imperfect if he had devised a social system which should not satisfy the needs and serve the happiness of every people, age and sex." [72] Owen also, it will be remembered, made this the starting point in his utopianism.

One and all believed that with proper environment man would be actually perfect. He was naturally good, but existing environment with its overwhelming imperfections and maladjustments destined him to evil and woe. Hence their utopianistic activities consisted mostly in educating man to a knowledge of this congenial environment and the devising of means to bring it to pass. As thinkers ahead of their time, they all saw the great value of education, and all with the exception of Babeuf, gave universal and compulsory education a very significant place in their methodology.

Without exception they believed in the abolition of that enemy of the very "obvious and simple system of natural liberty" —private property—upon which their predecessors had set their hopes; therefore, they were all exponents of the socialization of property. Private property was personal; it narrowed the feelings and sympathies; it prevented the utilization of a common gift for the common welfare; therefore, it must be taken out of the minds of individuals. Production also had to be socialized and supervised by society in its own

[71] Considerant "Destinee Sociale," ii, p xxxii.
[72] See "Nouveau Monde," p. 31, quoted by Gide, "Selections from the Works of Fourier," London, 1901, p 48

interests. Here the Utopian Socialists were true forerunners of the Marxians.

Nearly all anticipated some form of social religion. In their day these unprejudiced thinkers saw how ineffective current dogmatized religion was. The religion of their day was a matter of habit and form, and not a driving social force making for constant wholesome refurnishing of life. It encouraged reaction, and did not inspire to a fearless meeting of the future. It was a drag, a narcotic, a paralyzing system. The utopian socialists wove into their ideal schemes a new religion which recognized men as well as creeds, and social deeds as well as ceremonies, one which sought universal happiness and not universal conformity.

In certain other respects they did not wholly agree. There was no uniformity on the question of equality. Babeuf and Cabet had the idea of absolute equality, sheer dead monotony; Fourier and Saint-Simon-recognized differences in capacity, and had schemes of reward according to capacity; Blanc was the most advanced, accepting inequality; but demanding reward, not according to capacity, but according to needs. He struck the most adequately social note of all.

Nor did they agree on their views of the State. Fourier's idea of a central executive if one had to be was to domicile it nowhere nearer than Constantinople. Saint-Simon thoroughly believed in the State. Louis Blanc not only believed that the State was the main hope of good government, he took his ideals into the heart of political affairs and addressed a National Assembly in support of his views. Owen looked upon the State as an incapable institution that did not count very much one way or the other, that might be of small use temporarily for social purposes, but would gradually become obsolete.

But how feasible, then were the schemes of the Utopian Socialists? Their thought was of putting a perfect scheme before the world and then having it accepted. But their schemes were impossible with men as they found them; they, and all Utopians, dealt with men as they ought to be and "men as they ought to be" so far in history, is merely a glorious ideal. They were pioneers, nevertheless, creators of marvelously ingenious plans produced by much patient expenditure of brain labor. While these plans were in many respects dreamy products of highly imaginative, and in one case (Fourier) half-mad, Latins they called into being the social ideal, for their fancies challenged the rude reality of the surrounding world; they awakened the interest of the widest possible social circles in the realization of an improved plan of social life.

But the Utopian Socialists were practically the last of the Utopians. They had not learned that profound respect for history so essential in the conception of realizable social reform. For them the ideal state was a finished state and not a process. With them the Utopian spirit which had been enthralled with desire for perfection, vanished because it became bound up with a new doctrine, that of Hegel, which gave a hope of accomplishing social ideals. With the advent of Hegelianism, social reform began to acquire efficient and opportunistic tactics which gradually began to convert longings into reality. The ideal of perfection began to be influenced by a sense of possibility.[73]

The Utopian Socialists were "keenly critical, ingeniously suggestive, and contagiously enthusiastic." But their own direct attempt at solution came to nothing. One school after another flashed into popularity, only to disappear as rapidly. Only their ideas have persisted and served as a basis for new reform endeavors.

[73] This subject will be discussed at length in chapter X.

CHAPTER VI

THE RECENT SOCIAL ANTICIPATIONS—THE PSEUDO-UTOPIAS

The Utopian Socialists were the last of the line of the Utopians in the original and widely accepted meaning of the term. With the perfecting of theories of history and the growth of the idea of development or evolution, real Utopias ceased to appear, for men now had a conception of social growth and development, and were not confronted with the necessity of picturing a perfect substitute for but of making improvement in present society. Nowadays with our ideas of evolution we can have the same idealism, but it does not take such unreal form, because we have come to feel that amelioration may go on even if the ultimate goal is not yet in sight. Modern Utopias differ from the others discussed in that there is in them the feeling of forthcoming attainment.[1] They deal with men as they are and use familiar means, and the perfect consummation of their ideas seems to be just around the corner, an entirely realizable process, developing out of the near past and the present. There is in them little that could be construed as the product of unbridled and fantastic imagining. They are really pseudo-Utopias, and we are introducing them as samples of the kind of better worlds that take the place of the older Utopias in social thought.

We will not review all the more recent anticipations. Instead we will select for more particular attention three which are most representative. The first is Edward Bellamy's "Looking Backward," written in 1889. We select it because it is the best known and most famous of those written in the United States which has produced only a few. We have also selected.

---

[1] This essential difference and the causes responsible for it will be discussed at greater length in the second part of this work.

"Freeland—A Social Anticipation," written in 1890 by Theodor Hertzka, the eminent Austrian economist, because of the great following it had in Europe, innumerable associations being formed to carry into substantial effect its principles and institutions. Finally we will discuss briefly Mr. H. G. Wells' "Modern Utopia" written in 1905. We take it up chiefly because it was written by Mr. Wells, one of the most famous and most utopianistic of present-day social idealists. It also doubtless ranks highest among Mr. Wells' three utopian efforts.

In these works we find instances of the hypothesis stated above. Bellamy looking back upon the prodigious moral and material transformation of very recent times feels that he stands on a firm base of fact when he dares to anticipate certain changes in the near future. He states [2] that instead of looking ahead as some people do to "the progress that shall be made, ever onward and upward, till the race shall achieve its ineffable destiny," he will "find more solid ground for daring anticipations of human development during the next one thousand years . . . by 'Looking Backward' upon the progress of the last one hundred." In his addendum, he states progress will come soon. "Our children will surely see it, and we too, who are already men and women, if we deserve it by our faith and by our works." Hertzka makes no pretense of giving the outlines of an absolutely good order of society, but sketches one that is relatively best; one that best corresponds to contemporary conditions, and which is alone intelligible and attainable by man. [3] This will rest upon the law of evolution, to the principles of which he adheres. Wells was modern enough to realize that it would be folly for him to try to depict any lastingly perfect state. He saw that social improvement must be based on human nature as it is, so he expressly stipulates that in his Utopia people are fundamentally the same as those we know, [4] and that the new things are all an outgrowth of the thing that is, the difference is in the measure of the will and imagination that goes to make them.

These anticipations are not so rich in utopianism as those

[2] Preface, p. v
[3] Preface, p. ix.
[4] "A Modern Utopia," p 23.

already discussed. They were not so much high flights of the imagination as the calculated product of beneficent forces now at work. So our treatment of them will consist mainly of a brief outline of their characteristic features.

1. BELLAMY'S "LOOKING BACKWARD"

This work had an unprecedented vogue in the nineties, and called forth a score of books discussing its various institutions and principles. It is the product of careful economic analysis from the socialistic point of view and treats in an ingenious and thorough fashion present-day economic dilemmas. Some of Bellamy's ideas are not unlike those of Hertzka.

At the very start Mr. Julian West the fictitious narrator of the tale, speaks of some of the evils and insufficiencies of the late eighties. The accumulation and concentration of wealth in the hands of single families, its constant augmenting as the result of investment, and its transfer from generation to generation comes in for criticism. Interest, the abolition of which or an absolute limitation to the smallest possible rate, had been the effort of lawgivers and prophets from the earliest ages, he characterized as a "species of tax in perpetuity upon the product of those engaged in industry which a person possessing or inheriting money was able to levy." [5]

Society was marshaled into classes, particularly the rich and the poor. He likens the social order to a coach in which the rich are riding drawn by the masses. When the conditions of the road were unusually bad "the passengers would call down encouragingly to the toilers of the rope, exhorting them to patience, and holding out hopes of possible compensation in another world for the hardness of their lot, while others contributed to buy salves and liniments for the crippled and injured." [6] There were, however, frequent upsets which caused those on top to fall and take their place at the rope, while others rose. Those conditions are universal and thought to be permanent.

Strikes and labor unrest created constant chaos, which it was

[5] "Looking Backward," p. 9
[6] Ibid. pp 10, 11

felt would, unless a way out was found, finally ruin humanity. Men of the day felt that human history, like all great movements, was cyclical; society rises to the top and then takes the header into chaos. The idea of indefinite progress in a right line was a chimera of the imagination.

Bellamy differs from this point of view. He has his Mr. West of Boston fall asleep under the efforts of a mesmerist on Decoration Day, 1887, and wake up on September 10, 2000—more than 113 years later, aroused by men who discovered him in the underground cell in which he ordinarily slept owing to insomnia, now part of the ruins of an ancient house under a garden. He finds many profound changes, all illustrating a turn for the better.

He finds himself in a "city beautiful," not smoky, squalid, and shabby as the Boston of old, for in this new age there was "no destination of the surplus wealth so popular as the adornment of the city," which all enjoy in equal degree. What is more astonishing, it was a city without politicans, devoid of demagogism or corruption. Human nature had not changed, but conditions of human life, and with them the motives of human action, changed.[7]

There was no such thing as a labor question. Integration and syndication of capital had brought its logical result, the national control of industries. When the people through their rapid progress became ripe for it, they took over the tyrannous monopolies and capital aggregates. This solution came as the result of an industrial process which could not have terminated otherwise. All that society had to do was to recognize and coöperate with that evolution, when its tendency had become unmistakable.

The nation therefore assumed the responsibilities of capital. It was an extension of the functions of government to the economic welfare of all the people. Similarly, labor also was

[7] He says for example, "Nowadays . . . society is so constituted that there is absolutely no way in which an official, however ill-disposed, could possibly make any profit for himself, or any one else by a misuse of his power. Let him be as bad an official as you please, he cannot be a corrupt one. There is no motive to be   The social system no longer offers a premium on dishonesty " p 61

nationally organized, and this proved a true solution of what was regarded as the insoluble labor problem. When the nation became the sole employer all the citizens by virtue of their citizenship became employees to be distributed according to the needs of industry. There was no feeling of compulsion because it was regarded as absolutely natural and reasonable; in fact, there was contempt for the person who should need compulsion. Service was necessary to existence; not to serve would be suicide.

The state established a definite form of industrial service. The active period of service for each individual was twenty-four years, beginning at the close of the course of education at twenty-one and terminating at forty-five. After forty-five and until fifty-five, while discharged from labor, the citizen still remained liable to special calls in case of emergencies causing a sudden great increase in the demand for labor.

One may ask how the workers were divided up among the several hundred diverse trades and avocations. Bellamy's reply was that the industrial army was organized on the principle that a man's natural endowments, mental and physical, determine what he can work at most profitably to the nation and most satisfactorily to himself. Parents and teachers watched from early years for indications of special aptitudes in children, taking utmost pains to cultivate these, for knowledge of and a certain preliminary training for the national industries was part of the educational system.

By equalizing the attractions in the trades the supply of workers for each trade was kept equal to the demand. This was done by making the hours in the different trades differ according to their arduousness. Furthermore, the workers had second and third choices as to occupation, so that, if owing to the progress of invention or changes in demand, the worker was unable to follow his first vocation, he could still find reasonably congenial employment. The common labor group included all recruits, who had to do this work before being admitted to the liberty of the trades. During this period the young men were taught habits of obedience, subordination, and devotion to duty. During this period the young men also decided whether they would be brain workers or hand workers. If they decided to be brain workers they were given every educational opportunity to fit themselves for their art or profession. After these years at common labor they served an apprenticeship which differed in length in different occupations. Finally, they became full-fledged members of their vocation, being however, distributed in three divisions, distinguished by metal badges, according to the proficiency in their apprentice years.

Those who were too deficient in mental or bodily strength to be fairly graded with the main body of workers were in a separate grade, a sort of invalid corps, the members of which were provided with light tasks fitted to their strength. But they had the same income nevertheless, this depending upon the fact that they were men, and not on the amount of health, strength and mental capacity.

There were no wages in the sense of the wages of former days. The allotment of the worker was based on his humanity; all had the same share. It was demanded that all workers give their best, and "all men who do their best, do the same." The man of great endowments who did not do all he might, though he might do more than a man of small endowments who did his best, was deemed a less deserving worker, and died a debtor to his fellows.[8] A man who was able to work and persistently refused to do so, was sentenced to solitary imprisonment on bread and water till he consented.[9] Since industry was no longer self-service, but service of the nation, patriotism and passion for humanity inspired the worker, as they formerly did the soldier.[10] A man's rank depended upon the value of his services to society. There was another incentive of even greater significance, however. The highest of all honors in the nation, higher than the presidency, which called merely for good sense and devotion to duty, was the red ribbon, awarded by the vote of the people to the great achievers of the generation. Only a certain few could wear it at any one time. though every bright young fellow aspired to it.

8 Ibid. p 94
9 Ibid. p. 128.
10 Ibid p. 97.

The head of the nation was the head of the industrial army, called the president. He was selected from among former heads of the ten departments into which the public activities were divided. These heads had been elected from among themselves by the generals of the various guilds, and these had been elected through various stages by all who had served their time in some particular guild, into which the various vocations were divided, and who had been discharged.

There was, of course, international peace, for there was no desire "on the slightest international misunderstanding, to seize upon the bodies of citizens and deliver them over by hundreds of thousands to death and mutilation, wasting their treasures the while like water." [11] This perfect amity also simplified international trade. The business between nations was supervised by an international council and each nation had a bureau of foreign exchange which managed its own trading. A simple system of book accounts served perfectly to regulate their dealings, with balances struck in staples. There was no money, since all nations were on the same basis, nor were there customs duties. Nations supplied one another with goods at the same price they supplied their own citizens. Another international problem, that of emigration and immigration, was handled by having the nation to which a man emigrated pay an allowance to the nation from which he came to compensate for the expense of his maintenance and education.

Bellamy's method of carrying on distribution of commodities was most unique. There were no stores and banks, their functions now being obsolete since the business of production and distribution was no longer in private hands. [12] Since there was no money, he naively states, there was no use for banks. And since the nation was the sole producer of all commodities, there was no need of exchanges between individuals in order to get what they might require. Here everything was procurable

[11] Ibid. p 59.

[12] He states, "When innumerable different and independent persons produced the various things needful to life and comfort, endless exchanges between individuals were requisite in order that they might supply themselves with what they desired. These exchanges constituted trade, and money was essential as their medium." pp. 86–87

from one source, the national storehouses, and nothing could be procured anywhere else.

A credit corresponding to his share of the annual product of the nation was given to every citizen on the public books at the beginning of each year, and a credit card issued to him with which he procured at the storehouses, which were found in every community, whatever he desired. This obviated exchanges between persons, made credit personal, hence nontransferable. Incidentally it solved the problem of poverty, for the nation guaranteed the nurture, education, and comfortable maintenance of every citzen from the cradle to the grave.

There was a central store, a magnificent structure, in each ward. These were, however, merely sample stores, and there were no clerks trying to foist goods on customers. People made choices here and gave their orders. The orders were then phoned in to great central warehouses,[13] and distributed from there by a system of tubes running to all parts of the city. This was all done so quickly that goods arrived at their destination sooner than if shopped for by hand. The price of these goods depended upon the cost of the labor which produced the commodity, the cost of transportation and the scarcity of the goods.[14] This price was then subtracted from the credit accounts of the individual consumers. The type and quantity of goods needed at each warehouse was based on carefully prepared annual consumption statistics.[15]

Since land was publicly owned and business nationally conducted, and money wholly absent, there was no inheriting. There was nothing to prevent it, but also nothing to encourage it. Nothing had monetary value so accumulation of valuable goods and chattels in the hands of individuals was burdensome, for they were not salable and could not be used for personal purposes, and men would have to deplete their credit to hire houses to store these goods in

---

[13] Describing one of these he says, "It is like a gigantic mill, into the hopper of which goods are being constantly poured by the trainload and shipload, to issue at the other end in packages of pounds and ounces, yards and inches, pints and gallons, corresponding to the infinitely complex personal needs of half a million people " p 180.

[14] Ibid p 185.

[15] Ibid. pp. 181–183.

Housekeeping was entirely a community affair. Washing was done at public laundries at excessively low rates. The making and repairing of wearing apparel was done in public shops. The cooking was done in public kitchens, and the food was consumed in great community dining establishments, which were a sort of combination dining house, recreation building, library, and social rendezvous for the ward. Each family in the ward had its own elegantly furnished dining room in this great building. Meals were ordered the day before. The waiters were young fellows of the unclassified grade, who were assignable to all kinds of miscellaneous occupations not requiring special skill, but none are considered menial, for in this age people were willing to render any service and no one attached social prestige to any type of it. Whenever people needed assistance for special emergencies, such as extensive cleaning, or renovation, or family sickness, they called for it from the industrial force and paid the nation for it. A playful idiosyncracy was the fact that in inclement weather all sidewalks were covered so as to prevent the weather from having any effect on the social movements of the people. Bellamy has one of his characters say, "The difference between the age of individualism and that of concert was well characterized by the fact that in the nineteenth century, when it rained, the people of Boston put up three hundred thousand umbrellas, over as many heads, and in the twentieth century they put up one umbrella over all heads." [16]

There were no jails because there was no crime. He says, "In your day fully nineteen-twentieths of the crime, using the word broadly to include all sorts of misdemeanors, resulted from the inequality in the possessions of individuals; want tempted the poor, lust of greater gains, or the desire to preserve former gains tempted the well-to-do. Directly or indirectly the desire for money, which then meant every good thing was the motive of all this crime, the taproot of a vast poison growth, which the machinery of law courts and police could barely prevent from choking your civilization outright." [17] When the state took

16 Ibid. p. 152.
17 Ibid pp 200–201.

over all wealth, this ceased. As for the comparatively small class of violent crimes against persons, unconnected with any idea of gains, they were almost wholly the result of atavism, as he calls it, the work of the feebleminded or other degenerate types, and these were cared for in hospitals. The only crimes of the new day were those due to the outcropping of ancestral traits. Nor were there any laws or legislation, since heretofore ninety-nine per cent. of the laws were concerned with definition and protection of private property and the relations of buyers and sellers. Nor were there any lawyers, for there was no motive to color the truth, only to find it.

There was higher education on a large scale for everybody; not on a small scale for a select few. Nor did this new education unfit people for manual work, as had been the case with the old. The object of the education was to raise the general level. They felt that if they could not afford to educate everybody they would choose the coarsest and dullest by nature rather than the brightest, for these latter cannot dispense with aids to culture, while the naturally refined and intellectual can. Physical education was also included in this system. The object of this diverse education was to make it possible for each citizen to enjoy himself, to prevent communities from having to suffer the presence of coarse, boorish citizens among them, and finally to provide educated and refined parents for the coming generations.

Women were on an equal status with the men.[18] Women as well as men were members of the industrial army, and left it only when maternal duties claimed them. The result was that most women at one time or another of their lives, served industrially some five or ten or fifteen years while those who had no children filled out the full term. They had occupations to which they could best adapt themselves. The hours of women's work were considerably shorter than those of men, and the most careful provision was made for rest when needed. All the girls and women were ambitious for careers in addition to their maternal duties, which caused merely a temporary withdrawal.

[18] Ibid. p 256.

The organization of the female industrial army was the same as that of the men. The woman general-in-chief sat in the cabinet of the president. The women also received credit cards, just as the men, for "the maintenance of all our people is the same." Wives were not dependent on their husbands nor children on their parents.

Since women were economically independent, there were no marriages except love marriages.[19] Wealth and rank no longer diverted attention from personal qualities. Therefore, the gifts of person, mind, and disposition, beauty, wit, eloquence, kindness, generosity, geniality, and courage, were sure of transmission to posterity. The attributes that human nature admired were preserved, those that repelled it were left behind.

It was also an age of mechanical perfection. Music was centrally produced and enjoyed by any one by telephone connection in his own house for a small fee, thus making its enjoyment attainable by everybody instead of by the few as formerly. Sermons were also heard by telephone. Electricity was used everywhere.

It was a time of progress in every phase of life. The rise of the race to a new plane of existence with an illimitable vista of felicity, affected all its faculties with a stimulus, to which the mediæval renaissance could be but faintly compared. There ensued an era of mechanical invention, scientific discovery, art, musical and literary productiveness. Peace, amity, sufficiency and leisure had brought a new Golden Age. Men were no longer incurring the great wastes and making the ghastly blunders of the old age.

We have reserved comment or analysis because the naïveté, the shortsightedness, the misapplication, the very indiscriminating generalizations regarding the old order are obvious to the reader. Nor have we at any point called attention to certain of Bellamy's commendable anticipations of new institutions, and many changes which are already in effect some thirty years later, nor have we indicated the validity and possibility of most of his inventions. The reader has noticed these. We have merely attempted to portray in general outline this state,

[19] Ibid p. 267.

the time and location of which is just ahead, even though it was only a dream.

2. HERTZKA'S "FREELAND"

Dr. Theodor Hertzka, the author of "Freeland—A Social Anticipation," was a Viennese economist of some note, being a representative of those vigorous economists of the last decade of the nineteenth century known as the Manchester School as distinguished from the Historical School. His eminence as a writer and publicist rest partly upon the various honors he received, his output as an editor, and the books he published. In 1872 he became economic editor of the *Neue Freie Presse,* and in 1874 he with others founded the "Society of Austrian National Economists." In 1880 he published "Die Gesetze der Handels-und Sozial-politik," and in 1886 "Die Gesetze der Sozial-entwicklung." At various times he published articles which made him an authority upon currency questions. In 1889 he founded, and edited until his death, the weekly *Zeitschrift fur Staats—und Volkswirtschaft.* In 1890 he published "Frieland: ein soziales Zukunftsbild."

The publication of this book immediately caused a stir in economic and sociological circles on the Continent greater in significance than that of Bellamy's "Looking Backward" in America. By 1891, due to the immense demand, the book had been translated into many languages, and done into English by Arthur Ransom, to which we will make reference Of even greater significance, however, is the fact that the publication of the work immediately called forth in Austria and Germany a determination to put the book into practice. Nearly one thousand local societies made up of all classes, were organized in the larger towns and cities to provide the means and start the suggested colony. A central committee was organized, a suitable tract of land in British East Africa between Mt. Kenia and the coast was placed at the disposal of the societies, and in 1893 a start was actually made. Finally, however, the difficulties were found to be too great, and the plan failed.

In "Freeland" we have an economist's attempt to counteract the deficiencies of the present economic and social order, and in it we will find rather original and advanced ideas on production, marketing, banking, public service, consumption, and welfare, joined with a unique form of communism based on self-interest. In the preface Hertzka states that with the splendid advances in art and science and the subjection of the unlimited forces of nature, "a moderate amount of labor ought to produce inexhaustible abundance for every one born of woman" —"and yet all these glorious achievements have not been able to mitigate one human woe." In fact, "increasing facility in the production of wealth brings ruin and misery in its train." It resolves itself into the question "why do we not become richer in proportion to our increasing capacity of producing wealth?" He lays the difficulty primarily to what he calls "over-production" [20]

With the readjustment of production perfectly possible he feels that no positive obstacle stands in the way of the establishment of the free social order. He stresses repeatedly the idea that this is not fiction, but within easy reach; in fact, that the evolutionary tendencies are pointing in that direction. In the body of the book he discusses its fundamentals, and these rest on solid fact. It differs from other social anticipations, past and present, he says, in that it introduces "no unknown and mysterious human powers and characteristics; but throughout keeps to the firm ground of soberest reality. The scene of the occurrences (equatorial Africa) described by me is no imaginary fairy land, but a part of our planet well known to modern geography, which I describe exactly as its discoverers and explorers have done. The men who appear in my narrative are endowed with no supernatural properties and virtues, but are spirit of our spirit, flesh of our flesh; and the motive prompting their economic activity is neither public spirit nor

[20] He says, e. g., "We do not produce that wealth which our present capacity makes it possible for us to produce, but only so much as we have use for; and this use depends, not upon our capacity of products, but upon our capacity of consuming." p xviii Also, "I perceived that capitalism stops the growth of wealth, not as Marx has it, by stimulating production for the market; but by preventing the consumption of the surplus produce, and that interest, though not unjust, will nevertheless in a condition of economic justice become superfluous and objectless." "Freeland: a Social Anticipation," p xxi.

universal philanthropy, but an ordinary and commonplace self-interest. Everything in my "Freeland" is severely real, only one fiction underlies the whole narrative, namely, that a sufficient number of men possessing a modicum of capacity and strength have actually been found ready to take the step that shall deliver them from the bondage of the exploiting system of economics and conduct them into the enjoyment of a system of social equality and freedom. Let this one assumption be but realized—and that it will be, sooner or later, I have no doubt, though perhaps not exactly as I have represented—then will "Freeland" have become a reality and the deliverance of mankind will have been accomplished. For the age of bondage is past; that control over the forces of nature, which the founder of modern natural science, in his "Nova Atlantis," predicted as the end of human misery, has now been actually acquired. We are prevented from enjoying the fruits of this acquisition, from making full use of the discoveries and inventions of the great intellects of the race, by nothing but the phlegmatic faculty of persistence in old habits which still keeps the laws and institutions in force when the conditions that gave rise to them have long since disappeared." Therefore, Hertzka offers, in narrative form, a picture of actual social life as he conceives it possible.

The book opens in a unique but nevertheless realistic fashion. The International Free Society—as its name implies, an international organization for the furtherance of economic and social reforms—has notices posted throughout Europe and America to the effect that a great Congress is to be held at The Hague for the purpose of making plans for the actual attempt at founding this more rational and natural state. Delegates assemble from all parts of the world and it is but a matter of a few days before arrangements are completed for the undertaking. A colony is to be started in Masailand, Central Africa, between Kilmanjaro and Kenia. A pioneer company is organized at The Hague and sails for Mombosa, where the whole expedition of men, pack and riding animals, provisions and ammunition is assembled. It begins its trip into the interior and after a journey of about eight weeks finally arrives

at its destination.   Hertzka's description of this trip is vivid
and realistic.   It reads like Stanley's account of his expeditions, showing a remarkable knowledge of everything relating
to the topography, population, and fauna and flora of the country.

The pioneers founded their first colony in a large amphi-
theater-shaped valley, which they christened "Eden Vale."   As
population increments were added, they sent out smaller expeditions from this as the base into the surrounding country.
It was found to be rich in all kinds of raw materials including various woods and metals, and fish and game animals.
These various resources were soon brought under control and
Eden was established as a thriving community.   But how was
this new social and economic order systematized and harmon-
ized?

It was based entirely upon five fundamental laws; everything else in his scheme was merely the natural consequence of
a more detailed expression of these points.   These laws are:

1. "Every inhabitant of Freeland, has an equal and inalienable
   claim upon the whole of the land, and upon the means of
   production accumulated by the community."
2. "Women, children, old men, and men incapable of work, have
   a right to a competent maintenance, fairly proportionate
   to the level of the average wealth of the community."
3. "No one can be hindered from the active exercise of his own
   free individual will, so long as he does not infringe upon
   the rights of others."
4. "Public affairs are to be administered as shall be determined
   by all the adult (above 20 years of age) inhabitants of Freeland, without distinction of sex, who shall all possess equal
   active and passive right of vote and of election in all matters
   that affect the commonwealth."
5. "Both the legislative and executive authority shall be divided
   into departments, and in such a manner that the whole of
   the electors shall choose special representatives for the
   principal public departments, who shall give their decisions
   apart and watch over the action of the administrative boards
   of the respective departments." [21]

[21] Ibid. p. 137.

Unlike that of most Utopias, Hertzka's utopianism rests upon self-interest. The whole purpose of Freeland was to provide a means of removing all those hindrances that stand in the way of the free realization of the individual will guided by a wise self-interest.[22] Every attempt in the domain of economics to substitute public spirit, or any other ethical motive, for self-interest must immediately as well as in ultimate issue, prove an ignominious fiasco.[23] Therefore the object of the community is to concern itself with the affairs of the individual as little as possible in the way of hindering or commanding, but on the other hand, as much as possible in the way of guiding and instructing.[24] Combined with the principle of self-interest he would also have economic justice and freedom. This will differ in his perfect state from that in others in that he aims, not at establishing equality of poverty, which the others did, but equality of wealth. He says, "The equality of poverty would have produced stagnation in civilization. Art and science, the two vehicles of progress, assume abundance and leisure; they cannot exist, much less can they develop, if there are no persons who possess more than is sufficient to satisfy their merely animal wants.[25] This economic equality of rights has only recently been possible, for it could not be realized in earlier epochs of civilization because then human labor was not sufficiently productive to supply wealth to all, and equality therefore meant poverty for all. The one essential in this connection, however, is that every one enjoys the product of his own industry.[26]

Instead of abandoning private property he would have its ownership more widespread, for it is the best incitement to labor, and cannot be replaced by any substitute. The institutions of economic justice will cause private property to be a vastly different factor than it was under the exploiting system of industry. Thus with self-interest given full play, and every man securing the full profits of his endeavor, productivity

22 Ibid. p 104.
23 Ibid. p. 368.
24 Ibid p. 106.
25 Ibid. p 353.
26 Ibid. p. 355.

would be greatest and most profitable.[27] This would result in a real communism, for thus there would be a true solidarity of all economic interests.

Economic justice in this social epoch was best fostered by coöperative associations, organized by whole industries, indeed, along the lines of joint stock companies, composed of people interested in a particular kind of work.[28] Admission was free to every one. Unlimited capital was supplied by the Free Society without interest on condition that it be reimbursed out of the proceeds of production within a certain period of time, determined by the nature of the proposed investment. Every member's contribution of work was measured by the number of hours he worked. The highest authority of the association was the general meeting, in which every member possessed an equal active vote. The management was in the hands of a directorate of certain size and term of office, elected at and liable to recall by the general meeting. The net profits of the association were to be calculated at the end of the year of business, and after deducting the repayment of the capital and the taxes paid to the Freeland commonwealth, divided. Every member had a claim upon that fund of the net profits of the association proportionate to the amount of work he contributed. Every worker had freedom of movement and perfect freedom of contract. All salaried people were paid in "hour-equivalents" of mechanical work. Here there were no exploiters and the capital belonged to everybody or nobody, as you please. Profit and loss were equally distributed. Every one in the association was working for the same end because all received the same advantages in the end, depending of course upon themselves, their initiative and desires. Furthermore, the schedule of remuneration was so arranged that no family would receive less than was necessary for a very comfortable living, and most of them were able to establish a surplus, the goal to be sought for. The insurance department of the bank cared for other

[27] Hertzka admits that men would require a considerable degree of development along the lines of economic justice, but he does not doubt that it could be introduced anywhere if nations educated their people up to it.

[28] Individual producers were not forbidden, however.

chance contingencies.   Unlimited publicity characterized **every** phase of the system.   The fundamental law was, "No business secrets whatever."

As in Bellamy there were different associations which made it their duty to satisfy certain domestic needs.   For instance, one association had charge of the cleaning of a certain district including streets, lawns and houses.   Another provided meals, served in the private homes; still another furnished horses and carriages and a spring-driven horseless carriage.

Unemployment was avoided by having regular and automatic migration of labor from one industry to another, to correct disturbances in the relations between supply and demand due to natural causes.   Over-production, the bane of workers in an exploitive system, was non-operative here, because every product had to find a purchaser.[29]

Buying and selling of all conceivable products and articles of merchandise was carried on in large halls and warehouses, which were under the management of the community.   The public magazines offered such enormous advantages that everybody bought and sold there, though doing so elsewhere was optional.   "No fee was charged for storing or manipulation, as it was quite immaterial, in a country where every one consumed in proportion to his production, whether the fees were levied upon the consumers as such, or upon the same persons in their character as producers in the form of a minimal tax. What was saved by the simplification of the accounts remained as a pure gain."[30]

Government was also carried on in a unique manner. The governing body was a general committee composed of twelve men, each of whom was chief of one of the twelve branches into which the public administration of Freeland was divided.[31]   Each of these twelve executives was in turn se-

29 Ibid. p. 267.
30 Ibid. p 107.
31 The twelve departments were: 1. The Presidency or general supervision, 2 Maintenance, 3. Education, 4. Art and Science; 5 Statistics; 6 Roads and Means of Communication, 7 Postal and Telegraph Service; 8. Foreign Affairs, 9 Warehouses, 10 Central Bank, 11. Public Undertakings, 12 Sanitation and Administration of Justice.

lected by twelve representative bodies, the members of which were elected by all electors over twenty years of age, the object being to choose men especially fitted for their particular duties, whether it were the committee on education, foreign affairs, statistics, or sanitation. It may be remarked, that electors were of both sexes without discrimination. It is also noteworthy that the departments of justice, police, military and finance, which in other countries swallow up nine-tenths of the total budget, cost nothing in Freeland, simply because there was no need of such departments. The various public expenditures were met by deductions made through the bank from each individual's credit account. These contributions were exactly in proportion to his net income; "and as in Freeland there was no source of income except labor, and the income from this was exactly known, there was not the slightest difficulty in apportioning the tax." [32]

Education was free and universal. It was graded, advancing by degrees as in Plato's scheme, but differed in that it was open to all. Equal emphasis was placed on the development of mind and body. Until the age of sixteen boys and girls received the same training, although physical training was emphasized with the boys and musical training with the girls. At sixteen the girls either received training at home, or served as pupil-daughters under some highly cultured and intellectually gifted woman, or entered pedagogic training institutions where they received tutoring as teachers or nurses. The boys, from sixteen to twenty-two received military training which was universal, and at the same time attended industrial or commercial technical schools. The different sciences were nurtured and practically applied in Freeland's wide and varied domain. Music and art were cultivated and produced, great opera houses and conservatories being found all over the land. Everything was done to make Freeland a land of highly educated and superbly cultivated people.

Hertzka, as we have already noted, advanced the idea of the perfect equality of the sexes. This he had rest upon the mutual admiration which he felt the sexes had for each other. But,

32 Ibid. p. 109.

while he would admit women into various occupations, he felt of them all the only ones that were really appropriate for them were education of children and care of the sick and infirm. The most desirable state for women was matrimony. As in Bellamy, since women were supported by the state, marriages were pure and of love, and not "prostitution for maintenance." [33]

Vices and their dangerous results to the community were not punished; the community was otherwise protected. Besides, reformation was the best and effectual means of protection. To guard against widespread deterioration restrictions were placed on the consumption of alcoholic drinks. Casual criminals were considered as mentally and morally diseased persons, and were dealt with by both the Board of Medical Men and the Justices of the Peace.

We have, in brief compass, given some of the fundamental principles and institutions of Hertzka's anticipation. It rests, we see, upon the progress up to his time along scientific, technical, and economic lines, and is just an evolution from the present; an evolution, however, proceeding with the corresponding development of a new and higher morality, and the adaptation of economic institutions to the basic principles of social justice. This Hertzka felt would come when thoughtlessness and inaction ceased and when some great universal rationalizing force would break down the entrenched habits, selfishness, and conventionalities of the antiquated present order.

3.   WELLS' "MODERN UTOPIA"

This work is the product of a great imaginative writer as well as a sociologist and economist of note. But it is not so much a new creation of the imagination, forever removed from things prosaic, as an imaginative use of existing materials. Continuity with the present is preserved, and progressive minds can grasp this better state without any sense of strangeness or discrepancy.

This Utopia also like the other recent anticipations just dis-

[33] Ibid. pp. 139–140

cussed differs from all previous ones, in that a world Utopia
is pictured; not one confined to a small isolated portion of the
earth, or one on some strange planet. It is in touch with
reality, therefore, in that various climates, races and types of
culture can be presented. It is similar to Hertzka in that it
accepts humanity as it is at present, with both its capacities for
and its obstacles to improvement. Furthermore, Wells in it
considers Nature as an uncontrolled force incapable of subordination.[34]   But he does show his community of spirit with the
Utopians of old in the craving he feels for emancipation from
traditions, habits, legal bonds, property and especially in his
regard for human freedom, in his undying interest in the human power of self-escape, the mind to resist the domination of
the past, and the will to evade, initiate, endeavor, and overcome.[35]   Hence it is a masterful grappling with the present
Herculean problem of human advance.

He establishes his Utopia upon a very definite conception of
the necessity of freedom.   This he feels was something slighted
by earlier Utopians.   His freedom consists of that free play of
one's individuality which is "the subjective triumph of existence, as survival in creative work and offspring is its objective triumph,"[36] but which is not absolute; rather that chip-
ping away only of the spendthrift and socially harmful liberties
by the state, and the maintenance of all others, giving us the
maximum latitude of self-expression.   This greater liberty is
not to be won by the paring down of individualities to some common pattern, but by the broadening of public charity and the
general amelioration of mind and manners; it is to be a liberty
which comes of culture and consideration and not at the
expense of the strong.   In this recognition of individuality
we have another departure from the older Utopians, who accepted uniformity and stressed communism.   Since this liberty

[34] "We are to shape our state in a world of uncertain seasons, sudden
catastrophes, antagonistic diseases, and inimical beasts and vermin, out
of men and women with like passions, like uncertainties of mood and desire to our own." "Modern Utopia," pp. 7, 8.
[35] Ibid. p. 9.
[36] Ibid. p. 32.
[37] Ibid. p. 34.

is such a variable and relative matter, there can be no absolute
rights and wrongs, but merely qualitative, temporary adjustments.   He would also effect a compromise between freedom
of movement and the desire for privacy, this being not so much
for the sake of isolation, as for that congenial companionship
which may offer its greatest attractions apart from the crowd.
This privacy extends to private apartments and homes.   Travel
is encouraged as a means of broadening and making flexible all
individuals, and Wells permits his imagination to suggest ingenious forms of trains, ships and air service to make the constant migrations possible.   Since even in Utopia there will be
regions of mining and smelting with smoke and furnaces and
unsightliness,   the   transportation   facilities   will   enable
families to live far removed from these conditions.   Bacon's
House of Salomon will be a thing realized; men will be constantly experimenting and collecting knowledge to make man's
conquest over distance and unsightliness complete.

Of equal importance with the matter of freedom is that of
sustenance and working.   A necessary adjunct for both is
money, as Wells unlike most Utopians feels that money is both
a good and necessary thing in civilized life if it is used correctly.   "It is the water of the body social, it distributes and
receives, and renders growth and assimilation, and movement
and recovery possible.   It is the reconciliation of human inter-
dependence with liberty.   What other device will give a man
so great a freedom with so strong an inducement to effort?" [38]
Labor credits or free demand of commodities from a central
store offer far more scope for that native immoral drift in men
to exert itself than does money.   But gold is not used by Wells
as the standard of value; since its value is constantly changing
due to a number of factors, thereby causing a speculative element to enter into all types of business relations.   Instead he
would have salable productive energy as the standard.   This
energy is to be calculated upon the estimated total of energy,
periodically available in each locality and booked and spoken
of in physical units.   In a world having a very fluid popula-

[38] Ibid p 73.

tion as his, the price of the energy notes of these various local-
ities will constantly tend to be uniform, because employment
will constantly shift into the areas where energy is cheap.

All natural sources of power, such as coal, water power, and
the like, and all strictly natural products, are inalienably vested
in local authorities. They will utilize all these to generate
electrical energy, used universally, and its cost reckoned in
terms of units of physical energy.

In the modern Utopia there will be neither individualism
nor socialism, for both are absurdities; the way of sanity lies
somewhere between the two.[39] The World State presents itself as the sole landowner of the earth, with the local governments holding it, as it were, feudally as landlords. The State,
or these subordinates, hold all sources of food and power energy
and develop these through tenants, farmers and agents, and
render the energy available for the work of life. It or they
keep order, provide cheap and efficient administration of justice, maintain roads and cheap and rapid locomotion, pay for
and secure healthy births and a healthy and vigorous new generation, safeguard the public health, subsidize research, carry
on education, and so on.

In the matter of property he also takes an unutopian stand.
Property is necessary to freedom; in fact, the extent of a man's
property is very largely the measure of his freedom. Legitimate property is to consist of all the values that a man's toil or
skill or foresight and courage have brought into being. But
the State will limit the right of a man's property acquisition
lest his freedom curtail the freedom of others. A man's property will consist of all those things that are extensions and expressions of his personality,—clothes, jewels, tools, books, etc.;
all things he has bought with his money; perhaps also a house
with privacy that one occupies and uses; a man's household
furniture; and sums to insure special advantages of education
and care for the immature children of himself and others.
These things are also transmissible to the next generation.
He may also hold shares in business adventures, and also in

[39] Ibid. p. 87

various sorts of contracts, concessions, land leases, and factories. But these revert to the state at his death. He would
also have a periodic revision of endowments.

Unlike all but the most recent Utopias, Wells depends very
largely upon machinery to free men from the cramping thraldom of toil. This eventually will lift the burden from the
laboring classes, who then will be free from the life of servitude
and inferiority. Mechanical perfection eases, improves and
simplifies the life of the Utopian in every respect. Nor will
the machinery be unsightly and garish, it is to be artistic and
fitting in form as well as ingeniously efficient.

Wells has a chapter on "Failure in a Modern Utopia" in
which he also exhibits a radical departure from those that
have gone before him. The old Utopias were peopled with
citizens who were well-looking and upright and mentally and
morally in tune. But Wells is peopling his Utopia from the
actual population of the world, so among other things, he is
confronted with the task of handling the congenital invalids,
the idiots, the drunkards and men of vicious mind, the unteachable, spiritless, unimaginative and clod-like. These people will have to be kept under supervision and the bureaus
engaged in eliminating them; conversely, the people of exceptional quality must be ascendant; for Nature's process of having the strong murder the weak in cold blood will be substituted
the ways and means of modern men. In place of miserable
houses, uncomfortable clothes, and bad and insufficient food the
utopian state will force uncomfortable and unhealthful houses
to be condemned and demolished; for indecently or raggedly or
unhealthfully dressed and hungry and poorly fed citizens, the
state will find work, lend them money to conduct enterprises if
they have none, and if necessary serve as reserve employer of
labor. This public work, as a stimulus to individual effort,
would be onerous, but not cruel or incapacitating.

For the criminally inclined first offenders and for all offenders under twenty-five cautionary and remedial treatment would
be attempted in disciplinary schools in remote regions away
from cities. Capital punishment would not be, except that
in Utopia no doubt all deformed and monstrous and evilly

diseased infants would be slain.[40] Wells would have no jails either, for "no men are quite wise enough, good enough and cheap enough to staff jails as a jail ought to be staffed." [41] Islands would doubtless be used for isolation—one sex only on an island, to protect the state from the risk of progeny, and armed guards on duty to prevent boat building or the landing of boats. With the exception of the insane, who would have care and treatment, other misfits, such as drunkards, drug users and various criminals would carry on manufacturing and trade on their islands living as they pleased, for "you must seclude, but why should you torment?" [42]

There will be no need to fear unemployment for several reasons. In the first place, all Utopians will be reasonably well educated along utopian lines and there will be no illiterates unless they are unteachable imbeciles, no rule-of-thumb toilers incapable of learning the new, but only versatile beings. Second, there will be labor exchanges all over the world reporting the fluctuating pressure of economic demand and transferring workers from regions of excess to those of scarcity. If the excess is universal, the World State will either reduce the working day and so absorb it, or set in motion permanent special works of its own, paying a minimum wage, and allowing the works to progress as slowly or as rapidly as the ebb and flow of labor dictate. Between the two every citizen will be assured a sufficiency.

Another question of utmost significance in connection with progress is, "How shall we improve the quality of the people?" Wells does not depend on competitive selection entirely; that is too costly. He would prevent the birth of those who would in the unrestricted interplay of natural forces be born to suffer and fail.[43] He would not have state breeding as Plato advocated, for his state is one where individuality is the significant fact of life, and the supreme and significant expression of individuality lies in the selection of a partner for procreation. In-

40 Ibid. p. 143.
41 Ibid. p 144.
42 Ibid. p 147.
43 "The ideal of a scientific civilization is to prevent . . . weaklings being born." p. 181.

stead the state would enforce a few simple general conditions. The state should demand a certain minimum of efficiency of its parents, demonstrated by holding a position of independence and solvency in the world; they must be above a certain age, have a certain minimum of physical development, be free from any transmissible disease and any criminal act unless the offense has been expiated.[44] If individuals offend, the state will take very definite and drastic measures to prevent any repetition The children that are born, where public opinion welcomes the well-born child, will be better taken care of, and the death of a child will be almost unknown.   The mothers of these children, regardless of the wage of their husbands, will have a legitimate claim to a living, and the state will pay them wages as mothers, and an increasing wage if their children are above the minimum qualifications, physical or mental.   This mother wage would make unnecessary the industrial employment of married women or children and it would establish sound childbearing and rearing as a service to the whole community.

In Utopia furthermore it is necessary in order to secure good births and good home conditions that the union of the sexes should not be free nor promiscuous, nor practically universal throughout the adult population   Therefore there are very definite marriage laws.   The requirements mentioned above with regard to health, freedom from transmissible taints, and ability to secure an income above the minimum are emphasized.   In addition, a minimum age limit is set, about twenty-one for women and twenty-six or seven for men.   Wells also believes in each party having every item of information of significance concerning the other, and also in order to prevent hasty marriages, that plenty of time be given for contemplation before the state add its sanction   Since the purpose of marriage is primarily race continuance, if a marriage prove childless at the end of three or four or five years, it would seem reasonable to permit it to lapse.   But those unions that do result in children must endure, due to the general necessity for a home and for individual attention in their proper nurture.

[44] Ibid p 184.

Children must be brought up in an environment of sympathetic and kindred individualities, for no wholesale, character-ignoring method of dealing with them has ever succeeded.

The chapter on "Utopian Impressions" brings us a mass of heterogeneous conceptions. There are the residential quadrangles with all their mechanical perfections, there are the factories with their working rules drawn up by a conference of the Common Council of Wages Workers with the employers, a discussion of the vigor of the Utopian population and the absence of the fat, bald, bent or gray, the loose sensible clothing, the absence of animals because of their filth and their germ-carrying proclivities, the railway trains with their libraries, armchairs, couches, newsrooms, bedrooms, bathrooms, etc., going two hundred miles an hour, the scholar's conception of art, architecture, and learning in a utopian city. It all seems real and yet unique.

His discussion of government introduces the "samurai." [45] He states that he has perceived more and more clearly the weaknesses of electoral methods. So he has a class of voluntary nobility, the "samurai," identical with Plato's guardians.[46] This class of diverse beings is made up of reasonably healthy, diseaseless, efficient, intelligent adults, male and female, over twenty-five, volunteers in fact, who have lived according to the Common Rule, a rule which "aims to exclude the dull and base altogether, to discipline the impulses and emotions, to develop a moral habit and sustain a man in periods of stress, fatigue, and temptation, to produce the maximum coöperation of all men of good intent, and, in fact, keep all samurai in a state of moral and bodily health and efficiency." [47] They have passed through the Utopian educational system with its eliminating examinations which select those having steadiness of purpose and self-control and submission. They are forbidden to do certain things: they are forbidden to carry on such commercial transactions as tend to bring out unsocial human qual-

[45] He takes the name from the famous intellectual and ethical élite of old Japan
[46] Ibid. p. 259.
[47] Ibid. p 279–280.

ities; they are forbidden those activities which cause the mind to become foolishly dependent on applause, over-skillful in producing tawdry and momentary illusion of excellence; they are forbidden to play games or to watch them being played; they are also forbidden alcohol, drugs, smoking, servants, dramatic religion, etc. There are also a number of things they must do which discipline them, keep them clean mentally and physically, and broaden them. Women samurai who are married must bear children if they are to remain married as well as in the order. All samurai, male and female, must annually, for seven consecutive days, go into some wild and solitary place and have no intercourse with mankind, go without books, weapons, pen, and paper, or money, chiefly for the purpose of drawing their minds from the insistent details of life, its arguments and affections, and then in the great open of waste places think of one's self and the great external things of space and eternity, and what one means by God.

But when and how are the samurai used? Practically all political power is vested in them. Not only are they the only administrators, lawyers, practicing doctors, and public officials of almost all kinds, but they are the only voters. All the head teachers and disciplinary heads of the colleges, the judges, employers of labor beyond a certain limit, and all executive committees, and so forth, that play a large part in public affairs, are drawn by lot from them. A world ruled by self-disciplined, socially-minded and publically recognized experts!

In the discussion of "Race" Wells deplores the classificatory predisposition among men, in that it brings about a bias for false and excessive contrast, a tendency toward cliques, and an unwarranted exaltation of self. Among these objectionable aggregation ideas are those of nationality, self-centered religion, imperialism and race. He is chiefly concerned with those of race, which he considers utterly inane. So-called superior races, he holds, are merely the present politically ascendant peoples, above marrying with the non-ascendant peoples, who are thought unfit for any decisive voice in human affairs. This, he feels, to be all nonsense, because there are probably no pure races in the world. All we do is to take some quite arbitrary ideal as the type, and think only of that.[48] Do different physical and psychical characteristics necessarily render different races incapable of association upon terms of equality in a World State? Are not differences as wide as those indicated really found among extreme types of the same race? Admitting that anthropology has not spoken its last word, he feels, nevertheless, that there are no fundamental incompatibilities, and that there is ground for admitting all races into world fellowship. The viciousness of the half-breed is due to the fact that in an enormous number of cases he is illegitimate and disbarred from the normal education and refinement of either parent race. No all-around inferior race has ever been found. Wells would have a world-wide synthesis of all cultures and politics and races into one World State as the desirable end upon which all civilizing efforts converge. The existing collection of alternatives give no promise of permanent progress among men.

In the last chapter Wells comes back to the jaded, raw, wreck-strewn, discontented world of to-day, and in clever word pictures contrasts that which is with that which is within reach if men will but strive for it. He sees all about him the stuff that Utopia is made of, only it is in the rough and unrefined. To one who is in touch with advanced social and political and economic thought, Wells' ideas are entirely familiar, for they are based on it. He merely pictures a state in which everything the best thinkers are contemplating is in operation; in fact, in many cases, he describes as working in greater perfection that superior institution or doctrine already working imperfectly among us. The chief difference between our world and Utopia is that we are a bit undeveloped and out of order. But that is no cause for pessimism. Change is constantly going on. The sordidness and weakness of to-day is always imperceptibly but surely replaced by something else, and the future is recast in the spirit of what are now obscure and impalpable beginnings. The chief obstacle to this movement's taking a forward direction as it should are those who lack

48 Ibid. p. 331.

imagination and will, who have spiritual anemia, dull respectability, gross sentimentality, pettiness of heart, which prevents them from raising their eyes above the interests of the moment in which they are entangled.

As the result of our study of these recent characteristic anticipations we conclude definitely by way of summary that their writers were grappling with great present day problems, which were the result of contemporary advance along varied lines, intellectual, social, political and economic. Their solutions, while somewhat imaginative, are based in most cases upon proved potentialities, and depend upon normal evolutionary advance for attainment. We feel that if they are dreams, their dreamers at any rate were men with their feet firmly on the ground.

PART TWO

SOCIAL UTOPIAS: AN ANALYSIS AND CRITIQUE

—

CHAPTER VII

THE UTOPIANS AND THEIR UTOPIAS

The people of every age fall into three classes when we consider them from the point of view of their social outlook, and each type has its distinctive philosophy regarding race welfare. The relative predominance of one or the other of these groups is dependent upon a variety of social forces and conditions, and the ascendancy of one or the other causes a society to be static or dynamic, conservative or progressive in character. There three groups differ in placing emphasis on things past, things present or things to come.

The first of these groups is made up of those who look back and sigh for that which has been. They are the type who feel a certain kind of disquietude if they are often obliged to refurnish their minds and then, are seized by a frantic desire to get back to the old, because only then can they recover themselves and experience that at-homeness which gives inward peace. The present is permeated with evil, and with Tully they cry out "O tempora! O mores!" The future is uncertain and fraught with danger to society; the tried and proved past alone offers safe ways and means. The past is the ideal. It is this group who speak of "the good old days" and who constantly fear change lest it present situations with which they have had no previous experience. Furthermore, when they feel dissatisfied with the present, having become aware of its shortcomings, they say that only by reverting to the life of the past over which time has now cast its pale but attractive colors, can society redeem itself. Thus they register a protest which under certain conditions may contribute to social betterment, but the solution which they offer is reactionary and ineffective to a considerable extent, since they fail to recognize that there are forces over which society has no control which make for incessant change, and that the older an institution, practice, or dogma the more hopelessly out of adjustment it may be presumed to be.[1]

The second group consists of the army of world-as-it-is worshipers, largely unconsciously so, who constantly admire and defend institutions and practices as they exist. Unlike the first group they have a wholesome contempt for things past. Ancient codes, customs, proprieties, even institutions, are relics of bygone periods and are stumbling blocks to the activities of the present. The thoughts, the institutions, the activities of the present are ideal, the *summum bonum,* and in excellence are the highest and most complete. The past—ah, let it be; the future—we will wait for it; but in the meantime let us rejoice in the present!

The third group is composed of those who, looking ahead, hope for a more perfect society in the future. The representatives of this class have been in every age the prophets of a new and better but untried social order. Most minds are merely part of the interwoven spiritual fabric of their time and conditions; they are wrapped in a dense mesh of interests, customs, traditions and preconceived views and prejudices which bind them hard to the cheapest commonplace; their ideas are incorporated beyond recall into the mental whole which constitutes their society; they cannot escape from these bonds because they know not that they are bound. But ever and anon there have been the geniuses, the seers, the announcers of new ideas, the perceivers of new verities, intensely eager theorists,—the men ahead of their time,—independent spirits, magnificent pioneers, who, having conceived the higher possibilities of human happiness proposed to eradicate the social and moral shortcomings of the present, broke with their age, ignored the traditions, the theological and political prejudices, swept aside the heritages that thwarted and enthralled, untangled themselves from the humdrum of "that which is," and reached up and out of their time; proclaiming something above the comprehension of the mass, and creating anew. They are the objectors, the dissenters, the insurgents, the iconoclasts; they are always the men of the social opposition, the small but fiery and disturbing

[1] Ross, E. A., "Social Psychology," N. Y., 1908, pp. 203–204

radical minority who refuse to perish in the confusions of their time or to maintain a state of passivity. Imagination, foresight, vision, fantasy—be it what it may—gives them a picture of that which might be. This they prophetically proclaim to their generation.

Among these were men, who during the last thirty centuries, supported only by their own individual powers, challenged the control of the old world, arraigned the historical culture of a thousand years, called to account all creeds and convictions, and constructed out of the materials of their marvelously fertile minds and sympathetic natures those new and better worlds, the social utopias,—the most misunderstood of all suggested social structures. The hopes for the future of these Utopians have expressed themselves as a Kingdom of God, an Isle of the Blessed, an Utopia, a Great State, or some other social anticipation. They were all liberals, the champions of a better future, men who were not afraid of social change, above all, men of wonderful devotion. While few, they are of tremendous social significance; but this fact is not appreciated by the majority.

A somewhat more elaborate elucidation of the characteristics of this much neglected class of writers is essential. First of all *they were filled with that divine discontent which leads to larger things;* that spirit which is the inspiration of thinking men, which gives urge to the inventor, which gives boldness to the hater of injustice, which suggests to many a truer order. All mankind, at any rate the majority of mankind, desire to be moral and orderly; the great institutions of morality and the State are proof of these facts. But the difficulty with these institutions is that they crystallize and tend to become stationary or decadent and corrupt, burdened with various unsocial or anti-social elements. They do not change punctually with the needs of humanity, which are in constant flux. The Utopians are of that energetic minority which is in rebellion against these crystallized and perverted institutions and social practices. They imagine society under revised and perfected institutions and ideals. Their buoyant spirit rejects the dark fatalism which bids men regard themselves as the sport of fate.

their conditions beyond curing, their lot one to endure. The world about them fills them with a discontent which goads them on to visions of a better one beyond.

The Utopians are naturally also *critics of their age*, feeling that all is not well, and promulgating often with sharp satire a happy ideal for the future, which throws into bold relief the deficiencies and corruptions of the present; showing the wide gulf between present fact and future possibility. They, according to their nature, with bitter speech or by gentle contrast, show the deplorable effects of misgovernment, the evils of social laxity, the fruits of dense ignorance, and the results of oppression to their contemporaries, and look upon their respective ideal pictures as the embodiment of the teachings which they desire to give to the world as correctives. They condemn what they see about them as miserable because they conceive of a happiness which condemns it. But never have the people of any age accepted the criticisms and denunciations of these critic-prophets, nor have they been attentive to their prophecies. They have considered them as meddlesome trouble makers or muckrakers courting disaster. Prophets have no honor in their own country or in their own generation as another great Dissenter has said.[2] In every age they are derided as impractical visionaries, or denounced as heretics and radicals. It is only distant posterity who ever accept them, revere them, and give them the hearing and place they so fittingly deserve.

The Utopians stand out in their respective times almost without exception as *men of intellectual originality and constructive imagination*. Their pictures required imaginative gifts equal to any that ever inspired song or story, or the witchery of poet or painter; gifts, however, tempered by the constructive capacity which characterizes the real social technician. The Utopians have risen up and cried "It will be thus!" and pictured to us an age or place in which slander and crime, hate and war, avoidable pain and misery, injustice and persecution would be no more, and in which righteousness, love, peace, plenty and happiness would reign supreme. They all stand

[2] Matthew 13 57, Mark 6:4.

in the land of the future, and show humanity the fairer day that
was revealed to them.   They are all similar in their great inspiration and intense enthusiasm, their belief in their ideal,
and the strong desire to aid in world improvement.   At first
the reader sees merely what he considers to be the fantastical
imaginings of some idealist or inventive academician; but he
soon penetrates to the signs of deep suffering and the yearnings
of sympathy which lie underneath; the desire to tear away the
scales which bind the people to their short-sightedness or their
sufferings; and the suggestion of new and usually carefully
thought out devices for effecting that painfully longed for perfect future.   They were men, who, looking at a wilderness,
even as they looked, beheld a garden.

/ The Utopians also *have a commendable faith*.   It takes faith
of the intellect to anticipate a stage of society before it is
reached and it takes faith of character to launch oneself toward a goal before its tangible and profitable elements are in
sight.   It is said that Wordsworth, as he looked at his child
exclaimed: "Hope—and a renovation without end."   The
Utopians similarly picture the unclosed vista of a yet-to-be.
They have faith that there will be renovations without end.

While all men are inextricably bound to their time, it is true
that geniuses are able to lift themselves partially above it.
They profit by the geniuses that have gone before them, inheriting the best of the past.   But they put out this inheritance at
interest and get greater and more rapid returns than the average person.   They compose a sort of apostolical succession,
transmitting their superior knowledge on from generation to
generation.   It is also true that the genius can only work with
the material he finds ready at hand; he must employ the language and methods of thought prevalent at his day, and can advance only a measurable distance beyond his contemporaries;
it is that which makes him the genius.   He penetrates a step
or two beyond, and finds strange new meanings in what has
been inherited.   Here we also find the Utopians; men of their
generation and yet beyond it; a rare variety within the human
species, differentiated for a special function; evolved products,
and yet original moving forces in social evolution; men within

the society, and yet without it; feeling the "Zeitgeist," and yet dominated by the "Weltschmerz." Men to be expected, and yet unique.

Among the various Utopians, as among the thinking men of every age, two ideals have reigned—ideals seemingly negations of each other.[3] The one has been constantly gaining in emphasis and becoming clearer as the world's knowledge has increased; the other has declined *pari passu* but still remains a hope hidden in the hearts of men. The first ideal is the future of the human race in this world; the other is the future of the individual in another world hereafter. The one bespeaks a perfecting of our humanity in this mundane life; the other despairing of it in this world anticipates it hereafter. Both are powerful motives in life and both have had and have their adherents, the Utopians not excepted, as we have seen. There has been and is now an antagonism between the champions of one or the other of these ideals, a feeling that there is no common ground between them. The one group has felt that their ideal was the more disinterested and humanitarian, and that the other was essentially egoistic and vaguely transcendental. The other group felt that theirs was the "true and revealed ideal," while the first was materialistic and of the earth. However, they have many points in common. Both look forward to a perfect humanity and a perfect social state; both are born of the same psychological attitudes and emotional state of mind; the wishes and motives are the same; the specific end alone is different, and that is of minor significance. When men have learned to project their hope for a future either for themselves or for the world into the Ultimate Destiny the differences fall away; they are out for the same thing; they both resolve themselves into a fundamental identity in nature and destiny. Hence men may be allowed to make either of them the basis of their lives, according to their own individual character or temperament. There is as much faith in the willingness to work for an unseen future in this world as in another, and the same indefinite assumptions. Nor is

[3] I am partly indebted to Benjamin Jowett's introduction to his translation of Plato's "Republic," p. xciii, for this thought

it unbelievable that now and then an individual would arise who feels it his duty to devote himself to some future generation of men. Such in brief review are some of the outstanding characteristics of the men; now let us consider their products.

While the bulk of this volume has been devoted to a detailed discussion of the specific characteristics of various representative Utopias, certain general observations are necessary at this point to give completeness to the results secured from our analysis.

The prevailing conception of Utopias is practically uniform, definite and widespread, as current definitions from various sources in different languages demonstrate.[4] These new worlds of which the Utopians have dreamed and written have at all times been thought to be vain fantasies, the products of idle and even diseased speculation, mere mental driftwood of men otherwise sound. And yet the new age must appraise them differently and correctly.

We are coming to see that the course of civilization is the result of a vast complex of more or less dynamic physical and spiritual forces, some of which are gradually becoming distinguishable. Among these latter contributing elements are those tremendous recurring series or rhythmically undulating, successive waves of collective dissatisfaction which sweep first over one part of the world and then over another. Each of the series is due to the fact that the universe is not stationary; all is movement, shifting, and more or less rapid and incessant transformation, and men and institutions do not remain the

[4] "Any place or state of ideal perfection." WEBSTER'S STANDARD DICTIONARY.

"An ideally perfect place, realm, or condition; hence any imaginary region, or a book describing one." FUNK & WAGNALLS' STANDARD DICTIONARY.

"An imaginary conception of an ideal government." DICT. GEN. DE LA LANGUE FRANÇAISE.

"Utopias . . . are idealistic pictures of other worlds, the existence or possibility of which can not be scientifically demonstrated, and on which we only believe." ANDREAS VOIGHT, "DER SOZIALEN UTOPIEN," p 1

"An Utopia is a literary product of phantasy, which desires to show humanity the way to the betterment of its political, moral and social condition " SCHOMANN, "FRANZÖSISCHE UTOPISTEN UND IHR FRAUENIDEAL," p. 7.

same. Social readjustment instead of constantly taking place is delayed or in part prevented. Laws and institutions, once adequate, are no longer so; bonds that have held society together are strained or broken; customs as perpetuated have either interfered with changes, or miscarried and become instruments of discontent-producing oppression. Thus social idealists, half automatically, are stimulated by the instability about them to seek a new center of social gravity; and not being able instantly to procure what will bring concord and contentment, the imagination brings before their minds the thought of re-making the world as they would like it to be.[5] Of such are the Utopias, the foam-flecked crests of these waves, voicing the best and highest thought the natural products of their time. Actually most of the Utopias stand at the head of their age, express its profoundest hopes, and represent the quintessence of its most advanced thought. This is shown by the fact that the majority of the Utopian writers share the preconceptions which underlay the thinking of the political and religious radicals of their day. Their minds can well be compared to concave mirrors which attracted and caught the best thought of their times and reflected it back with concentrated force.

The Utopias are bulletins suggesting the introduction of new elements into social life, new ways of doing things, calling for new training, and requiring new ways of living to which the people would have to be accommodated. And yet even such startling inventions or creations contrary to current opinion, are not the results of individual talent or genius.[6] As Bald-

---

[5] It is thought by some, and the recent Utopias bear out the idea, that Utopias also arise at another point in the social cycle "As soon as the mental progress of a people has reached a point where wants are to some extent antiquated, the mental life begins to expand beyond the immediate present, and the imagination on the basis of certain social experiences constructs an ideal world, where desires quite remote from economic wants receive satisfaction "
Hayden, "The Social Will," p 13 Our analysis in Part I, however, shows that in but few cases does this apply to Utopias

[6] For example, G. C. M Smith, the editor of "New Atlantis" (Cambridge, 1900), tells us that it is possible that Bacon was partly inspired to create his great college of Research, the House of Salomon, by the Academy of the Lincei of Rome, founded in 1603 for the common prosecu-

win says, "No effective invention ever makes an absolute break with the culture, tradition, or fund of knowledge treasured up from the past." . . . "To invent a social thing without using material current in his environment would be as impossible to a man as to think anything without using the materials of his own memory and past imagination." [7]   Behind all individual genius is something greater, more creative, more powerful, more intimately in touch with the sources of life, something which accounts for his product; and this is the collective mind, crude and largely dormant, though it may be. But even though the Utopias are such advanced expressions of the social imagination, this fact does not invalidate what we have previously said regarding the unique character of the Utopians. The Utopians, as all inventors, are variations; they took this spirit of advance, which but few felt, and instead of permitting it to waste itself as an emotional effervescence, developed it into something concrete and comprehensible, even though not feasible.   This genius and their commendable departure from the stereotyped, evidence their emancipation from the thought of their time and their masterly presentation of a goal is their condensation of the superior thinking of the time. The Utopias incorporate the best element of their age, which creation, however, is an act of ingenuity and originality. Most people use the existing materials in the traditional or conventional way; the Utopians used them in a new fashion. And yet this reorganized plan was so progressive that it was beyond the comprehension of the mass; the Utopians were giving audible expression to murmurings so faint that but few even noticed them.   These voices were so far in the van of their age that their conceptions were received as fantasy and their owners dubbed "Utopians."   The Utopias are merely Utopias from the point of view of the great unawakened masses and the shortsighted individuals of their day, and the Utopians are only "dreamers" in the sense that such is a popular description of

tion of researches in physical science and mathematics, and also by the efforts of an Edmund Bolton, who, in 1616 proposed the foundation of an "English Academe," to be called "King James his Academe or Temple of Honour," p. xxi.

[7] "Social and Ethical Interpretations," p. 180.

any man who is wide awake, and a hundred years or so before his fellows. It is only given to a few to look beyond the accomplished. It is this advance guard who proclaim the ideas that within a generation, or a century or five centuries would percolate down into the masses who by that time are ready to accept them.

Not all of any of the Utopias has been realized, but as much of them have been, as is the case in any improvement scheme; they have not been wholly realized because realization requires a full century after the conception of the ideal, and conditions change in the meantime. Furthermore, at the time of their conception society has developed no means of bringing their ideas into practice, nor would people generally have given their consent, if it had. In other ages Utopias come true. Thus we see that Utopias are not tangential departures from the social base, but that each has a historical background and a newly developed idealism upon which to work. If all men of a given age were capable of the same forelook, and graced with the same realistic imagination, and capable of sounding the depths of the social idealism of their age as the Utopians were, the world would never have known the derisively used word "Utopia." Utopias are merely relative.

Another reason why the Utopias were ridiculed by their contemporaries, is doubtless because of the well-recognized fact that all great inventions are at first rough-hewn, and to a degree angular and unassimilable. Steadier and more painstaking men modify them into better conformity to the actual demand which society makes.[8]

The third probable reason is that leaders and the governing classes often find it to their personal interest to keep the social life as nearly static as possible. Hence, they frequently interfere through control of social institutions with the social mechanism by which conscious changes are brought about, or by propagandist methods cause to fall into disrepute anything which by contrast criticizes or accuses them.

A fourth reason, and perhaps the most significant one, is because despair is now habitual of attaining what these Utopias

[8] Baldwin, Ibid. p. 189.

described.[9] This thought was echoed by Francis Bacon, the scientist and Utopian, when he wrote in his "Novum Organum": "By far the greatest obstacle to the progress of science and the undertaking of new tasks . . . is found in this, that men despair and think things impossible. . . . If therefore any one believes or promises more, they think this comes of an ungoverned mind." What has been needed at all times is a resolute spirit of control and a will to do. Bit by bit as we learn to do this, and cease to despair, we shall make for ourselves a better world; we shall then accomplish in reality on a large scale what Ward anticipated when he wrote, "The environment transforms the animal; man transforms the environment." [10] Here is the beginning of real civilization, the conscious control by man of man and nature.

[9] Lord Macaulay: "An acre of Middlesex is better than a principality in Utopia" "Essays," Montague Edition, Vol. II, p. 213.
[10] Ward, Pure Sociology, p. 16.

CHAPTER VIII

UTOPIANISM AND THE RÔLE OF IDEAS AND IDEALS

In the first part of this work we noted that the very essence of the various Utopias was the delineation of the means whereby the writer's vision of social perfection is to be realized. This spirit of hope expressing itself in definite proposals and stimulating action, we have called "Utopianism," meaning thereby the rôle of the conscious human will in suggesting a trend of development for society, or the unconscious align-ment of society in conformity with some definite ideal. We may also think of it in its working out as the realization in life of ideals seemingly incapable of attainment, for we know now that there is a potency about inspiring ideals that prompts men eventually, and yet unconsciously, to make them real; they breathe a spirit which gives hope, and encourages action. In this chapter we are analyzing the Utopias as ideals, and are examining the technique of the process of individual and social progress which comes as the result of the efficiency of ideas and ideals. Let us first consider the Utopias as stimuli to imagina-tion and idealism.

The Utopians when they constructed their ideal worlds were building better than they knew for up to three-quarters of a century ago their Utopias were among the most important symbols and carriers of social idealism, means whereby new truths were disseminated and impressed upon the race generally, in a new and fascinating fashion.[1] Thomas Carlyle in his "Sartor Resartus,"[2] had this idea when he wrote: "In many a painted Device, or simple seal-emblem the commonest Truth

[1] It is true, however, that some of the anticipations spoken of by their authors as Utopias, particularly those of the last half century, have been so ridiculous and fanatical that men have passed them by in disgust.

[2] Ginn Edition, p 199.

stands out to us proclaimed with quite new emphasis. . . .
For it is here that Fantasy with her mystic wonderland plays
into the small prose domain of the Senses and becomes incorporated therewith."

Most of the Utopians by the exotic character of their utopianistic projects stirred the imagination of men, and we know
that imagination is prerequisite to social reform.   Every great
scheme for the improvement of societal life first had its outlines shape themselves in some one mind's eye; the mental
optic always comes into play before the physical instrument.
But they played a still more marvelous rôle, for by capturing
public imagination they created centers of imitation and
injected new ideas and ideals into the group mores.   They also
introduced the minds of men to mental freedom; they tended
to loosen the dead hand of the past, and encouraged that fearless
groping and searching out after something better, always better,
that transcending of the limits of the actual, that desire for
social experimentation, which prevents stagnation and assures
progress.   They induced the human mind to hold before it
the favorite device of the Utopian Francis Bacon: a ship passing through the Pillars of Hercules out into the unknown
sea, and over it the words, "Plus Ultra." The Utopias as
they have come on age after age, have served as goals constantly receding, which led the race onward and upward, for
most of them have represented the most advanced thought of
their age on social questions.   They have been, along with
certain other social elements, great inciters and quickeners,
leading and wooing society on the way toward the goal of
perfection.[3]   Probably no Utopia if it could be completely

[3] Spargo and Arner, "Elements of Socialism," p. 199, in writing in this
connection of the Utopian Socialists have said: "They have rendered
a great service by their criticisms of existing society, and by holding
out the inspiration of a definite ideal   It has always been too common
for men to accept things without questioning them, to assume that whatever is, is right, and that what is must continue to be. The Utopians
have bravely challenged this conservation and forced millions of men and
women to move in the direction of progress, who otherwise would not
have moved at all   It matters little that their plans were impracticable,
nor even that any serious attempt to carry them out would have brought
about a worse condition than that which their authors sought to remedy.

realized in all its details would be entirely workable, but it provides the will to experiment with proposals which after trial enable still newer ideals for humanity to be projected.

Like all ideas and ideals we must trace the Utopias back to one man's mind, for all germinal processes originate that way. The inventions, mental and mechanical, that have transformed modern life, go back to individual men of genius, very often lonely, neglected and almost unknown thinkers, perhaps even never dreaming how they would now as "sceptered soverigns still rule us from their urns." [4]   These ideas and ideals are a mixture of suggestion, memory and constructive imagination within the individual; they are the result of contrast with present reality, and with the ideas of an earlier time, and come from exceptional, intellectual, foresighted individuals. During such periods the social inventors alone of the dissatisfied thousands, gain a clear conception of both the old social evils and of new remedies; they see clearly both the goal and the path to be traveled in order to attain it; they set forth a proposal which suggests a whole new social adjustment.   Among them as among all effective idealists the imagination forms strange new combinations out of the actual details of existing situations, and feels new human possibilities. It is a process of discovery, of achievement above the scope of mere imitation and absorption with the current social custom and tradition.   It is something different, something more vital and transforming made out of existing materials.

Individually conceived, these ideas once launched, spread and some become incorporated into the fabric of social thought.

The inertia of conservatism and the inexorable forces of social evolution made the acceptance of their plans impossible, but nothing could prevent mankind from seeing the evils which these prophets of a better social order decried, and so, even though we speak of the 'failures' of dreamers, like More and Owen, it must be confessed that much of the progress we have made has been directly inspired by them   Their success lay in other directions than they dreamed "

[4] Wundt says   "Even the life of primitive peoples of nature is not entirely unaffected by individual personalities, whose influence may be more or less permanently operative even after they themselves have been forgotten." "Elements of Folk Psychology," Schaub Translation, Macmillan, 1916, p. 514.

They become public property, as it were, part of that social heritage which is constantly available because transmitted from one generation and age to another, and, in the process, revised to date by each in turn. And who can say that they are not as truly a part of history as actual events or the acts of eminent men themselves and that they play the same rôle.[5] We have come to realize that human life and conduct are affected by ideals in the same way that they are affected by the examples of eminent men. Who can say that the world has not been different for Jesus or Napoleon or Lincoln having lived in it, and by an infusion of their lives into others of a later day have changed succeeding ages? Similarly the social dreamer does not live in vain. Having presented the vision of a city beautiful or a regenerated society, he has suggested the social possibilities of mankind.[6] Neither the lessons from the life of the great man, nor the ideals of the dreamer are immediately applicable in practice, but there is a spirit flowing from them which tends to raise individuals above the common routine of society or trade, and eventually elevates groups and nations. There is about the work of many a dreamer an impetus, which, by transforming certain elements of the real into the ideal, eventually tends to transmute the ideal into the real; an optimism which breeds optimism; a resolve which translates itself into practice.

But we must not overlook the fact that the acceptance of ideals is the ending of a long process. The idealist's thought may be great, but it, like every proposal for reform, has to fight for acceptance before it receives a place in social belief and usuage; and not all are taken in. For some time, perhaps for an age prior to its final acceptance, it is subjected to critical discussion, which develops various arguments for and against. If in this way the favorable judgments, eventually after a generation or century or several centuries, out-

[5] "Ideas are our most precious heritage, for they guard us from more evils and lead us to more goals than all other devices and powers." Patten, S N , "The Social Basis of Religion," N. Y., 1911, p. 49

[6] "Moral evolution has consisted almost wholly in the increasing liberation of the imagination." Starke, "La famille dans le différentes Societes," p. 272.

weigh the unfavorable it becomes part of the general opinion of the group and we have the basis of a new social policy or institution.   These ideas eventually develop into action which produces social change.[7]   Thus Baldwin says,[8] that these ideas are generalized, discussed, pared down, made available in form and content, by social processes, and then finally pass over to the domain of the accepted and socially selected.   But the acceptance has been first here and then there.   Even though there is great opposition at first the new idea has a subtle quality, hidden from the many, which makes it esteemed by the few   And it must be acknowledged that it is not the hidebound, shortsighted intellectual underling, nor is it the genial, fiberless, unstrenuous individual who is first impressed and moved to act by ideals and upbuilding ideas.   It is upon the great "men of spirit," the transcending spiritual and moral seers among society that their new beneficent light first shines, and from these pinnacles is reflected upon the mass of men. It is these great ideal-receivers who transmit the message to the masses.

The method of transmission and agency of acceptance is primarily exposure to constant suggestion and ensuing unconscious imitation; choice plays a minor rôle.   Where ideas are in the air, as the saying goes, men catch them by a sort of infection, and often without any notion whence they came. But in most minds some struggle goes on before the idea is assimilated; in some, it is tardy, but with most it is comparatively speedy, for social pressure to adopt and follow is largely unconscious.   The average man is not primarily influenced by his rational nature; he is largely the creature of his senses and instincts.   Man cannot and does not live by thought alone.   He is simply the depository in an individual unit of the various thoughts, memories, and feelings that make up the mental substance of his time.   He is the creature of his time, and as his time absorbs new motives and a new spirit

[7] It is worthy of mention at this point, even though it is discussed at length in the next chapter, that a surprisingly large number of the ideas of the Utopians have been accepted and translated into fact by later generations.

[8] "The Individual and Society," pp. 152, 153.

he breathes these also. Ideologically considered, life is a constant unfolding process, an eternally swelling stream everlastingly admitting new ideas, and he who floats with this stream cannot expect to escape getting wet. He may well oppose bringing his viewpoint and life into conformity with a certain ideal, and yet in spite of himself, may inadvertently fall into the new way of life, too, because others have been doing so.[9] As an average man, he has been thoroughly molded by society; he is his society individuated, so far as he is an individual at all. He has accepted the ideas, and does not know it.

The adoption of new ideas comes with the unfolding of social needs. The eventual and complete acceptance may and usually does come, however, in a time of stress or strain, such as results from profound religious, political, or economic changes in national life. And thus with the differentiation and development of society new measures and institutions will prevail. Then society examines its accumulated stock of unused ideas and puts in control those which now offer the greatest advantages. If the idea or ideal is efficient, it will survive and gradually become a race heritage; then it will be converted into practice, and finally become an established social institution. It is possible, of course, that the reformer's thought is so advanced that only centuries afterward will society attain to it; but eventually, if his project is sound in principle society will catch up with it [10]

Therefore, who can say that an ideal is incapable of realization? Since the ideas and ideals of the Utopians were of

---

[9] A. D. Innes in "Ten Tudor Statesmen," London, 1906, p. 86, writing in a somewhat different vein, has said, "Sir Galahad is not a practical model for the British citizen, who would take warning from the career of the Knight of La Mancha. Yet the conception of Sir Galahad is worthy of serious contemplation by the British citizen who may therefrom divine not a little practical direction in the conduct of his life To condemn the presentation of avowed ideals as impractical is merely to display a complete misapprehension of the meaning and use of ideals "

[10] Many of the great leaders of men have well understood the fact that worthwhile ideas are often too new, and before trying to put their ideas into execution have either waited until the times became ripe through the natural course of events, or have sought to develop in the public mind a point of view that would support their plans.

the same kind as those discussed above, who can say that the
schemes of the Utopians are unattainable or that their utopianism is impotent? After all, is it not perhaps a matter of
mistakes in dating the consummation of our ideals? As man
succeeds in discovering the ideals of the past, does he not
find many of them realized about him? Can any one living
in the twentieth century with miracles being constantly per-
formed before one's very eyes, with the ideals of a century or
a millenium being realized, say that anything is utterly impossible? No, the dreamer may be the prophet after all! As
Wells says, in his "Modern. Utopia," it is not bad to dream
dreams, because the dreams may be realities when you and I
are dreams. Who would deny indeed, that our present day
sciences, observations and deeds daily bring into being things
which the dreamers of the past hoped for? Our grandfather's
Utopias have become our commonplaces. That which was
ridiculously improbable yesterday is truth and reality to-day.
Another age will find our Utopian conceptions inadequate or
even untrue.

Such a study therefore also teaches us that social ideas
and ideals do truly serve as goals and assist in social control
As goals they serve as the basis of a more comprehensive social
organization; they give hope and inspire courage, and through
these lend vigor to life; and after being assimilated they lift
men to a higher and better plane of social life. Much of the
advance that society makes is the result of new ideas that are
instilled into the minds of great masses of people. The classic illustration of this is the Renaissance, which achieved the
entire transformation of mediæval society. Society takes its
color and form from whatever engages the attention and holds
the minds of its people. Reforms are indeed largely the expression of new ideas permeating the minds of the majority.
Mr. Harper [11] in discussing the opposition to this conception
has said, "Just because idealism sets up an altogether worthy
goal in the efforts to attain which, mankind is ever becoming
better and better, its opponents imagine that they have successfully disposed of its claims when they describe it as Utopian.

[11] "The Social Ideal," p 282.

This epithet is easily used, but it is generally employed by the shortsighted." Fortunately there are great historic movements, as for example, the abolition of slavery, which prove that ideals once confidently pronounced as Utopian, have in the evolution of society been realized,—and not only to the satisfaction of those who always believed them to be possible of realization, but also those who opposed them. As the result too, of their power of indirect suggestion, the Utopias arouse people and eventually bring action, without antagonizing many—a most significant quality. As suggestions for social control they also serve a beneficent purpose, since they are newer and higher forms in harmony with the best of the future. Inasmuch as they have come from superior individuals, and have passed through the sifting process, they are usually vastly superior to the existing forms of control; they tend to be more definite, more elastic and inclusive, to do away with harsh and external authorities in favor of control resting on enlightenment.

A study of Utopias and ideals should also teach us not to scoff at the dreamer and the hopeful reformer. Even though some people hold to ideals which the world contradicts we dare not upbraid them or despise or persecute them, for it is not certain that they are deluded or demented or perverted; they may have something rare and precious which the rest of us cannot yet behold. We should have a deep sympathy with these efforts as with every effort to rise above the everyday world, to judge the present by the future, our own times and fortunes by an all-including purpose in human life. A new idea is not necessarily fatuous; it may be one with a place in the march of events. Some day the procession will have caught up with it.

It is given to us as individuals now and then, in our better moments, to formulate ideals. A perpetual selective process goes on through the interaction of these sublimated desires of ours as individuals (for this is what ideals are in the last analysis) which forms a collective desire in the group mind that we call the social ideal. This social ideal is generally much less distinct in its features than the more sharply conceived ideals of the individual. Although it works differently the social ideal is a powerful stimulus to action. Social emotion lies back of it. This common social ideal is the ideal of *social perfection*. Unlike the Utopians, average men do not go so far as to attempt to analyze perfection, or determine the factors involved in it and the means of attaining it, nor can they any more than they can analyze or define perfect beauty or perfect truth. Yet they yearn for and direct their efforts toward this ultimate aim. But the general idea has always been a simple hope. Its presence is an indication of social consciousness, the fact that society realizes its own existence, and recognizes that it must have a destiny. The ideal of perfection, therefore, is not in conflict with the realistic tendency of the age, it calls attention to a neglected phase of reality. Its presence is highly promising. It lifts humanity into its true sphere and presents the highest aim for its realization. This ideal, this common utopian anticipation, must depend for the approach to its consummation upon the strengthening and speeding up of those occasional movements for the better thing, those temporary exhibitions of a different social disposition entirely which at times occur, before we are again thrust into the hungers, the jealousies, the prejudices and habits which sway us daily. This idealism is a shining, scintillating thread running through the confusion, ignorance, harshness and dogmatism of the ages. It evidences that all men share in a measure the Utopian hope. It makes the acceptance of utopianism less difficult.

Ideals have great utility in themselves. Even if we had no evidence of the realization in time of ideals they would be of value to us, just the pure ideals themselves. Plato already had grasped the thought that man is controlled not only by what he sees, but by what he imagines as desirable, when he expressed the opinion that if a man has once found the image of an ideal state in which justice and happiness prevails, and in which life reaches fuller and higher possibilities than it has yet attained, the ideal has not been conceived in vain. He says in speaking of his ideal "Republic," "In heaven, probably there is a model of it, for any one who inclines to contemplate, and on contemplating to regulate himself accordingly; and it is no matter to him whether it does exist anywhere, or shall ever exist here. He does the duties of this one alone and no other." The very existence of ideals in the mind may inaugurate an endless process of social amelioration.

Principles and ideals are always with us, and serve as a criteria by which we may ' judge actual conditions. This is the great function of ideals, that even if they cannot be realized, they yet enable us to understand the real, they give us a comprehension of the character of the immanent truth; they give us a norm whereby we can ascertain the defectiveness, the abnormality, the perversion in existing institutions and conditions, the perfect standards to which conduct ought to approximate. That which is always begs comparison with that which should be, and the discrepancy is obvious. A guiding star does not lose its value as a guide because it is never reached. The ideal is a guide as well as a goal. Therefore, while the actual may differ far from the ideal, we know that the actual will not go far unless it has a high ideal set before it, and as George Herbert says,

> "Who aimeth at the sky,
> Shoots higher much than he that means a tree." [12]

Utopians and utopianism, regardless of type, furnish ideals of this character; ideals of extraordinary effectiveness as means and standards.[13] The Utopians helped to make a soul for the world. By their spirit of optimism which prevented men from seeing the world with a.jaundiced eye, they counteracted that vicious philosophical cynicism and that subtle, social hopelessness which neutralizes social effort. They surmounted the barriers of egoistic and blind self-interest and held up an ideal of social relationships whereby human capacities

[12] Quoted by Barker, "The Political Thought of Plato and Aristotle," p 160.

[13] "In this respect the Utopian dreamers of social justice . . are, in spite of their impracticability and non-adaptation to present environmental conditions, analogous to the saint's belief in an existent kingdom of heaven They help to break the edge of the general reign of hardness, and are slow leavens of a better order" James, W., "Varieties of Religious Experience," London, 1908, p. 360.

were to be infinitely elevated and enlarged; they spoke of desires ennobled and rationalized, and motives broadened and humanized. They felt a responsibility for the welfare of humanity; they were men influencing man for the sake of mankind. They painted a social harmony, that to all intents was the realization upon the part of the individual of his own highest worth, and the realization by society of his truest service. Truly a lofty sphere of contemplation.

Looking back we see that civilization has largely been built up through invention and discovery, in both the physical and intellectual realms of life, the products of thinkers and idealists; almost wholly intellectual achievements. This sustains us in the belief that while Utopias may never actually appear and Utopians may be forgotten, yet there is an enduring element about their ideals which causes them to live on and on. They do not wholly die!

It is perhaps true that, even though no utopianistic thought had ever been expressed, and though no Utopia had ever served as a lure, the progress of the world would have continued just as it has, due to the scores of other progressive factors constantly at work. But the presence of these utopian elements has, without a doubt, tended to accelerate and stimulate human advance in accordance with the technique already analyzed, and along the lines specifically to be described in the ensuing chapter.

CHAPTER IX

THE UTOPIANISTIC CONTRIBUTION TO CIVILIZATION

The value of an ideal depends, not upon its novelty, but upon its power to contribute to social betterment. Those ideals may assuredly be reckoned the most precious which have given the world noble lives, provided strong social motives, or incarnated themselves in effective social institutions. Such superior and successful ideals are to be found in most of the Utopias. Auguste Comte has said "There is no Utopia so wild as not to offer some incontestable advantages," [1] and peering into the life about us we cannot help being convinced that these words breathe a profound truth. Everywhere we see utopianism become reality. The Utopians and their utopianism have a great rôle in shaping the social evolution which came after them. In this chapter we shall consider briefly some of the more significant of the utopianistic ideals which are to-day current and also explore the relationship of certain of the more outstanding elements in utopianism to social evolution; in this way we shall weigh the concrete evidence for utopianism translated into reality. Of course, ideas and ideals are not always put into effect in just the form that the thinker conceived them. Occasionally society in applying them changes them somewhat, but the kernel is recognizable, nevertheless. Moreover, we cannot say that the Utopias were the only stimulating agencies nor were their creators the only prophets and oracles, for as we have shown, they were part of the advance movement of their respective ages. But none can deny that they were tremendously potent in the cases cited. Let us proceed to their analysis.

[1] "Positive Philosophy," Martineau Version, II, p. 25.

The utopianism of the prophets and Jesus has come to dominate the moral and spiritual life of men as no other ideals have been able to do; the very fundamentals of successful social life and happy human relations have come to be based upon it.   Jesus' utopianism stressing the individual in particular, nearly two milleniums ago attracted attention to the necessity of proper personal conduct as the basis of succesful social life; he felt that as individuals do right, become virtuous, and are regenerated, the world will progress toward righteousness and peace.   This emphasis upon individual integrity and strength this discerning of the key to the old problem, this devotion to fellow-men through careful self-culture, are ideas which have become wonderfully effective in history, and are penetrating and permeating the inmost recesses of the life of the world. But it is not the content of Jesus' utopianism that is so important, it is its spirit; and it is a spirit which constantly leads onward.   His utopianism was a growing principle, a perpetual, onflowing, constantly changing one.   Just as Paul adapted Jesus' spirit to his age, so the best thinkers of every age have learned to adapt it to theirs; it is the great reconstructive spirit of every age.   That realization has always fallen short of the ideal is due to the subtle genius of ideals, for they are a continually effective court of appeal whatever the age by which they are approached.   The Christian spirit in its power will doubtless be the stimulating element in the spiritual evolution of the ages.

The Messianic state of the prophets, the catastrophically founded era of the apocalyptists, and the Kingdom of God of Jesus, aggressive, fantastic or transcendental each cultivated a splendid hope of emancipation, of social peace, of future justice and fraternity, and tended to keep the souls of the people alive amid the vast internal decay and the crushing sorrows of the foreign rule of the Assyrians, Persians, and Romans.   Similarly, they have been the ideal and inspiration of different groups of men at various times through the ages since,—an ever-glowing goal.

More's Utopia [2] stands out as the inspiration, not only of

[2] The tremendous influence of Plato's "Republic" has been previously discussed   See chapter on "The Republic."

the whole train of later Utopias, but of the whole trend of social reform. It doubtless suggested such treatises as Campanella's "City of the Sun," Bacon's fragmentary "New Atlantis," Hobbes' "Leviathan," Harrington's "Oceana" and Filmer's "Patriarcha." In suggesting universal and compulsory education More launched a thought which has not yet run its course. While his conception of penology and his plea for religious tolerance appeared to his contemporaries as preposterous, yet his explanation of crime and its remedies is in harmony with our advanced modern policy, and the religious freedom which seemed a chimerical vision at the time of his death has been enjoyed for generations. Speaking of his industrial scheme Miss Scudder says, "If the industrial system on which his society is founded is still confined to Utopia, communication between that commonwealth and England is at least more frequent than in his day. One is inclined to suspect certain of our economists, even, of occasional trips into that land of vision; while as for dreamers,—Ruskin, Bellamy, Morris, Howells,—they have sojourned there long enough to bring back full reports, which differ sometimes in detail from those of Hythloday." [3] As an advocate of the short working day with its opportunity for cultural growth and its abolition of drudgery and degradation, he still stands in the lead among the myriads of reformers. Many of More's ideals still represent the height of social anticipation. Mr. Wells tells us that it also bore fruit in the English Poor Laws.[4] It was a broad-visioned, masterly work. It compelled attention; it wrought itself into wise men's thinking; it became one of the instruments of a progress which by the close of the nineteenth century had purged English society of the greater number of the evils mentioned therein. The fact that it has been three times translated into English from the Latin, and also into many other languages, testifies to the eagerness with which men have read it and sought its ideas.

The Utopianism of Robert Owen is commonly recognized as the stimulating element underlying some of the most significant

[3] Scudder, Vida D., "Social Ideal in English Letters," Boston, 1898, p. 60.

[4] "Outline of History," II, p. 211.

reforms and newly created social institutions of the last century. As we have already indicated in a previous chapter, Owen through the publication of his humanitarian ideas with regard to labor under the new mechanical régime in industry, and by means of spirited agitation, was influential in bringing to pass the first labor legislation, the British Factory Acts in 1819, which, as Wells says, was "the first attempt to restrain employers from taking the most stupid and intolerable advantage of their workers' poverty." [5] The coöperative buying societies among the poorer folk beginning with the Rochdale pioneers are also the direct outgrowth of Owen's experiments of New Lanark. He was one of the pioneers of the trade union movement, and laid down the first plans for labor bureaus on a national scale. Owen was a man who in every way through his ideas and acts left his impress upon his own and succeeding generations.

And so we might go on with each Utopia or Utopian, but it is needless; let us rather attend to various specific forms of contribution which the Utopians have made to civilization.

The Utopians first of all *assisted men of later generations in avoiding social disaster.* Themselves witnesses of the accumulating forces of social distress and maladjustment, and through their utopianism proposing a solution of those very difficulties, they showed how revolution and other social disaster might be avoided. They were and are announcers of a regimen making for social health, security and peace between classes. They breathe a sort of philosophy of history,—an interpretation which enables men to profit by the mistakes of past generations.

Among the Utopians one finds *a commendable fearlessness.* They acknowledged social evils, which few do, and then went further and dared to suggest changes and picture a state where such changes had been carried out. Most men still hesitate to do this. We are afraid of the unknown perils of disturbing our accustomed ways; we prefer to endure the evils we know, but rather would not combat. The Utopians were willing to

---

[5] "Outline of History," II, p. 404.

suggest the use of untried forces.   They were the venturesome men who because they dared did much to achieve necessary change, quietly and rationally.[6]

The Utopians centuries ago *discovered a new criterion of human value.* They rejected the subjective individualistic standard of value, which still largely prevails and set up the conception of the social good, and of the development of society as a whole. They sought after a unified and coördinated group, based on brotherly coöperation.[7]   As far back as the Hebrew prophets, they recognized a social self as well as individual selves; they perceived the inter-dependence and solidarity of all society.   Only recently has this solidarity come to be widely realized.   Theirs were ideas and ideals by which society, and not individuals, merely, were controlled.   They advocated unity and coöperation as against the domination of individual ambition, selfishness and rapacity.   Their Utopias anticipated *social* destiny not *individual* destiny, and were and are effective as their content and spirit are grasped by groups. If some of them, as for example Jesus, seemed to stress unduly the individual, it was because they saw that progress in human society depends on the production of finer and finer strains of men and women, and that the best will be the more social.   The Utopias surely were always composed of ideally socialized individuals.   We of to-day have everywhere obtained our conception of unified society from some of the Utopians; the communists and socialists in theory and practice apply theirs narrowly, the sociologists and social workers theirs in a broader and less specific form as the basis of their general policy and endeavor.

The Utopians, especially the Utopian Socialists, also *anticipated other social thinkers, in their appreciation of social laws,* for on the whole, the bare idea of undeviating law, physical or social, is one of the late products of reflective thought.

[6] "The first task of the social reformer is to confront this doubt which paralyzes social theory and makes the advocacy of far-reaching social enterprises the monopoly of the rash." Jones, Henry, "The Working Faith of the Social Reformer," London, 1910, p. 14.

[7] Especially the Utopian Socialists.

They constantly sought out these generalizations of human and social reactions and conduct, which they made the basis of their reforms.

It was in this way that Fourier gained *a conception of the theory of the instincts,* only recently receiving prominence in social psychology. Groping about in his mind for an explanation of human conduct he hit upon the idea of the "passions." What he meant by "passions" was really "instincts." He was the forerunner of our present day "instinctivists" who see in these natural endowments of the race, evolved long ago as part of its equipment for survival, the motivating factors in conduct.[8] While he did not express it clearly, yet it is very evident that he had this in mind. In reacting violently against the influence of intellection and civilization, he came to perceive the importance of the instinctive and automatic reactions of man. He felt that the thwarting of the instincts was something which interfered with human happiness; it was a crowding in, a cramping of the self. Therefore, he wanted a "natural" life—one which would bring harmony between the race and its environment. He grasped what Graham Wallas[9] has called the "master-task of civilized mankind"—the adjustment of social life to human nature.

---

[8] McDougall, Wm , "Social Psychology," Boston, 1909, p. 44 — "We may say . . . that directly or indirectly the instincts are the prime movers of all human activity; by the conative or impulsive force of some instinct (or of some habit derived from an instinct), every train of thought, however cold and passionless it may seem, is borne along towards its end, and every bodily activity is initiated and sustained The instinctive impulses determine the ends of all activities and supply the driving power by which all mental activities are sustained, and all the complex intellectual apparatus of the most highly developed mind is but a means towards these ends, is but the instrument by which these impulses seek their satisfactions, while pleasure and pain do but serve to guide them in their choice of the means "

"Take away these instinctive dispositions with their powerful impulses, and the organism would become incapable of activity of any kind, it would lie inert and motionless like a wonderful clockwork whose mainspring had been removed or a steam engine whose fires had been drawn. These impulses are the mental forces that maintain and shape all the life of individuals and societies, and in them we are confronted with the central mystery of life and mind and will "

[9] "The Great Society," p. 68.

This led him to become the father of *scientific management and present day employment management*. He recognized the evils of monotonous and fatiguing labor, and felt that something in the industrial system was responsible for the irksomeness and displeasure which every worker felt. By adapting work to the individual's peculiar makeup, attempting to get the round peg in the round hole and the square peg in the square hole, so that work would be agreeable, he sought to increase the happiness and efficiency of the worker, and the productivity of society. He played on the instinct of workmanship and of rivalry, and by contenting his workingmen created good will now recognized as absolutely essential. More recently, Hertzka and Wells started with "men as they are" in building the conception of the ideal social state.

The Utopians also were adaptationists in that they attempted *to assist in adapting social life to the time;* or better still, to create a perfect social life for all time. They aimed at social self-preservation, self-enlargement, and self-perfection. By proper adaptation of mankind to environment and vice versa, the Utopians would attain collective fullness of life. They were, with a few exceptions, handicapped, however, by a limited knowledge of the fundamental aspects of human nature and society, and by a lack of means for changing environment. Where they did attempt to change environment it was in a superficial way. They, however, arrived at certain conclusions as to what adaptations were desirable that became for them working hypotheses. These have since been verified, corrected, or repudiated. It is those that have been verified or corrected that we deal with in different portions of this chapter.

The question of determinism or free will has long been a controverted matter among social thinkers. Did this issue present itself to the Utopians? Assuredly! Some of the ethico-religious Utopians, especially the prophets and Jesus. proclaimed the doctrine of free will both for the individual and for society as a whole. The individual, as such, was capable of self-regeneration. He was not bound by experience or circumstances, but was a free moral agent, author of his own destiny. The same held for society as a whole; the group could change its life as it pleased; it also was the result of the expressions of the free will of its component individuals. The apocalyptists, on the other hand, were absolute determinists. Men, both good and bad, had nothing to do but wait for the next act in the divine drama.

But among the Early Modern and Socialistic Utopians we meet with another view. They were determinists as far as the individual was concerned. While they all desired a free expression of will yet they all insisted that the factors of environment, both physical and social, constantly overwhelmed the individual, and made him their plaything, their sport. They recognized the individual self as a servant of the human will, but the will was socially determined. They saw that what we call "social environment" envelopes individual character more closely than aught else. It penetrates the most intimate recesses of man's life, and molds it more vitally than any physical circumstance. The Utopian Socialists held that the actual morality of the individual is largely a product of the social environment. They saw the self as a social product just as Jean Paul had done when he expressed it in the words, "No man can take a walk without bringing home an influence on his eternity." Therefore, they insisted that bad environment was a check upon social perfection, and that good environment was an indispensable, if not all-important, aid. One motive to re-creating the social environment was to provide favorable surroundings so that the human soul could attain a better and nobler condition. This idea is borne out by repeated expressions upon the part of nearly all the secular Utopians. Fourier, in particular, as we have previously shown, insisted that there must be a harmony between the race and its environment. The only notable expressions of attempts to control or direct physical environment are found in Bacon's "New Atlantis," the forms of which the reader will recall.

On the other hand, the doctrine of free will held good with regard to society's activities and this we might call a social will. While the actions and thoughts of the individual, beyond the natural, were determined almost exclusively by his physical

and spiritual milieu, society's was not; it was characterized
by a freedom of activity and susceptibility to change under
the dominance of strong human wills consciously rebuilding
it according to new truth.   And this the Utopians intended
to do, for they were all dissatisfied with the haphazard, unconscious and halting advance of their times.   They desired
to utilize the proceeds of human achievement in a workable
program of human advance.   These feelings are prominent
in the writings of the Hebrew Prophets, of Jesus, Augustine,
More, Campanella, Harrington and the recent Utopians.   They
were pessimistic as to present conditions, and optimistic as to
the possibilities of society in the future.   They were anticipating worlds in which the civilization would be rational, self-
motivated, and definitely willed.   And yet they were not disposed to maintain an ability in the race to immediately shake
off an existing state or semi-determined condition in which
it found itself.   They, however, had the idea that contemplating an ideal would eventually lead to its adoption and translation into fact by society and not by individuals here and
there   They were interested in *social* progress rather than
individual welfare and *individual* processes.   This social pre-
occupation of the Utopians and utopianism should be stressed.
For the *laissez-faire* attitude, so common with respect to the
future, they substituted a partial control of society by social
ideals and social idealists.

The Utopians felt that *society by its own free will could
reconstruct its methods of direction and control,* and here lies
another significant aspect of Utopias.   While they do not act
as effectively as the customs of the past in bringing conformity,
yet they have a marked potency.   They serve to bring about
an ascendancy of the future over the present.   They develop
a control which looks ahead and prepares for that which may
be.   This is noticeably the case in a dynamic society where
the look backward is more and more the sure sign of decay or
denotes some other attitude which has fallen into ill-repute.

The Utopians, one and all, from the prophets on, *recognized
the ability of men to surpass themselves.*   In the collective
human will they beheld a power, which, if set in motion along

superior lines will determine the course of humanity. They insisted that human beings may achieve happiness and greater perfection if only they will so to do. They saw that social advance is artificial, the fruit of purpose and design. They all recognized the need of a higher moral and spiritual development, and with a rare optimism felt that this was possible. All of them would create an environment where man could attain his true spiritual and mental stature. This is the very essence of the best constructive thought of to-day.

Their utopianism 'all breathes the spirit that *there is nothing we cannot do if we but strongly enough will to do it.* They are full of the "will-to-transformation" as Todd calls it.[10] But, again, it must be a willing which contemplates means as well as ends. The Utopians nearly all had the idea that society was responsible for environment; especially the spiritual environment; they believed that the individual erred because of defective social inheritance and environment. But they also saw that if proper surroundings were provided even relatively mediocre stuff could be made into a desirable social element. Therefore, they demanded a careful organization and use of the means we have pointed out in our search for utopianistic elements. Centuries ahead of their time they realized that not only do individuals sin against society, but that society also sins against the individual. They, by deliberately devised telic agencies would convert this detrimental aggression into one of mutual benefit and constructive effort.

Plato and More, and Campanella and Bacon after him were *the prophets of the modern eugenics movement.*[11] Handicapped by the absence of a theory of heredity, and upheld only by a strong social idealism, they regarded the supreme impulse of procreation as a sacred function, to be exercised in the light of scientific knowledge The future welfare of the race demanded that only physically perfect, valorous and high-spirited individuals should procreate. Plato and Campanella both

10 "Theories of Social Progress," p 506

11 Plato's was the first comprehensive scheme of eugenics in the history of social or biological philosophy, but Theognis, another Greek antedating Plato by nearly two hundred years, clearly perceived the principles of eugenics as applied to the human race

went so far as to advocate the making of unions for the end of procreation with the assistance of the elders or the "great Master" or physician aided by the chief matrons. These Utopians saw the necessity of sound physique and mentality as a basis for perfection; they saw that the quality of a civilization is to a large extent determined by breed; they saw that the foundation must be sound if a lofty superstructure is to be reared. They vaguely conceived this auto-evolution,—human selection based on acceptable parentage, as against natural selection—as a means of improving human kind and hence bringing about a more rapid social advance. This luminous conception of racial betterment, is only now beginning to stir men to action. Yet, it, like most of the other elements mentioned, was of Utopian origin.

The Utopians from Plato onward, almost without exception, *advocated the equality of the sexes.* For them society could not afford to thwart and by custom enthrall half the population and lose its superior services. They made women not only the companions of men, but also the religious, political and civil equals of men, permitting them to enjoy the same opportunities of achievement, and to make their contributions to social advance. At the same time most of them recognized the profound physiological differences of the sexes and made due allowance for them. In these respects also the Utopians anticipated what is only coming to be recognized by the progressives of our day.

In Plato, and it is hinted at in others, especially by More, one finds the *first advocacy of preventive medicine.* He encouraged gymnastics and the care of the body because they rendered resort to medical art unnecessary. Consequently he felt that the primary purpose of the physician was not to cure diseases, but rather the establishing of a program of exercise and the advocacy of such diet as would make diseases and ills impossible. He anticipated the conception that prevention is better than cure, and set up a standard for medical science which it has only recently adopted. More, in advocating the elimination of crowding in cities, the playing of games, the prohibition of all places breeding vice and disease, and his supreme emphasis upon good health in general also tended to substitute preventive measures for remedial medicines. It may be said that the various eugenics programs of the Utopians also were directed to this end.

Another broad heralding of a form of enlightenment which men have lately adopted was that of *religious toleration.* Early Modern Utopians, especially More and Harrington, in a time of religious absolutism and enforced uniformity, dared to advocate the toleration of all religious views, not manifestly anti-social. Most of them had religions of reason, which discarded false beliefs and useless forms and permitted the native force of religion to shine forth. The bases of morality were alone safeguarded. They foresaw what men have only recently established as a working method after they have suffered centuries of inquisitions, persecutions, excommunications, bigotry and intolerance.

Akin to this is the conception of some form of *social religion* which we find among the Utopian Socialists, particularly Saint-Simon and Cabet. They saw the stiltedness and hollowness of a dogmatized and partly moribund religion,—one which had come to consist of forms and ceremonials and creeds. They saw that religion must be regenerated, made human and helpful, a driving social force and an invigorating stimulant to social conduct, inspiring a fearless meeting of the future; not a drag, a social soporific, a thing which makes men cringe and fear. Stressing brotherhood and socialized ethics, they sought universal happiness rather than universal conformity. We cannot fail to recognize their influence in present day thought.

The *social theory of property* now coming to be held doubtless also goes back in considerable part to some of the Utopians, who emphasized it in rather a crude way. Nearly all of them were exponents of a socio-economic philosophy which vested the ultimate sovereign power of ownership in the state, both for land and most other forms of property. They held to this because the Utopian state was one of a fraternal coöperation aiming at the common good. This utopian conception may in part at least have been responsible also for the prevailing interpretation of property rights as residing only in the state.

To-day we hold that nothing can be owned in any absolute sense. Property, inheritance, and income taxes, the police power, the right of eminent domain are all evidence of this. Neither the money a man earns nor the property he holds is his own. The fact that the state usually though not always pays compensation for the property it appropriates in no manner invalidates this principle. In time of war, food, crops, clothing, industries, etc., are seized by the state. In time of disaster everything can be taken lawfully. The state refuses to recognize private property rights if the general welfare demands that it be made available for public use. The essence of property lies in the good will of the state   The Utopians originated this idea and made it current mental coin.

An Utopian contribution of great importance is *their recognition of the utility of social institutions.* To be sure, this was not true of all of them. With the prophets and Jesus utopianism was individual and subjective. It was the secular writers, including Augustine, however, who perceived that redemption may, in fact must, be objective or institutional, since only thus can the resistance of highly elaborated systems be overcome, and the new saving doctrine be promulgated and put into effect. They sensed the need of definite agencies to mold the social will and bring social changes to pass.

The most significant institution and the most powerful utopianistic measure of the Utopians was *education.* They felt that it was possible by this means to turn thorny, unproductive, selfish, shirking, exploiting, sinful, cross-grained human beings into righteous men, coöperators, good citizens, members of a great united human brotherhood, or as in the case of the ethico-religious Utopians, into members of a great theocracy. Their philosophy was a constructive optimism based on the amenability of the individual mind to proper direction. Among the prophets we first note the careful efforts at instruction of the people; in Plato we see that the realization of the Idea of the Good is the ultimate condition of a proper State animated by true justice, and it is education which is necessary if this realization is to be attained; the ministry of Jesus was for the purpose of inculcating a socialized ethic; the early modern Utopians all emphasize education hard—Bacon even creating an extensive system; similarly the Utopian Socialists made it an integral part of their schemes of social regeneration.

To the Utopians education was one of society's main instruments for realizing its destiny. The types of education which they stressed were not repetitive, memoriter, pedantic, and therefore non-progressive, but a dynamic culture, of a functional and social nature, practical withal and fitting for life, —one which developed the perceptive powers, physical endurance, domestic qualities, skill and the powers of social discipline. Their educational systems were active factors in maintaining the perfect worlds they described. The Utopians, as most later social thinkers, saw that education was a marvelously efficient agent of social control and social direction in that it made for self-control and discipline, in that it suggested rewards and penalties for conduct; they saw it as a means of incorporating new ideas and ideals into the group intelligence, so that they would become convictions, and lead to new socialized activity; they saw its effectiveness in fitting human beings for the performance of those daily industrial tasks for which they were best fitted, and in training for family life; they saw it as a method of fitting men for the tasks of citizenship and participation in public affairs. Judging from the spirit of their discussions of education they considered it a process whereby perfect social units might be created. It was an agency which not only enabled men to adjust themselves to their environment, but which also enabled men to adjust their environment to meet their physical, social and spiritual needs. It was a means whereby progressive ideas of morality and social obligations, government and law could be grafted upon the mind and determine its development. It was an effective means for the social manipulation and control of ideas, standards, values, habits of thinking and acting, and indirectly even of industrial processes. It was the utopianistic measure *par excellence*.

Among recent social philosophers we have an exalted exponent of this idea. According to Lester F. Ward social progress is not determined entirely by evolution as Spencer and the scientific socialists have maintained, for evolution can be manipulated and accelerated through the rôle of the mind and will. By bringing full educational opportunities within reach of all, society would be enabled to capitalize all of its latent assets of human capacity, and perfection would be attained. In maintaining this principle, Ward had support which the Utopians did not have, because he was in the presence of a universal press, a national, free, compulsory educational system, libraries, etc., to point to, and from which he could receive encouragement. All the greater marvel that the Utopians should have dared to entertain such ideas!

The most notable example of a Utopian institution for the *advancement of knowledge* and the benefit of the race was Francis Bacon's House of Salomon, a College of Research, previously discussed, which he had himself thought of trying to create if he could become master of some existing foundation in Cambridge and Oxford. This research idea is not in his "Novum Organum," his greatest work, which embodied his scientific methods, a book that had almost no influence upon his own time nor the seventeenth century; it was only the eighteenth century which read and discussed it. The conception of the research body was woven into the utopian fragment "New Atlantis" embodying many of the same ideas. His immediate purpose in writing this was doubtless to move King James to found a Salomon's House in England. Yet much as James had affected the character of a second Salomon, he took little or no interest in the intellectual reformation urged by his Chancellor. The fact that Bacon left the work unfinished, and without even publishing the fragments and turned his hand to other things, shows that he had no sanguine hopes of producing any immediate result.

And yet such a luminous and valuable conception could not remain unnoticed. Shortly after Bacon's death the general principle was already being put into effect in England and it eventually spread to many European countries. Prof. Nichols [12] writes: "It is admitted that the suggestion of the 'College of Philosophy' instituted in London (1645) and after

[12] In "Francis Bacon, his Life and Philosophy," Vol. II, p. 236.

the Restoration extended into the 'Royal Society' (1662) was
due to the prophetic scheme of 'Solomon's House' in the 'New
Atlantis.' Wallis, one of the founders of the Society, exalts
him by name, along with Galileo, as their master. Sprat says,
'It was a work becoming the largeness of Bacon's wit to devise and greatness of Clarendon's prudence to establish.' Boyle
credits for its inauguration "that profound naturalist . . .
our great Verulam' Dr. Thomas Sprat, just mentioned,
bishop of Rochester, and first historian of the society writes in
his 'History of the Royal Society'" (1667) [13] "I shall only
mention one great Man who had the true Imagination of the
whole extent of this enterprise, as it is now set on foot, and
that is Lord Bacon." [14] Joseph Glanvil, in his "Scepsis Sci-
entifica" says, "Solomon's House" in the "New Atlantis" was
a prophetic scheme of the Royal Society." Henry Olden-
burg (c. 1615–1677) one of the first secretaries of the Society,
speaks of the new eagerness to obtain scientific data as "a
work begun by the single care and conduct of the excellent Lord
Verulam " [15]

Bacon thus through the "New Atlantis" provided the model
for the Royal Society which eventually developed into the
British Research Society, and his predominating influence was
thus firmly established in the generation which succeeded his
own.

But his influence extended far beyond the boundaries of his
own country, and is active in the foundations of most all the
scientific societies. Mr. M. C. Adams [16] says, "Even in Italy,
Galileo's own country, in 1714 Count Marsigli founded an
institution at Bologna in which, says Fontenelle, people thought
they saw the accomplishment of Bacon's 'Atlantis,' and in 1806
when this institution had to be reëstablished, it, was placed once
more 'under the auspices of the great Englishman, the great
Chancellor of England, the pillar of a straight-forward, social

[13] P. 35

[14] Thomas Tenison in his "Baconia," p. 264, says practically the same
thing

[15] All quoted by G C. M Smith, editor of "New Atlantic," Pitt Press
Series, Cambridge, 1900, pp xxviii–xxxii

[16] "Philosophie de F. Bacon," 1890, p 343, quoted by Smith, op. cit

and solid philosophy.' Bacon, therefore, certainly had a happy and fruitful idea, and above all, he had shown that Governments and private individuals have every interest in realizing it."

The "New Atlantis" not only led to the foundation of the Royal Society and similar academies abroad, it was one of the inspiring causes of that mighty work of collaboration, the French "Encyclopedie," in which the savants of the eighteenth century gathered all the results attained by science up to that date and used them as a battering-ram against established abuses in Church and State. Speaking of the "tree of human knowledge" which he and his fellow Encyclopædists had constructed and the chain of ideas which had guided them in that vast undertaking,—Diderot writes in the Prospectus,[17] "If we have come at it successfully, we shall owe most to the Chancellor Bacon, who threw out the plan of an universal dictionary of sciences and arts, at a time when, so to say, neither arts nor sciences existed. That extraordinary genius when it was impossible to write a history of what was known, wrote one of what it was necessary to learn."

Bacon's "New Atlantis" can truthfully be said to be the basis of all modern research and human benefit foundations. [18]

[17] Diderot—"Oeuvres Completes" (1876) XIII, p. 133, quoted by Smith, op. cit.

[18] Smith on pp. xxvi–xxviii, says

"There are indeed many points in which modern science seems to fulfill Bacon's anticipations. Our scientific expeditions and consular reports serve the purpose of the missions' sent out from the 'New Atlantis' in enlightening us with regard to foreign countries. Our observatories take the place of the high towers for the study of atmospheric conditions We concern ourselves much with the problem of applying the force of waterfalls as a motive power Where Bacon speaks of 'Chambers of Health where we qualifie the Aire . . for the cure of diverse Diseases,' Mr Spedding tells us that the experiment has been tried and some relief has been obtained in cases of phthisis by the inhaling of oxygenated air. Some of the greatest results in modern medicine have been obtained by those experiments on animals both in the way of surgical operations and treatment by drugs which Bacon advocated in the 'New Atlantis.' . . The development of new varieties in the animal and vegetable world by cross-breeding is now systematically pursued as Bacon recommended. Mr. Spedding tells us that when Geoffroi St. Hilaire was attacked for advocating the study of 'monstrosities,' he invoked the authority of Bacon. Telescopes, microscopes, microphones, speaking tubes, have been in-

Thus has Bacon's utopianism lived on. Though productive as a scientist yet his greatest contribution lies in the impetus which his advocacy of inductive and experimental methods gave to future scientific investigation. As he himself said, he rang the bell which called the other wits together.[19]

Another institution of social improvement stressed much by the Utopians was *the State*. From Plato on most of them made the State supreme, though they differed in the degree of sovereignty they would give it. Insofar as they accepted or advocated it, it was as a social institution erected by the people for their own welfare. Plato, for example, conceived the State, not as a governing and corrective body, but as an association of ethically minded individuals bound together by thoughts of a common purpose and all serving in their proper places. It was for all of them a means to an end, a definite agency, the purpose of which was to surround the individual with those influences which will make him most happy and cause him to be of greatest service; a means of providing liberty and equal opportunity to the individual. Some, especially the Utopian

vented or improved according to the dreams of the philosopher The imitating of smells is, as Mr Ellis points out, an achievement of modern chemistry. 'The oil of pineapples and that of bitter almonds enable confectioners to imitate perfectly the scent and flavor of pineapples and bitter almonds respectively and both . . . are got from very offensive substances.' One of Bacon's sentences suggests to us the Maxim gun. We can say of ourselves 'wee have some Degrees of Flying in the Ayre . . . wee have Shipps and Boates for going under Water . . . wee imitate also Motions of Living Creatures by Images of Men etc.' We have not only an army of investigators in the different laboratories of Europe, we have learned societies which discuss and coordinate the results arrived at, and journals in which approved results are published. Our great inventors receive statues in public places with as fully recognized a right as our princes, soldiers and statesmen Finally the results of scientific research, —especially when they have a direct bearing on the general interests— are often published officially One Government Department issues prognostications in regard to the weather, coming storms, etc ; another gives counsel as to necessary measures in time of plague to man or beast In these many ways did Bacon forecast the course of scientific research, even though it cannot be said that Bacon had himself developed the methods of modern investigation "

[19] Lee, Sidney, "Great Englishmen of the Sixteenth Century," N. Y., 1904, p. 250.

Socialists, stressed the State particularly as a means of providing the proper sort of environment. All saw it as an instrumentality, and not as an end, even though most of them lived during times when the State was worshiped and government was absolute and by the few. The democratic movements have caused us to conceive of the State in the same manner as did the Utopians. We, like the Utopians, are sure that much of the welfare and progress of society depends on the character and management of the State.

In the case of our most notable political Utopia, Harrington's "Oceana"—which dealt almost entirely with the machinery of an enlightened state—we have a brilliant example of utopianism coming true. Professor Dwight writing some thirty odd years ago [20] traced the potency of Harrington's ideals in shaping political institutions and thought in America. John Adams, we are told, was perfectly familiar with Harrington's "Oceana" and much influenced by his teachings, as his writings show. The principles of the "empire of laws" and rotation of office in the Constitution of Massachusetts were taken directly from the "Oceana." The secret ballot was made part of the first constitution of New York State but a hundred years after Harrington voiced the thought. The idea finally, in 1872, triumphed in England when it was applied to parliamentary and municipal elections, the greatest precautions being taken to preserve Harrington's cardinal point of secrecy. The sentence from "Oceana": "The exercise of all just authority over a free people ought to arise from their own consent," was uppermost in the mind of Thomas Jefferson when he drafted the declaration of American Independence; in fact, he made use of its very words in maintaining that governments derive their just powers from the consent of the governed. Both American and British statesmen were attracted by Harrington's unique proposals and finally embraced them.

The Utopians were the source of suggestion and perhaps also the *founders of the modern communist and socialistic phi-*

[20] Dwight, Theodore W., "Political Institutions and Political Thought," Political Science Quarterly, Vol II, pp. 1–44

losophy and the movements based upon it, as many writers of importance will testify.[21]   More's "Utopia," and to a certain extent, Plato's "Republic," have become a sort of source book to which all socialists go for many of their fundamental principles.   In fact, the foremost modern exponent of scientific socialism says, "With the 'Utopia' modern Socialism begins "[22]   In the first place, as we have repeatedly indicated, the Utopians were protesters against the existing order, and awakened the fire of agitation.   Then with the evils of the dawning of the capitalistic organization of society in sixteenth century England already acute, More felt it to be a system productive of unavoidable injustice, inequality and misery. And its continuance, even with palliatives, offered vain hope of social betterment.   More and his followers therefore absolutely condemned private property which they thought to be the basis of the capitalistic system, and embraced the social conception of property, making all productive property socially owned and controlled.   From them has been derived the socialistic theory of property current to-day.   He also, and most of his followers down to Louis Blanc, would have absolute control of production by the state in order to do away with the exploitation and the economic wastes and the social chaos which intermittently appear in society conducted on the basis of private enterprise.   This in the interests of social welfare.   Furthermore, "The problems which every socialist state builder since has felt it his duty to solve, the problems of population and marriage, of hours of labor, of the use of money, of a possible decreased productiveness, are faced frankly and discussed with a quaint ingenuity and a broad human sympathy which have made 'the golden book of Thomas More' with Plato's earlier dream the most imperishable of all socialistic visions."[23]   It finally remained for Robert Owen about 1835 to give the name

[21] See, for example, Guthrie, "Socialism before the French Revolution"; Kautsky, "Die Vorlaufer des Neueren Sozialismus"; Muckle, "Die Geschichte der sozialistischen Ideen im 19ten Jahrhundert", Spargo and Arner, "Elements of Socialism"; Engels, "Die Entwicklung des Sozialismus von der Utopie zur Wissenschaft "

[22] Kautsky, op cit , p 466

[23] Skelton, "Socialism, A Critical Analysis," p 7.

"socialism" to the movement, though, to be sure, his efforts were of a benevolent rather than democratic nature.

The *study of sociology itself* may owe much of its original impetus to the influence of the Utopians. Saint-Simon in his "Nouveau Christianisme" laid down the principles of a collective condition of society, a new fraternalism, which while dreamy and idealistically humanitarian, yet attracted attention. Futhermore, he developed in connection with his utopian thought a policy or "politique" of observation and experiment on the collective condition of society. These ideas particularly influenced Auguste Comte, a disciple of Saint-Simon, and the inventor of the term "sociology," who, since he was dissatisfied with Saint-Simon's analysis, was led by it to work out a better scheme of social analysis and organization in his "Positive Philosophy," which served to outline roughly the field of sociology.[24] In general, it may be said that the Utopians with their recognition of society as an object of necessary study, with their comprehension of social phenomena, with their partial analysis of social processes, with their conscious attempts to provide a happier world to live in, were approaching sociology as we conceive of it to-day. It remained, however, for the propounders of the doctrine of constant change or evolution, such as Hegel, Marx, Darwin, Huxley and Spencer, with their ideas of origin and development, and the insight into telic processes which later men derived from this form of writing, to place the study on a working basis as an agency of social helpfulness.[25]

We might continue by examining various other ideas and ideals presented by single Utopians, such as More's and Bacon's conception of the importance of the family, or Saint-Simon's emphasis on the expert as an agency of advance, noting their widespread influence to-day. We might also discuss at length the Saint-Simonian Church with its broad organization and its missionaries, and the Fourierist, Owenite and Icarian movements in America, or the influence of Blanc on Guild Social-

[24] Bogardus, E S, "A History of Social Thought," Los Angeles, 1922, pp 210–211

[25] This fact will be discussed at greater length in the following chapter.

ism and French Syndicalism,[26] to add emphasis to what we have been advocating in these pages, but it is unnecessary. Utopianism is not expressed in vain; sooner or later, in some form, it becomes fact. Nothing is wholly lost.

[26] The idea that organized trades will eventually supplant the State.

CHAPTER X

THE LIMITED PERSPECTIVE OF THE UTOPIANS

While many of the ideas and ideals of the Utopians transcended their age and even later ages, while the Utopians were geniuses and inventors, men in many respects ahead of their times, they were, nevertheless, men of their own times also, with the limitations in social perspective which all men have. No man, however great, can foresee all the social changes of the future. Some changes can be anticipated, to be sure, else the study of history would be of no avail, but society is the sport of ever-changing forces intermittently accelerated and retarded. No man can have at his command all knowledge, for knowledge is gradually unfolding. We of to-day, millenniums or centuries afterward, with our fuller knowledge of society and our sounder social philosophy, are able to discern in the schemes of the Utopians weaknesses and limitations of which they were unconscious. To review these is the purpose of this chapter.

The Utopians *failed, in a broad way, to see the necessity of a sound physical basis for social advance.* The ethico-religious Utopians were entirely ideological in their schemes—utterly removed from the earth. Nor did the Early Modern Utopians perceive the necessity of supplying economic sufficiency for the whole group. Only with the Utopian Socialists do we have a dawning of this truth, and even they overlooked the tension between population and resources. It took the Industrial Revolution to arouse men to that problem. We see now that the greater the productive power of society and the fuller the equipment of life on its physical side, the more time there will be for leisure and culture, the more social and spiritual capital there will be to invest, and the broader will be the opportunities for conceiving and perfecting means of social advance.

None of the old Utopians gave this a thought, and only few of the Utopian Socialists grasped its significance. It is only more recently that men, stimulated doubtless by the enormous economic advance of the last century, have seen how fundamental to all other activity are well organized, efficient economic institutions.

While the eugenics conceptions of Plato, More, Bacon and Campanella were marvelously potent, they were the only ones to comprehend even vaguely the importance of the individual's physical and psychical makeup, and to recognize that in large measure it reflects the makeup of his parents. In brief, most of them had not caught the significance of heredity; they failed to see the individual physical basis of social perfection.

It was *impossible for the Utopians to obtain a correct view of human nature.* Hence frequently they went astray. In the first place, they assumed that men were originally perfect, born angels, as Rousseau said, after corrupted by the social environment due to the lack of education or because of deficient and badly operating institutions, or to the knavery and ignorance of the past; in brief born to be the pawn of environment. But as Professor Ross says,[1] "Nothing is more foolish than to imagine that all the defects in people flow from defects in society and will vanish if only we organize society on right lines." The removal of evil suggestions and evil institutions will not leave men saints. In spite of the fact that they were courageously groping for them there were human traits which the Utopians wholly failed to comprehend, and others which they pitifully misconceived. And it is the control of these which is fundamental to any movement for social perfection. For example, tendencies developed in man hundreds of generations ago must be included, for they are not buried but will continue to break out and make trouble for centuries in the future.

With the exception of Fourier, the Utopians *did not recognize the importance in social life of these instincts, or the social forces developing out of them.* They were thinking exclusively of what human beings ought to be and ought to want And yet here are powerful innate traits, tendencies or pro-

[1] "Principles of Sociology," p. 4.

pensities, slowly evolved through an immense period of time to assist in individual survival, primary social forces motivating man's conduct constantly, assisting him in his undertakings and in molding his institutions, which cannot be ignored because they are so absolutely basic and practically unchangeable. They did not face this greatest problem before human society, that of the rational control of human instincts in accordance with social advantage; the harnessing of these impulses so that they will work with and for civilizing endeavors. They did not do it, because they knew nothing about them.

It was due to this dead load of ignorance that many of their schemes were better never carried out; they would have repressed or checkmated these native forces, and consequently would have cramped people's lives. Human nature cannot be laced in a strait-jacket; reforms that consciously or unconsciously attempt to do it are foredoomed to failure. To be sure human tendencies may be redirected and sublimated, but in any case they may not be left out of the reckoning. Among some of the suggestions of the Utopians doomed to futility on the above grounds are the following: In proposing the communism of goods they flouted the deep-seated instinct of self-interest. Recent attempts have shown the utter folly of doing this, and the social disaster which results. They erred also in lightly doing away with private property, the greatest and most natural inducement to individual effort and achievement. Deny it, and your scheme fails. An ordinary man has to have a personal stake in his job; and no idealism we can inculcate holds out a more effective lure. Ownership appeals not only to the acquisitive instinct, but also to the parental and self-assertive instincts. Fostered and diffused, it makes for social contentment; repress it and disaster follows.

Plato and Campanella advocated a communism of women, which would doubtless run counter to the deep-seated monogamic sense among Western peoples and would be a constant source of jealousy. The over-riding of the parental instinct in the breeding schemes of Plato and Campanella also runs counter to human nature as we find it. The barrack life offered in several Utopias denies that seclusion which all people desire for the private functions of life. The uniformity of apparel also runs counter to the native desire for self-adornment and self-distinction. People rebel at being all run in the same mold; they cannot be brought to conform absolutely to one rigid standard of life conduct, because, owing to hereditary factors each individual is distinct from all others. Individuals always will differ in capacity, which is in large measure hereditarily determined. Individuality and character, while partly the result of social environment influencing the individual to assume certain mental attitudes and control his feelings and emotions in certain ways, are primarily inherent and unchangeable, the products of congenital transmission. The Utopians, in many cases, held a view of society entirely too artificial; in building their ideal social order they thought nothing of over-riding natural affections and balking natural desires and impulses. They did not see folks as we, with our better knowledge, see them.

The Utopians *did not perceive that life is a constant struggle and probably will always be.* Hear Mr. H. G. Wells speak through his "Modern Utopia," which is essentially a rational discussion of conceivable social progress. "The old Utopias— save for the breeding schemes of Plato and Campanella—ignored that reproductive competition among individualities which is the substance of life, and dealt essentially with incidentals. The endless variety of men, their endless gradation of quality, over which the hand of selection plays, and to which we owe the unmanageable complication of real life, is tacitly set aside. The real world is a vast disorder of accidents and incalculable forces in which men survive or fail A Modern Utopia, unlike its predecessors, dare not pretend to change the last condition; it may order and humanize the conflict, but men must still survive or fail." [2] "There must be competition in life of some sort to determine who are to be pushed to the edge, and who are to prevail and multiply." [3] "Whatever we do, man will remain a competitive creature, and though moral and intellectual training may vary and enlarge his conception

[2] Wells, "Modern Utopia," p 135.
[3] Op. cit , p. 137.

of success and fortify him with refinements and consolations, no Utopia will ever save him completely from the emotional drama of struggle for exultations and humiliations, from pride and prostration and shame. He lives in success and failure, just as inevitably as he lives in space and time." [4]

These various difficulties may have arisen out of another limitation of the Utopians, namely, their *over-social view*. They contemplated men too exclusively in the mass; with a few exceptions they failed to perceive that individuals must be considered *alone* as well as *together;* and that these characteristics are far different than those of groups. Above all, they did not see that, to be successful, social reform must begin with individuals. Mr. Henry Jones writing of the successful social reformer has said, "He knows that every individual of them all has his own internal life, intensely real and significant to *him;* and society is not to him a general term, but a system of personalities, every one of them unique. And he has the gift of sympathetic imagination, to construct their experience from within." [5]   We are not criticizing their social point of view in general, or their contributions to the conception of social will. We merely insist that in order to offer a workable Utopia they ought to have considered the individual more.

In support of the contention that the Utopians failed to grasp the full significance of the life about them, it can be said that in their projects of reform *they failed to start with things as they are.* This was partly the result of a too limited social experience, partly, the by-product of an over-luxuriant imagination. They permitted a gulf to develop between the Is and their To Be. Moral enthusiasts make no headway with their reforms unless they propose changes continuous with the social processes that have brought society thus far on its way. Men must start with what they find and build up from that; if they find good, make it better; if bad, eliminate it, or improve it. Humanity can never transcend the conditions of its existence. Movement toward Utopia calls for a conception, not of the best imaginable world at the moment, but the best possible

[4] Op cit , p 137.
[5] "The Working Faith of the Social Reformer," London, 1910, p. 7.

world. We must focus our efforts on the scientific and the practicable. The fulcrum for raising society must be found in things as they are. The ideas that you expect to disseminate and use as the basis of your reform may not be too far removed from the current thought of the time, nor may the discrepancy between what you want and what is be too great.

It may also be said in criticism of some of the Utopians [6] that *they failed to see how to use the spirit of protest for reform purposes.* They understood only vaguely the possibilities of directing society; their potency, as we have seen, lay in the ideals they proposed, not their measures. They were weak in that they left their ideals merely as ideals, and did not attempt to set in motion agencies of action. As idealists they were great; but if they had been agitators as well as idealists they might have been greater. For quicker effect there must be propaganda and action along with the ideals. Moreover, some of the Utopians removed their perfect states so far from earth that one wonders how they could have had the potency they did. Their schemes lacked the attractiveness necessary to win adherents to their cause and give society a definite direction.

The Utopians, with the exception of the most recent pseudo-Utopians, *erred in assuming that their ideal states were the "ne plus ultra,"* the last word in social speculation, the final goal of social endeavor. They could conceive of no progress beyond their projected state. As early as Plato we find this fault, since he pictures his state an unshakable, unchangeable order founded upon the highest righteousness, improvement on which is not only unnecessary, but impossible. We find the same defect in most of the others. To-day we recognize this as untrue to life. Complete and lasting human happiness is irrevocably denied; it is the nature of the race to be forever dissatisfied. Furthermore, the Utopians seemed to have forgotten, or perhaps never recognized that only he finds happiness who is always anticipating and striving for something better

They also *erred in presenting their Utopias as going concerns.* They, especially the Utopian Socialists, felt that it was possible to work out beforehand in the most minute detail

[6] Not the prophets, Jesus and some of the Utopian Socialists.

a scheme for the complete ordering of social, political and industrial affairs,—schemes which might be realized by their
contemporaries.   While they should be praised without end for
grappling with society's most vexing problems and for pro-
pounding a new social dispensation, it must be confessed that
they went to a ridiculous extreme in these laudable endeavors,
laying down rigid specifications for every contingency, omitting
no least detail.   They made human nature over into a depend-
able regularity, leaving no room for spontaneous growth.   The
long sought social order leaped complete from the brains of its
devisers.[7]   They were dominated by the idea that a condition
of social quietism can be reached and maintained.

In this connection we contend that the Utopians, as many
other social idealists, *were wrong in thinking a state of social
perfection possible*.   There is an idea common that social motion is toward an absolute form of society, a forever fixed
social state.   But as Huxley says, "The theory of evolution encourages no millennial anticipations."[8]   Social perfection is an
illusive ideal, always receding as we advance.   Humanity's
perfection will never be attained; it is only possible to work toward it.   However far evolution, even directed evolution,
should take us, we will always be merely approaching Utopia;
Utopia is forever a becoming.   As Nordau contends, "All
known facts compel a reason which is closed against mystic
reverie to assume an eternal, regular, cyclic movement, perpetually passing through similar phases, and to reject as ir-
rational the idea of a goal to which the earth is constantly approaching.[9]   History shows that society is ever moving toward
something different from anything yet realized or even compre-
hended.   Nothing endures, nothing is precise and certain, the
present state of social life or social thought is not final, there is
no abiding thing in all we know.   Our ideals or social perfection are merely the best thought of our own age.   All is meta-
morphosis.

What we must think about is social progress—a constant be-

7 Skelton, op. cit., p 83.
8 "Evolution and Ethics," p 85
9 "Interpretation of History," p. 328.

coming on the part of ever restless, changing human beings. The Cro-Magnon doubtless had an ideal of social perfection, and how it must have differed from those of to-day! In thinking of social advance we should allow for thousands of years yet to be lived. Hence we dare not limit the height to which the vital flux of nature through man may rise.[10]   The social idealist should have a critical and elastic mind, and recognize that his ideal is merely one of the moment, defective to-morrow, and positively useless day after to-morrow. The thing to strive for is social progress, not social perfection; incessant becoming, not stagnant being.

This critical view, however, ought not in the least to weaken social endeavor, or the functioning of constructive social institutions. Instead of holding up the "good," or the "best" of the moment, as the goal, it holds up the best that the race at its best will ever conceive. At the moment we follow the "best" as we see it, but we must be willing to admit that it presently will be different. And we must be willing to permit, in fact, must encourage, the constant revamping and improving of social ideals. What we yearn for is that social order which will realize the greatest good for perennial humanity.

Because of the limitations discussed above and others which will be discussed, the last century saw the passing of Utopias. The Utopians prior to the Utopian Socialists had no surety of certainly realizing their hopes. Their states were perfect, utterly devoid of change and development, and far removed from this world. While they had luminous ideas of reconstruction, they lacked precedent to give substantial foundation to their views. They were thus spinners of an ideal social fabric, which they hoped might be, and yet which they rather felt would not be, at least to any great extent. This thought as expressed by Plato, with regard to the existence of the ideal republic in heaven, has been discussed under several different

[10] "I see no limit to the extent to which intelligence and will, guided by sound principles of investigation, and organized in common effort, may modify the conditions of existence, for a period longer than that now covered by history" Huxley, op cit , p. 36.

heads previously in this work.   The same idea is rather humorously expressed by More.   We are told that there was no doubt about Hythloday having told More and Peter Giles of the exact situation of the island of Utopia, but unfortunately at the very moment their attention, as he is reminded in a letter from Giles, was drawn off by a servant, and one of the company coughed so loud, as the result of a cold caught on shipboard, that they were prevented from hearing, and the secret perished with Hythloday and to this day the site of Utopia remains unknown.   For the Utopians society was an uncontrollable beast, with its evil tempers, diseases, and ungovernable natural forces, distorted bodies and souls, and its perverted institutions.   And they had no conception of how to begin converting what they saw about them into something better.   Because of the supposed impossibility of attainment, they chose the form we customarily speak of as Utopian.   Only with difficulty could they conceive of these pictured perfect states as possibilities; instead they thought of them as fantastic insubstantial imaginings, for society could not be immediately changed as the result of conscious and arbitrary construction.

On the other hand, the Utopian Socialists were students of Rousseau, and imbued with the spirit of the French Revolution.   For them anything was possible if men would but resolve to have it so.   The French Revolution demonstrated in dramatic fashion that things could be accomplished if men would but sufficiently will their accomplishment.   Therefore, the Utopian Socialists, while we think them visionary thought themselves practical, and as we have seen, felt that their schemes could be imposed with ease upon their contemporaries.[11]

[11] Skelton in writing of these unavoidably short-sighted and circumscribed points of view of the Utopians and their contemporaries says: "It leads in the planning for the future, to suggestions for the erection of new social structures, built to scale from carefully worked-out plans, wherein every detail of front, rear and side elevation has been provided beforehand.   There is little conception of social growth and development: once Nature's ideal system is discovered it may be stereotyped without limit.   Nothing can show more completely the difference between the preconceptions—or prejudices—of their time and of our post-Darwinian day than the sentence quoted from Cabet (Voyage en Icarie, p 64):

Both of these assumptions, while natural, must be branded as weaknesses to-day; they were unscientific and unreal. Proposals to remake the whole social structure on a rational pattern, were merely the logical outcome of the absolute and unhistorical thinking of the time. The Utopias were rather fantastic intellectual products because intellect and history had not yet learned to coöperate in anticipating future society. Because they lacked the historical point of view, they lacked knowledge of social movements, or how to originate them. With the rise of a theory of history and the thrifty growth of the idea of development or evolution, real utopias in the original sense have ceased to appear, for the necessity of supposing an unrealizable state, or the necessity of superimposing a perfect society upon an imperfect one, has ceased to be. This change dates from the birth of Hegelianism, and became difinite later with the work of Marx, Spencer and Darwin along the lines of evolution. History, before Hegel, offered an explanation of isolated phenomena, while rejecting almost altogether the notion of a universal story. There were theories of history before Hegel to be sure. The Christian or religious theory, of which we find some evidence in the writings of the Apocalyptists and in Augustine, held that development follows a preconceived plan, proceeding from the will of God, a sort of pathway of mankind determined by God. Herder exchanged the religious theory of development as the basis of history for a naturalistic theory of human continuity but even so there was a predetermination in it. Among other less clear sources, in Vico, for example, one gathers that even before Hegel it was dimly realized that all human existence is a unified process in which the concrete events, which are the subject of written history, are but incidental features; but this dim conception was not strong enough to color social thought, it had not yet reached the stage where it gave hope. It was merely a gestating principle.

'And yet how could the social organization escape being vicious since it was the work, not of a single man and a single assembly creating a complete and coördinate plan, but of time, of successive generations adding piece by piece.' To the Utopian this was valid and serious criticism; to the men of the twentieth century it is sheer irony." Op. cit , p. 73.

These nebulous conceptions were finally given concrete form in Hegel's famous "Lectures on the Philosophy of History" and in the works of other nineteenth century philosophers. History was not the expression of a predetermined plan, but was the result of laws immanent in historical life itself.[12] History was a sort of unfolding of the human spirit-cycle, repeating itself in different ages, a sort of inherent self-development.[13] The Hegelian school of history concerned itself almost solely with the spiritual and moral forces in history, conceiving of history as the conflict, triumph, defeat and mutual adjustment of human wills.[14] This idea of continuity and fluidity, once incorporated into social thinking, gave a conception of human progress. And with the spread of such an evolutionary idealism, social idealism ceased to be full of ingenious fancies of fertile minds; its elements had to be incorporated into the general process of social development, or they were useless. When the doctrines of the Utopian Socialists, for example, became blended with Hegelianism they ceased to be "utopian" and became "scientific." The Hegelian conception of evolution found in the writings of Karl Marx as early as 1848, marks the turning point in social theory.

Nowadays, with our ideas of evolution, we can take the same idealism, and weave it into a romance, yet somehow it does not seem preposterous, because we now have the conception that such things are possible, even probable. It is likely that each generation of the future will have its social ideals, a little more certain and complete, and more real—constantly better working

12 "History had by this time come to be regarded as a strictly self-dependent development of ideas in which each advance proceeds with rigid logical necessity from that which went before." Wundt, "Elements of Folk Psychology," N. Y, 1916, p 520.

13 Hegel took the metaphysics out of the conception of history and gave it a sound basis of natural development. "Hegel hatte die Geschichts-auffassung von der Metaphysik befreit, er hatte sie dialektisch gemacht—aber seine Auffassung der Geschichte war wesentlich idealistisch. Jetzt war der Idealismus aus seinem letzten Zufluchtsort, aus der Geschichts-auffassung, vertrieben, eine materialistische Geschichtsauffassung gegeben, und der Weg gefunden, um das Besusstsein der Menschen aus ihrem Sein, statt wie bisher ihr Sein aus ihrem Bewusstsein zu erklaren." Engels, "Die Entwicklung des Sozialismus von der Utopie zur Wissenschaft," p 25.

14 Thesis, antithesis, synthesis.

plans, instead of dreams. But the Utopians could not appeal to a spirit which recognized historical development. To-day in looking back we can see how Utopias and Utopianism have accelerated and assisted in redirecting the social movement, because we have become accustomed to the idea of development; but others before us could not do that. The so-called Utopias of the present are not Utopias in the sense of those which we have described and analyzed through the bulk of this work; they are merely a collection of the best modern thought on a variety of social, economic and political subjects, in many cases merely carrying a step or two further movements already under way. They are scientific and based on attained or attainable facts, and they are worked out in accordance with the natural order or sequence from existing conditions, true also to the law of cause and effect and duly regarding the limitations of nature, both human and physical.

Another fact has greatly contributed to the passing of Utopias. Even though the Utopias were themselves the products of accelerated intellectual advance, the Utopians, excepting Bacon and the recent pseudo-Utopians, failed to anticipate the startling progress on the way in human knowledge. The unprecedented intellectual activity with the splendid advance in physical science, in knowledge of human affairs, and the development of mechanical invention during the last century or so, has completely revolutionized man's conception of social progress. As man penetrates into the hidden intricacies of human consciousness and sub-consciousness, as he learns to utilize more and more of nature's resources and conquer the elements one after another by ingenious inventions in chemistry and mechanics such as the years now passing have seen produced, men are not forced to set their perfect states on distant isles or planets. No, the better thing is almost available; human ability applied in that direction will in the course of a few years or decades make it possible. This tremendous development of knowledge and through it of machinery, has bred in us a new spirit of faith in our own ability to conquer. We who within a decade have seen the political destinies of two of the world's greatest nations reversed, who have seen the air and depths of the sea conquered, who have been able to send messages across oceans by wireless, hear concerts hundreds of leagues away, who have seen cures found for such dread diseases as leprosy and tetanus, who have marked the stupendous advance in diabolical devices for dealing death and destruction (the same ingeniousness could be used for constructive purposes), are ready to assert that nothing is impossible. What would have been a revolutionary invention in the days of Thomas More, to-day gets only a few inches in the daily newspapers. Expectation has come to be the common attitude.

With the reign of the evolutionary principle, and of the conception of controllable forces, with human productive power magnified a thousandfold by machines, with the ability to shape opinion and direct the course of society, the hard-and-fast conception of the perfect state of society of Utopian philosophy has disappeared. But we need not deplore it; for it is still incumbent upon us to increase our store of the advantageous elements discussed in the previous chapter. The same spirit is still expressing itself, only now it is operating with this effective evolutionary principle. We now have been able to develop a technique of social change, which we trust, will in time make it possible more and more to correct man's faults and remedy his weaknesses. We have had demonstrated for us an improvement in life before undreamed of. To be sure individuals will continue to have limitations, and life must continue to be a continual adjustment, but we see that the more we secure a scientific control of the physical and social environment, the less radical and unpleasant these adjustments are likely to be, and the more can the orderly step-by-step process of advance be speeded up.[15]

But in spite of these weaknesses and limitations, we must

[15] "The Modern Utopia must be not static but kinetic, must shape not as a permanent state but as a hopeful stage, leading to a long ascent of stages. Nowadays we do not resist and overcome the great stream of things, but rather float upon it. We build now not citadels, but ships of state. For one ordered arrangement of citizens rejoicing in an equality of happiness safe and assured to them and their children for ever, we have to plan a flexible, common compromise in which a perpetually novel succession of individualities may converge most effectually upon a comprehensive onward development." Wells, "Modern Utopia," p. 5.

not discount the Utopians over much. We cannot expect men of five centuries or a millenium ago to have the same social knowledge that we have. While they were visionary, while some of their ideals were impracticable and their own concrete efforts at realizing them almost *nil,* their work has been worth while. Their writings have been a force, stimulating here, holding forth a temporary goal there, and suggesting untold possibilities beyond, if they did claim perfection; so that to-day if we observe closely, we see their influence on every hand, obscured and sometimes not easy to recognize, but present nevertheless. Considering the difficulties that confronted them we marvel that their weaknesses and limitations of perspective were as few as they are. As thinkers they were truly great. Some of their ideals may have been illusory, the products of an ungrounded optimism, and some of their ideas may have been fitted only to their own time, but nevertheless they have played a stupendous part in shaping human history.

Utopia never will quite come we may be certain, because it is always just beyond immediate attainment. Utopia is always a fleeting state. Its author encountering his principles realized would not know them, as we of a future generation do not recognize them as a Utopia come true. After all Utopia is not a social state, it is a state of mind.

THE END

INDEX

A

Abraham, Apocalypse of, 60.
Absolute equality, 206.
Absolute state control, 206.
Adaptationists, 285
Amauret, 153.
American Revolution, influence of, on French thought, 183
Amos, and Hosea, difference between, 15; as Utopian, 9; denunciation of his time, 12-13; social conditions of time of, 9-12; Utopia, 13-14; utopianism, 12-14.
Apocalypse, characteristics, 52; factors responsible for, 51-52.
Apocalypses, non-Jewish and non-Christian, 50 footnote.
Apocalyptists, 281; period, 50; sociological appraisal, 64-66; Utopias and utopianism, 50 ff
Aristocracy of education, 156
Artificial view of society, 162.
Astrology, 164
"Atéliers sociaux," 210.
Augustine, "City of God," 86-7; conception of Church, 92-3, life, 84; meaning of "City of God," 91-2; philosophy of history, 86; social and political background, 84-6; sociological valuation, 94, Utopianism of, 87-91.

B

Babeuf, François Noel, 188 ff ; life, 189; critic and idealist, 188; "Code de la Nature," 189; communist, 189; community of goods and of station, 190, dissensions through inequality, 190; mutual compact, 189; national organization of labor, 190; social mediocrity of, 191
Backlook, people with, 257.

Bacon, Francis, 146 ff.; life, 146-7; communism of knowledge of, 152; eugenic measures, 150, family the foundation of society, 148-9, House of Salomon, 293-6; influence of science, 147-8; marriage, 149-50; "New Atlantis," 146 ff.; relation to other works, 147-8; quoted, 266; college of science, 150-2; social will ordering progress, 152-3; welfare of people, 148.
Ballot, secret, 172-3.
Ballou, Adin, characterization of Robert Owen, 221.
Barker, Ernst, 102, quoted, 114.
Baruch, Book of, 59.
Bellamy, Edward, "Looking Backward," 225 ff.; absence of money, 232; community housekeeping, 233; distribution, 231; education, 234; equality of sexes, 234; industrial service, 229; integration of capital, 228; international peace, 231; jails, 233; labor credits, 232; labor question, 228; marriage, 235; nationally organized labor, 229; social order, 227; strikes, 227-8; supply and demand of workers, 229; wages, 230.
Black Death, 122.
Blanc, Louis, 208 ff ; life, 208-9; influence of Saint-Simon on, 209; "atéliers sociaux," 210, certainty of work, 210, fraternity, 210; happiness, 210; industrial centralization, 210; "Organization du Travail," 208; practical accomplishments, 212-13; practical nature, 209; social hierarchy, 211-12.
Bosanquet, Bernhard, 102.

315

British Research Society, 294.
Brotherhood, 207.

C

Gabet, Eltienne, 204 ff.; life, 204-5;
absolute equality, 206, absolute
state control, 206; brotherhood,
207, education, 207, influence of
Thomas More on, 205; new era,
205-6, state religion, 207.
Campanella, Thomas, "City of the
Sun," 153 ff.; life, 153-5, city-
state, 156; common dwellings and
dining rooms, 160, communism,
159; controlled mating, 162-3;
educational scheme, 158; elective
government, 156, equality of
sexes, 161; experts as rulers, 156-
7; influence on Saint-Simon, 193,
no classes, 161; state as devised
product, 158; Utopia and uto-
pianism of, 153 ff.
Capital, integration of, 228
Capital punishment, 130
Carlyle, Thomas, quoted, 268-9
Centralized political power, 180.
Certainty of work, 210
Change, influence of, 273.
City beautiful, 228.
"City of God" of Augustine, 84 ff.;
effect of ideas of, 93; valuation
of, 94
"City of the Sun" of Thomas
Campanella, 153 ff
City-state of Campanella, 156, of
Plato, 102, of More, 138
Civilization based on invention and
discovery, 278
Classes, alignment of, as result of
French Revolution, 183-4.
Cleanliness, 163.
Clothing, sensible, 251.
"Code de la Nature" of Morelly,
180 ff.
Common dwellings, 160
Common meals, 137
Communist, 189
Community of women, 303-4; Plato,
107.

Communism of knowledge, 152.
Compulsory marriage, 188.
Conventionality, worshipers of, 258.
Coöperative associations, 241.
Copernicus, 125.
Credits, labor, 232
Criminals, treatment of, 248-9.
Critics of age, 260
Crusades, 122.

D

Daniel, Apocalypse of, 53 ff.
Demosthenes quoted, 20.
Determinism, 216, 285-7.
Deutero -Isaiah, 42 ff., brother idea
of, 46, individual redemption, 45;
message of, 43-4; Utopia of, 44-
5· utopianism of, 45-6.
Diffusion of knowledge, 178
Disappearance of Utopias, 225
Discontent, significance of, 259.
Discoveries and explorations of
fifteenth and seventeenth cen-
turies, 124-5.
Dissensions through class inequality,
190.
Distribution, 231; common, 242

E

Early Modern Utopians, 121 ff.; con
tributing events, 121-5, general
nature, 125-7
Economic and industrial conditions,
importance of, 180
Economic justice, 240-1.
Education, 234, 291-2; Plato, 112-
16, More, 140, Campanella, 157-8,
Harrington. 175-6, Cabet, 207,
Owen, 217-18
Educational schemes of Early
Modern Utopians, 179.
Election, indirect, 173.
Enclosures, 131.
Encyclopædists, 182.
Engels, Friedrich, quoted, 220-1.
Engrossing and forestalling, 132.
Enoch, Apocalypse of, 55 ff.
Enoch, Secrets of, 58.

Environment, influence of, 216-17, 222.

Equality of sexes, 243, 289: Campanella, 158, 161; Plato, 110.

Eschatology, 52.

Eugenics, Plato, 107-9; More, 139; Bacon, 149-50; Campanella, 162-3; Early Modern Utopians, 180; movement, 288-9

Evolution, ideas of, 311

Exercise, value of for mothers, 163.

Ezekiel, 35 ff ; social background of, 36; conception of individual responsibility, 38-9; determinism, 38-9; emphasis on ritual, 36-7; personality, 35-6; theocracy, 40-2; Utopia and utopianism of, 35-40.

Ezra, Apocalypse of, 59.

F

Faith of Utopians, 261

Fourier, Charles, 197 ff , 284; life, 197-8; free love, 203, method of payment, 202-3; passionate attraction, law of, 198, "passions," 198-200, phalanx and phalanstery, 200-2; sociological laws, 197.

Fraternity, 210.

Freedom, necessity of, 245.

"Freeland—A Social Anticipation" by Hertzka, Theodor, 236 ff.

Free love, 203

French "Encyclopædie," 295.

French Enlightenment, 182.

French Revolution, 181

G

Government, 242-3

Guelph and Ghibelline, 160.

H

Happiness theory, 215.

Harrington, James, "Oceana," 165 ff., life, 165-7; balance of property, 170-1; general education, 176-7; indirect election, 173; laws, 170, national religion, 175; political utopianism, 177; property and social stability, 171-2; religious toleration, 174-5; rotation of offices, 173-4; secret ballot, 172-3; tract for times, 168-9; two-chamber parliament, 174.

Health, 163.

Hebrew prophets, compared with Plato, 119, practical nature, 47; problems, 48, purpose, 49, social vision, 47; unit of rehabilitation, 48-9; Utopias and utopianism, 7 ff , 280-1.

Hegelian theory of history, 209, 224; influence, 310-11.

Hertzka, Theodor, "Freeland—A Social Anticipation," 226, 236 ff.; coöperative associations, 241, common distribution, 242, education, 243; equality of sexes, 243; Freeland's fundamental laws, 239; government, 242-3; property, 240; self-interest, 240; unemployment, 242; works of, 236.

Hosea, and Amos, difference between, 15; and Gomer, 17; as Utopian, 14; doctrine of love, 15, 18; social background of, 15-17; Utopia of, 18-19

Housekeeping, community, 233.

Human nature, 302.

Human value, criterion of, 283.

Humanism, 147

I

"Icaria" of Cabet, 205.

Ideas, assist in social control, 274; consummation of, in time, 274; incorporation of, in social fabric, 270-1; rôle, 268 ff.; survival, 273; utility, 276-7

Ideals, as criteria, 277; rôle of, 268 ff.

Imagination, necessity, 269.

Individualism, 247.

Individuals, originators of thought processes, 270.

Industrial contralization, 211.

Industrial Revolution in England, 213, influence on Utopian Socialists, 183.

Industrial service, 229

Instincts, 302; theory of, 284.

Intellectual enlightenment, 125-6; originality of Utopians, 261.

Inventors, 265

Isaiah, 19 ff., personality of, 19-20, compared to Amos and Hosea, 19-20; conditions of time, 20; conception of judgment of, 23, denunciation of conditions of time by, 21-2, idea of progress of, 24, idealism of, 27; potency of idealism of, 28; theory of social reconstruction of, 23-4; Utopia of, 24-7; utopianism of, 19-24.

J

Jails, 233

Jeremiah, 28 ff ; comparison with other prophets, 28-9, impending disaster, 31-2; influence of life on ideas, 33-4; life of, 29, social conditions of time, 30-1; time, 29-30, Utopia and utopianism, 28-34

Jesus, 66 ff , ideas of, outgrowth of those of predecessors, 69-71; Kingdom of God of, 71-4; life and family of, 66-7, product of "Bad Times," 67-8, recognition of law of development by, 71-2; sociological and revolutionary, 68-9; utopianism, 74-83, 280-1

John, Revelations of, 60 ff

K

Kingdom of God as seen by Jesus, 70-5

Knowledge, advancement of, 293.

L

Labor Bureau, 218; national organization of, 190, 229, question, 228

Laissez-faire philosophy, 184

Laws, supremacy, 170, written, 170.

Life, a constant struggle, 304; of reason, 126

Louis, XIV, 181; XV, 182, XVI, 183.

Luxury and poverty according to More, 132.

M

Maccabees, 51.

Machine process, 183

Machinery, importance, 248

Man perfectible, 185.

Manchester School, 236.

Marco Polo, 122

Marriage, 235, laws, 250

Marriage relation in early modern Europe, 149.

Marx, 209.

Massachusetts, Constitution of, 297.

Mechanical perfection, 235.

Messianic hope, 49.

Modern Utopias, 225.

"Modern Utopia" of H G Wells, 244 ff.

Money, absence, 232, and precious metals repudiated, 135-6, 161-2, need, 246

Moral training, 137

More, Sir Thomas, 127 ff , 208-1, life, 127-8, conditions of time, 130 3, reflected spirit of time, 129, anti-war, 142, city-state, 138, common meals, 137; community of property, 134-5; concentration of political power, 138; dress and jewels, 136-7; educational system, 140; equal opportunity, 138, hours of work, 141-2, indictment of his society, 129-30; money, 135, pleasures, 140, public honors, 141, religious toleration and worship, 143-6; sanitation, 142, state-controlled family, 139, Utopia, 128, utopianism, 133 ff

Morelly, Abbé, 186 ff ; compulsory marriage, 188, maladjustment of social forces, 187, private property and misery, 187; study of soul, 186-7, universality of work, 188

Mutual compact of Babeuf, 189.

N

National organization of labor, 190.
Nature, 222.
Necessity of unity in the state, 179.
"New Atlantis" of Francis Bacon, see Bacon
New Era of Cabet, 205-6.
New social order, prophets of, 258.
New York, Constitution, 297.

O

"Oceana" of James Harrington, 165 ff., see Harrington also
"Organization du Travail" of Blanc, 208
Ottoman Turks, 123
Over-social view. 305.
Owen, Robert, 213 ff, life, 214; characterization of, 221; works, 215 footnote; determinism of, 216; education scheme, 217-18; happiness, the aim of religion, 215-16, influence of environment, 216-17, Labor Bureau, 218; as prophet, 220; Utopia, 219; utopianism, 281-2

P

Paper and printing, introduction, 125
Parliament, two-chamber, 174
Passing of Utopias, 223, 308 ff.
Passionate attraction, law of, 198-200
Passions, human, 186
Payment according to services, 202-3.
Peace, international, 231.
Peter, Apocalypse of, 59.
Phalanx of Fourier, 200-2.
Physical basis, necessity of, for advancement, 301-2.
Plato, "Republic," Chap III; father of idealism, 99, comparison with Hebrew Prophets, 119; aim to develop superior men, 116; all individual interests forbidden, 106; assimilation of individual in state, 105, city-state idea, 102; community of women and property, 107, educational program, 112-16; ethical aristocracy, 104-5; equality of sexes, 110; eugenics, 108, Idea of Good, 104-5, 116; idea of, on scientific mating, 109; social classes of "Republic," 103-4; sociological significance, 119-20; state of, unrealizable, 100-1; truth, 117, Vision of Er, 117.
Political romance, 168
Population, improvement, 249
Potency of schemes of Utopian Socialists, 223
Preventive medicine, 289-90.
Private property, abolition of, by Utopian Socialists, 222; Early Modern Utopians, 179.
Process of idea acceptance, 271-2.
Progress in science and knowledge, 312
Property, 159; balance of, 170-2; community of, 107, 111, 134-5; social theory, 290-1; widely diffused, 240
Prophets, see Hebrew Prophets.
Pseudepigraphic writings, 52.
Public worship, 144-5
Puritanism, 168.

R

Race, 252.
Reformation of man, 244.
Religion and brotherhood, 146
Religion, national, 175.
Religious toleration 290; More, 143-6; Harrington, 174-5.
Renaissance, 147, 169; influence of, 178
"Republic" of Plato, see Plato.
Ritual, social significance, 37.
Roman Empire, 84, 101.
Ross, E A, quoted, 302.
Rotation of office. 173-4.
Rousseau, 182, 183, 309, influence of, on Robert Owen, 220.

S

Saint-Simon, Henri de, 191 ff., life, 191-2, constructive viewpoint, 192-3; government by experts, 194-5; hierarchy of talent, 193, influence of, on theories of Blanc, 209; men naturally unequal, 196, rank and reward according to capacity, 195; social religion, 196-7; tripartite social control, 194

"Samurai" of Wells, 251-2.

Savonarola, Florentine theocracy, 94 ff.; Florence under, 96-7, time of, 94-5; decline of, 97-8

Science, 150-1

Scientific college of Bacon, 150.

Scientific management, 285.

Self-interest, 240.

Sexes, equality of, 234.

Shakespeare, 147

Social consciousness, 276.
    control, 274.
    destiny, 283
    determination, 288.
    dreamer, 271
    ethics, 149
    evils, source, 152.
    evolution, effect of Utopias on, 279.
    forces behind Utopian Socialists, 181-4
    forces, maladjustment of, 187.
    free will, 287
    hierarchy of Blanc, 211-12.
    ideal, 275-6.
    idealism, 268
    institutions, utility, 291.
    inventors, 270
    laws, appreciation of, 283-4.
    mediocrity of Babeuf, 191.
    movement, acceleration of, 312.
    order, 227.
    perfection, ideal of, 276; gradual process, 38; possibility of, 307-8
    religion, 216, 290; anticipated by Utopian Socialists, 223
    science, 146
Socialism, founders of, 297-8.

Socialized science, 153.

Sociological laws, 197.

Sociology, dependence of, on Utopians, 299.

Spirit of protest, 306

Stael, Madame de, 195

State, 296; family controlled by, 139-40, Plato's conception of, 102; religion, 207.

Strange inventions, 151.

Strikes, 227-8.

Suggestion and imitation, 272, 275.

T

Theocracy, 49, of Ezekiel, 40-2; of Savonarola, 94 ff.

Theory of history, 310-11.

Thievery, absurdity of punishment for, 131.

Thieves in sixteenth century England, 130.

Todd, A J, 288.

Tolerance for reformers, 275.

Trade unions, 219.

Tully, 257.

Turgenev quoted, 151.

U

Unemployment, 242, 249.

Universality of work, 188.

Utility of ideas, 276-7

Utopia a state of mind, 314.

"Utopia" of Sir Thomas More, see More; origin of word, 1

Utopian philosophy, disappearance of, 313.

Utopian Socialists, 181 ff.; difference between, and other Utopians, 184, ideal states to be superimposed on all, 184; not of proletariat, but men of affairs, 221, social background, 181 ff.; were in deadly earnest, 185

Utopians, Chap. VII, 259, 260, 265, as inventors, 265, assisted in avoiding social disaster, 282, determinism of, 285-7, faith of, 261; fearlessness of, 282.

Utopianism, contribution of, to civilization, 279 ff., definition, 268; political, 177.

Utopias, as carriers of social idealism, 268-9; as going concerns, 306-7: as inventions, 264; assumed to be last word, 306, conceptions of, 263; definitions of, 263 footnote; of sixteenth and seventeenth century, 178, passing of, 308 ff ; relativity of, 265-6; sociology's interest in, 2

V

Villages of unity and coöperation, 219.

Voltaire, 182.

W

Wages, 230.

Wallas, Graham, 284

War of Roses, 130.

Wells, H. G., "Modern Utopia," 226, 245 ff ; individualism, 247; importance of machinery, 248; improvement of population, 249; marriage law, 250; necessity of freedom, 245, need of money, 246; race, 252; "Samurai," 251-2, treatment of criminals, 248-9; unemployment, 249.

Women, communism of, 107, 303-4.

Workers, supply and demand of, 229.

CPSIA information can be obtained
at www.ICGtesting.com
Printed in the USA
BVHW041832081021
618571BV00010B/253